LEGALIZED KILLING

The Darker Side of the Castle Laws

by John R. Wright

Legalized Killing: The Darker Side of the Castle Laws
Copyright © 2010
John R. Wright

Cover art by the author: "Forensic Questions"

Library of Congress Control Number: 2010913372

ISBN-13: 978-0-615-40165-2

Cotter's Cliffs Publishing LLC
P.O. Box 4
Cotter, AR 72626-0004

**To Faron and his daughter,
and to all the children deprived of a parent
through violence.**

"...all these moments will be lost in time, like tears in rain."
- The last android of *Blade Runner*

Cover Art: Forensic Questions

Who is the one over here? Is it the intruder, who apparently added murder to the crime of burglary? Or is it the homeowner, who tried to defend himself? Was this bloodshed avoidable? Are we wrong to assume a simple case of self-defense?

Acknowledgements

This book is meant to be educational, hopefully to save a few lives. Much earlier, during my career as a chemist, I had contributed to two science symposium volumes, and over half of volume five of the *Biochemistry of the Elements* series (Plenum Press) was my work. After the latter task I had sworn never to be involved with another book, but in the year 2008 I became motivated to write *Legalized Killing*. I had thought at first, "Well, this ought to be an easier kind of writing." It wasn't.

My wife was patient and understanding during the period of researching and writing that resulted in this book. Far too many hours were spent at the keyboard of a computer, time that might have been better occupied doing the simpler things of retirement.

Various individuals provided information, offered suggestions and critically reviewed parts of this book. Those doing so were lawyers, law enforcement officers, some of my prior students and several friends. Their input is anonymous, for obvious reasons, but I thank them, too.

Disclaimer

The author is not a lawyer, and the information presented in this book should not be viewed as legal advice. If legal advice is needed, seek a lawyer.

The book does contain practical advice about the self-defense situation, which could be summarized thus: Be mindful of the other person's property so that you will not be viewed as an intruder, and pay more attention to the security of your own property, so that the likelihood of a hostile intrusion is minimized. In any case, never use deadly force on anyone unless you or those you care about are in *mortal danger*. Using deadly force just because someone happens to be on your property but is not actually threatening you is *morally wrong*. A court cannot award a death sentence for mere trespass, and neither should a property owner. If you intend to have a gun for self-defense, *become proficient and safe with it*. Enroll in a proper firearms training program.

Preface

After hearing my stories of suspicious shootings in Oklahoma a certain lawyer here in Arkansas, who would rather not be named, suggested that I write this book. I am not sure if he was entirely serious, but I took his suggestion to heart. He also recommended that I read a book by John Grisham, *The Innocent Man: Murder and Injustice in a Small Town*, but I did not open that book until *Legalized Killing* had reached the second-draft stage. There is no influence from Grisham in my manuscript. However, when I started reading *The Innocent Man* I ran into *deja' vu* at almost every turn.

Grisham's non-fiction story characterized a certain Oklahoma prosecutor as arrogant. I've personally experienced that kind of arrogance, but the problem isn't just an attitude. The historical record shows a pattern of incompetence, arbitrariness and corruptions in Oklahoma's law enforcement and criminal justice systems. These failings are well-documented, and they range from prosecutors pilfering the evidence vault in northeastern Oklahoma to a sheriff's sexual corruptions in western Oklahoma. Law enforcement officers have been heavy-handed, used deadly force when it could have been avoided and allowed a lynch mob mentality to prevail at times. The natives of southeastern Oklahoma -- at least some of them -- even believe that their courts are in bed with an entity they call "Little Dixie Mafia." That may be a myth, but it's what they think. Such problems occur *everywhere*, but there is a feeling that southeastern Oklahoma has more than its share of trouble.

John Grisham's bestseller is about jurisprudence gone crazy in Ada, Oklahoma. It tells the true story of a brutal rape and murder of a young woman. A man was charged with her murder, tried, convicted and sentenced to death on flimsy evidence and dishonest witness testimonies. Meanwhile a more likely suspect was overlooked, and blame was thus placed on the wrong person. The man was almost executed but was later found not guilty. His exoneration happened more than a decade after his conviction and imprisonment, but when the prosecutor was confronted with DNA evidence proving the man's innocence, he refused to admit the mistake. He even filed a lawsuit against Grisham.

Also in Oklahoma, in a town not far from Ada, a young man, unarmed, was shot to death a few days before his court date as a critical prosecution witness. The crime he had witnessed and would have testified about was a drug-related murder, one involving interstate drug trafficking. The one who killed him freely admitted that he shot the witness, but he claimed that he did it in self-defense. Given this intriguing setting, the district attorney, the same prosecutor that would have used the victim as a witness, released the killer. She obviously reached a decision only a few hours after the killing; the man was set free on the very day of the shooting. She had applied Oklahoma's self-defense law, which Oklahomans refer to as their "Make My Day" law. But was it actually self-defense, or was it a murder passed off as self-defense?

This book is a critical evaluation of the self-defense laws in America. It does not take a position against those laws but raises questions about instances where the laws appear to have not been applied prudently or where citizens misunderstood them, and in researching for material it was found that there were *many* such cases on record. The witness' death was not unique, and Oklahoma is not the only place where this kind of thing is happening. Chapter one of the book thus begins with the homicide of the prosecution witness, described above, and the facts about that incident are examined in depth. Chapter two tells the story of the associated drug-related violence that put him in danger. America's so-called "castle laws" are presented in Chapter three, and they vary quite a bit across the land. Chapter four evaluates evidence of the *effects* of those laws. The drug problem in our country is a significant factor in many home intrusions, and that is the subject of Chapter five. Chapters six and seven go into gun ownership and how guns are used by people who do not wear a badge or a uniform. Chapter seven also examines the behavior of armed criminals, because that is what a citizen has to deal with when a dangerous intruder comes into a home. A forum of public and professional opinions from the ongoing self-defense debate is found in Chapters eight and nine. The quotations are *exact*, including spelling and grammatical errors. Finally, Chapter ten takes a hard look at how individuals are caught up in the classical self-defense situation and how they handle it; some do the right thing while others make a mess of it. It appears that every outcome that one could possibly imagine actually happens. Misconceptions and bad judgment have indeed lead to tragic outcomes, and many more are ahead unless some corrective actions are taken.

The subject is controversial, and I have placed myself near the heart of the controversy. My perspective will not please everyone. Readers should draw their own conclusions. But if the book causes the reader to be more aware of the way legislators, courts and citizens view the so-called castle laws, along with a sense that things are not quite right and that a new danger has been created, then its purpose will be accomplished.

Awareness of that danger can actually save lives. Similarly, if those who think the castle laws give them a license to kill are caused to realize that a court's decision of *justifiable homicide* is not a sure outcome, perhaps better judgment will be used.

The book is referenced to relevant background literature, and endnotes are used when the amplification of an idea would disrupt the continuity of the story. They are pertinent, and they are there for those who want to know more. References to chapter endnotes are shown as superscript lower case letters, and the literature citations are denoted by superscript numbers in parentheses, italicized. This superscript referencing method is not a standard style, but it was used to avoid confusion with the many quoted passages from state statutes, which are full of number and letter paragraph headings.

John R. Wright, Ph.D.

CONTENTS

Introduction: self-defense and justice

"...With liberty and justice for all." - From the flag pledge

The concept of justice for everyone is very noble, but in the year 2010 -- in America -- it is not really true. For one thing, some individuals can't afford lawyers, which excludes them from access to what they perceive to be justice. The troubled kid from a slum is not on an equal footing with the celebrity. The justice of the real world, whatever it is, has a price tag. There *are* public defenders, but what is their actual record of success? A lot of people are too well off to qualify for a public defender but not rich enough for the best counsel; they can end up financially ruined and convicted, too. *The weak link in access to justice is the legal system itself,* and it has, in the minds of a lot of people, come to a point where it isn't trusted because it appears to be unable to deal *fairly* and *consistently* with issues of right and wrong. It is more about winning or losing, and it *is* preoccupied with *money and politics* to an extent that some find decidedly uncomfortable.

In one case a man commits the murder of just one person and receives the death penalty. He is executed twelve years later after many costly appeals. Another man kills someone and claims self-defense even though it wasn't. The prosecuting attorney doesn't file charges, and the man walks away free. In contrast, during the 1960s an elderly woman in St. Louis, Missouri shot and killed a burglar. The burglar had a long background of criminal activity, including violence, but she was sent to jail even though her action was a genuine case of self-defense. Serial killer Henry Lee Lucas received a death sentence for murdering eleven individuals out of an undetermined larger number that he *actually* killed, but he was never executed (Lucas' death sentence was later commuted to life by Texas Governor George W. Bush.). Lucas' first victim was his own mother.

The problem is international in scope. Where was justice in August of 2009 when a Scottish judge, Kenny Macaskill, released terrorist Abdel Basset Ali Mohamed Al-Megrahi on grounds of "...*compassion and mercy...*," sending him home to Lybia for a hero's welcome? Abdel had been sentenced to life imprisonment for his role in murdering a total of 270 innocent people, including every soul aboard Pan Am Flight 103 and others on the ground, the latter killed by falling debris. Flight 103 crashed at Lockerbie, Scotland in 1988. The convicted terrorist was dying of prostate cancer, which was the stated basis for setting him free, but talk of a possible oil deal between the UK and Libya raised a question of corruption in many minds.

Justice is not altogether blind when big money comes knocking. Compassion and mercy were not issues when the terrorist bomb tore Flight 103 apart at 35,000 feet altitude. Convicts die in prison all the time, and the exception made for Al-Megrahi was outrageous.

It also happens in cases that you never hear about on CNN or NBC or FOX news. The April 23, 2009 issue of *The Baxter Bulletin* (Mountain Home, Arkansas) carried a story about the conviction and sentencing of a 70- year old man who held up a Gassville, Arkansas branch bank with a "toy cap gun." He *got four* life sentences! Bank robbers shouldn't be free to walk the streets, and the one in question was a repeat offender. However, *four life sentences are fairly meaningless for someone already living on borrowed time.* In such cases the penalty is symbolic. Another dastardly old man, Bernie Madoff, *got only three life sentences* for wreaking a multibillion dollar hell on unsuspecting investors! All things considered, Bernie may have been the more destructive of the two in terms of the number of individuals impacted and how their lives were affected.

It was said that the Gassville cap gun robbery was terroristic and that the perpetrator had kidnapped the bank staff; but a cap gun does not have the *substance* of violence. It seems that what terrorism originally meant has changed, and that became evident when an apparent Islamist zealot shot over a dozen soldiers to death and injured many more at Ft. Hood, Texas. Mainstream journalists and political leaders would not use the word "terrorism" to describe that incident. Such stories are in the news all too frequently, and they are not well-received by ordinary citizens.

The castle laws, which this book focuses upon and which were intended to spare homeowners from prosecution for assault, manslaughter or murder and further civil lawsuits if they kill or injure a dangerous intruder, will also lead to the same kinds of wild variations in justice, as in the cited examples. The legislators who wrote the laws didn't take into account that some people will do things that are either stupid or devious. While these self-defense laws hopefully will protect innocent individuals that are forced to defend themselves, they will also be used in ways not intended, and one effect will be to further de-value human life. The protections should apply *only* to those who are genuinely threatened by intruders, who have not invited trouble and who have to shoot or die. Even in those cases a shadow is cast upon the life of the one who had to resort to the ultimate violence. There will always be that nagging thought: *Was there a way to avoid it?* Hindsight always brings things into better focus. Good people have a conscience.

But the shadow is even darker if something beside self-defense was involved. These laws create zones of potential lawlessness if they do not have criteria for disallowing motives other than self-defense, and while a substantial number of citizens have already defended themselves in the way *intended* by the applicable castle laws, others have escaped prosecution for senseless or highly suspicious killings. When such laws are misapplied, justice takes a vacation. The accumulating injustices of this type are especially malignant.

In writing this book I have been aware that the subject is largely in the domain of law, and I am not a lawyer. Offhand, it would seem that a lawyer ought to be writing this type of book. The subject involves legal language, and the ordinary citizen reads statutes from a perspective that is different from a lawyer's. That deficiency must be acknowledged. But I am intimately familiar with one situation that involved a so-called self-defense shooting. There were disturbing facts associated with the incident that cause one to doubt that self-preservation was the shooter's real motive. Also, I grew up with guns, and I have some understanding of firearms, gun safety and how a gun should be used in self-defense. That aspect will be treated, too. This subject needs to be examined from every corner.

Clearly defined operating rules are paramount when lives are at stake. The safeguards written into the castle laws across the land vary quite a bit, and that ought to be a concern among legislators. In researching the available castle law literature it became apparent that many citizens do not know what the laws allow or disallow, and unnecessary killings have already taken place because people thought they could do things that were not actually permitted. For example, one individual offered this anonymous comment at a blog site: "*I live in Texas. I can tell you that most Texans never realized that there was any duty to retreat* [before they had a castle law]. *That duty was added to the law around 1973 with little fanfare as I recall...Most Texa*[n]*s already thought that they had the legal right to protect themselves under those circumstances anyway.*" The comment was written about two years *after* the Texas castle law went into effect and the duty to retreat had been removed.

A friend who knew that this book was being written asked me for a copy of the Arkansas self-defense law, because he had never read it. At least one Texas legislator has been dismayed by misapplications of the law *he created*. That kind of frustration happens mainly because of three factors: *a law that was poorly written in the first place; court officials that ignored or misapplied parts of the applicable laws; and citizens that do not know their limitations. It's a bad mix.* Many more examples could be cited.

The collateral effects of homicides ruled to be in self-defense are life-shattering. Using the case of the cap gun bank robbery, if the court thinks the bank staff suffered the mental crimes of terrorism and a form of kidnapping in the *absence of an actual physical threat (i.e., a real firearm)*, how does it suppose that the loss of a life under very questionable circumstances -- supposedly a homicide in self-defense -- will affect a victim's spouse, children, parents, grandparents, cousins and others who were close friends? Common sense says that the tellers at the Gassville bank have already recovered from their encounter with the cap gun robber. They hardly remember it. In fact, I asked the opinion of a Gassville bank teller, one who was actually caught up in the incident, and she agreed that such a loss had to be much worse than her own discomfort when an alleged lunatic attempted to rob her bank.

The issue is about *criminal justice.* A simple definition of justice was presented during a commissioning program at Medina Air Base in San Antonio. I was an Air Force officer trainee at that time (in 1961), and it came from a staff judge advocate, who was instructing the class concerning the Unified Code of Military Justice. He said justice was "*...seeing that the* *person brought before a tribunal got what he or she actually deserved.*" The statement sounded perfectly reasonable at the time, but from the examples cited and other experiences, what is the success rate? It would be worthwhile to know. Fifty percent? Seventy-five percent? Ninety-two percent? For sure, it isn't one hundred percent. The stigma of a "homicide in self-defense" is severe. One's death becomes comparable to that of a road-killed animal, whether or not the killing was actually a justifiable homicide. Miscarriages of justice of that type are just as pernicious as the execution of an innocent man for a murder he didn't commit.

The basic reasoning *behind* the castle doctrine *is valid.* Homes *are* invaded. Businesses *are* robbed. Lives *are* threatened. A woman who served a military tour in Iraq and who had actual combat experience returned to civilian life in Jonesboro, Arkansas. She worked at a Papa John's Pizza, and when two robbers came in she was *shot at.* They got away with $15 and a pizza bag! The traumatized woman concluded that "*...home is more dangerous than Iraq.*"[1] You want to think that your life is worth more than fifteen dollars and a pizza supreme! There *is* a crime problem in America, and people need to be able to defend themselves from dangerous intruders.

But putting the idea into action is a different matter. There are a few hotheads out there who are more than eager to apply the law, thinking it gives them a license to use deadly force as they please rather than take options to avoid trouble. The more volatile ones will kill when they are not actually threatened or when they could have side-stepped a confrontation. Others kill or injure themselves, family members or neighbors because of their ignorance concerning guns. These laws even present opportunities to commit premeditated murder under the guise of self-defense, and that is why legal vigilance is so necessary.

Proponents of the castle laws will not want to hear about such detractions, but the reality of those situations will be justified with documented accounts of actual incidents throughout this book and especially in chapter 10. This problem needs to be faced, not ignored. The focus of this book is *mostly upon what has actually happened, not what might take place.* It shouldn't be necessary to disarm an entire population just because a few with wrong motives mess things up. Punish the ones that do the serial killings, public shootings, twist the intent of self-defense laws, etc. Make unenviable examples of them.

There is a tendency to be black or white on the guns and self-defense issues. It's usually "*Guns are evil, so confiscate all of them*" versus "*Every household should be armed.*" Read your history of Germany of the late 1930s to find out what it's like when the state holds all of the power. Similarly, guns for *everyone* will incorporate even the homicidal individuals, including quite a few that have thus far escaped notice. *Reality comes in shades of gray.* And remember this: self-defense does not always involve guns.

I was one who originally accepted the castle doctrine as being entirely valid. My views are now modified. Those who are anti-gun will not like hearing that people have a right to defend themselves with lethal force, if necessary, but at the same time, neither will the pro-gun people care much for the assertion that the castle laws pose serious problems. The anti-gun crowd will say, "*You are being inconsistent, contradicting yourself,*" while the other camp will ask, "*Why is he doing this, now that we've just acquired self-defense laws that work for us?*" I realize that I am at the heart of a controversy.

To the first group the response is that self-defense is a natural trait among *all* living creatures, and it can't be ignored. Test the idea if you wish. Try to take hold of a stray cat. Would you wear a garland of poison ivy on your head? Even plants fight back. "*Don't mess with us. We'll get you with thorns or poisons.*" Self-preservation is a built-in property, and humans are not different. On a microscopic scale the leukocytes and macrophages and lymphocytes, specialized cells of our immune system, wage a constant war against invading pathogens. It is programmed into the very tissue that we're made of. No one has the right to barge into your home and take your life or the life of someone you love. You ought to be justified in killing to keep from being killed. Granted, the anti-gun group is not wrong to think that some individuals should not be allowed to have a gun (such as felons, reckless people and the mentally deranged), but there are *many more* responsible citizens that *can* be trusted with guns. They will not use a weapon defensively unless they absolutely have to. We will no longer be a free nation if the Bill of Rights is destroyed. This is not a black or white issue; there are indeed shades of gray in it.

To the second group the response is that you need to be aware that the intention of the legislators who wrote the laws is one thing and the way the public and district attorneys and courts will use them is quite another. The disasters that have already taken place have come from lack of common sense and not knowing the intended limits of the castle laws. I believe that a lot of well-meaning legislators and citizens, *including legitimate gun owners*, are going to be dismayed as time passes. Chapter one will examine the shooting death of a young man in Oklahoma as an example of how a castle law can be evoked even under questionable circumstances.

The issues of why responsible citizens might bear arms, the various ways guns can be used other than for shooting people, gun safety, decisions of when and when not to use a gun in self-defense and practical nuts and bolts information about choosing and using a gun should not be ignored in a book that purports to examine the self-defense laws. Chapters 6 and 7 focus on these subjects. It is a fact that states and locations that allow the citizens to have guns also have lower crime rates, while those with restrictive gun laws are indeed dangerous places, because the criminals are armed and law-abiding citizens are not. This shows us clearly that criminals will have guns in spite of oppressive gun laws. The hypothesis holds that a would-be armed intruder (burglar, etc.) might be more hesitant in a state where there are guns in most of the households, seeing that they might be shot by someone dwelling there (i.e., the mere *existence* of armed citizens intimidates the criminal), and it probably works that way to some extent but certainly not in all of the cases. After all, burglaries and robberies still occur in states like Oklahoma, Arkansas and Texas.

There are numerous possibilities inherent in the castle laws that could allow a genuine murderer or the perpetrator of a completely senseless killing to escape justice. There is no statute of limitations for murder. So how do you proceed if at a later date something surfaces to indicate that what had been attributed to a homicide in self-defense was actually a genuine, premeditated murder? How does that fit with a law that prevents any further litigation? Will the original decision be allowed to stand? The reluctance to re-open such a case would be daunting even if a legal means could be found. District attorneys and judges do not like to see their decisions overturned. Would a prosecutor want it known if someone he or she turned loose subsequently killed two more people in another state? That would be political dynamite. My belief is that the system would simply allow the failure of justice to go by. In fact, it happens all the time, and we see examples in the murder convictions that were eventually overturned by DNA evidence. These errors of the court must pervade the whole spectrum of crimes, from minor to the most heinous.

It is evident that the statute puts a lot of power in the hands of a district attorney and does not take into consideration that a district attorney might yield to *inappropriate motives or bad judgment* in his or her decisions. It's a worse situation than what you get in a trial by jury, because in a trial more than one mind is involved in the decision process; and yet, even a trial can lead to erroneous results. With only one person deciding, an obvious murder might be allowed to pass because of a heavy workload. Obtaining a *disposition* by evoking a castle law looks even simpler than plea-bargaining. The prosecutor applies the presumption of innocence and takes the easy way out. Why shouldn't the prosecutor take that route? After all, the presumption of innocence decreases the likelihood of a successful prosecution from the outset. But the law doesn't absolutely rule out a murder charge if the prosecutor wants to take on the burden of proof.

Maybe the prosecuting attorney just didn't like the one that was shot, or there had been an error in a prior prosecution of the deceased, and embarrassing information is best laid to rest. The prosecutor could even be genuinely corrupt, willing to take a bribe -- not unheard of.

The lawyer told his client that he would take the case for $25,000. The prospective client responded, "I don't have that kind of money," which was the truth. There was a brief pause, then the lawyer said, "Well, I'll do it for $3,000." The rather large gap of $22,000 thus omitted would have been "incentive" for several cooperating members of a corrupt system, the lawyer being one of them. He did essentially nothing to help his client, and if the client hadn't found the paper trail that proved his own innocence he would have been convicted. This is a true story without names and places. Situations like that are grounds for more than disbarment, but they actually thrive in some systems.

Perhaps the shooter had an influential friend in high places, and that friend warned the prosecutor to go easy. After all, a prosecutor's career is distinctly political, and with that in mind another motive is recognized: a prosecutor might favor what he or she believes the voters want to hear rather than follow what morality suggests doing.

Fear of violent criminals is another factor. The Oklahoma District 19 prosecutor, who had been a charter member of the now defunct Durant-Texoma Evening Kiwanis Club, carried a .38 revolver and told some of the club members that he was concerned for his safety because of *who* he had to deal with. The danger is real, but it goes with the career. It must be accepted just as a soldier accepts his risks.

In any case, the prosecutor who *knowingly* allows a murder to be passed off as a homicide in self-defense becomes the moral equivalent of an accessory-after-the-fact. I'm told that a more appropriate legal term is "obstruction of justice," Court officials are indeed capable of obstructing justice, and they are no more above the law than the next man or woman. A decision not to prosecute might seem to be perfectly legal because of a wording of the law, but it certainly would be a failure of justice if a reason to doubt exists. *The castle laws more or less compel the one that is supposed to prosecute to decide for innocence. It is a bad concept.*

And this question *must* be asked: is a state law that denies a survivor access to legal redress even valid under the United States Constitution? A statute shouldn't put innocent citizens lower than enemies of the state. Terrorists that have attacked the United States -- who are not even citizens -- have been given the right to a trial. It is a worthwhile question, and it needs to be addressed; parents of homicide victims suffer post-traumatic stress and are frequently secondary victims of the criminal justice system. [2]

One is right to assert that public ignorance and errors of the legal system are the weakest links. A lot of citizens do not know what they can or cannot do (the legal perspective), or better said, what they should or should not do (the moral perspective). Some of the legislators did not do a good job of anticipating the problems that these laws have created. Criminals and their defense lawyers are sure to exploit the loopholes. The legal process is where the wisdom ought to be and where the long-lasting decisions are made. Its failures are the worst ones. From a legislative issue that had nothing to do with the castle laws, a judge who should know about the process said this: "...*having reviewed cases as an appellate judge, I know that when the legislature has the chance to include a definition and refuses, then what we look at is the plain meaning of those words."* We thus ask, what has become of common sense and the spirit of the law? If we are going to have good laws, legislators need to recognize the attitude of court officials and write the laws accordingly, hopefully so that what was intended is what will actually happen. Legislators should get around their mistakes by amending or starting over, or simply repealing bad laws.

But even if that's done, will it actually make a difference? Many individuals have serious doubts about the integrity of our courts. You hear it discussed over coffee and in other settings where people feel comfortable about saying what they are thinking: *"Was that judge out of his mind? He threw out most of the evidence that favored the defendant's innocence."* or *"The prosecutor focused attention on the father and mother and let the real killer get away."*... and so forth.

Maybe there is an ego problem bordering on pathological among *some* judges and prosecutors. If *any* person has a consuming ego and also has life-or-death power over the lives of others, it is likely to lead to *malevolent behavior.* The vicious excesses of historical figures such as Caligula, Nero, Hitler and Stalin come to mind. George Armstrong Custer is counted by

28

many to be an American hero, yet he made comments suggesting that he would have "...*pushed*..." the Native Americans "...*clear off the Earth*..." if necessary. One of three reasons given for his success at the Washita River Massacre was this: "...*the women and children offered little resistance*...;" in fact, his troops were killing Indian women and children at the Little Bighorn when his luck ran out. Abuse of authority is a *perversion* of powerful and influential people. Some fall into it; other do not. Exemplary leadership is a rare thing. Unless a person possesses sound mental health and moral integrity, too much authority over the lives of others can lead to actions that are simply *insane*.

Then my conscience said to me: "See here, you shouldn't think like that!! It's too much like contempt of the court and of authority. It's...disrespectful." But respect is a two-way street. All of us are subject to the law. Court officials are no exception. Most of us have heard the question put to prospective jurors when they are called to the stand for screening, and it goes something like this: "Do you believe in the American system of justice and in trial by jury?" It's as if everyone thinks the answer has to be "yes," but the response to the question could be "no." What if I'm having trouble believing in the system? Don't I have the right to say "no" to such questions? Thoughts like these seemed rash even to me, and I felt guilty about them until an opinion voiced by a Justice of the United States Supreme Court was brought to my attention:

"Commentary and reporting on the criminal justice system is at the core of First Amendment values, for the operation and integrity of that system is of crucial importance to citizens concerned with the administration of government. Secrecy of judicial action can only breed ignorance and distrust of courts and suspicion concerning the competence and impartiality of judges; free and robust reporting, criticism, and debate can contribute to public understanding of the rule of law and to comprehension of the functioning of the entire criminal justice system, as well as improve the quality of that system by subjecting it to the cleansing effects of exposure and public accountability."

This opinion came from Associate Justice William J. Brennan, U.S. Supreme Court, June 30, 1976. Justice Brennan was mostly a liberal when he joined the Warren Court, and I've been mostly a conservative throughout my life. Brennan's opinion, however, transcends the various political colors. It is the foundation on which this book rests.

REFERENCES CITED -- Introduction
1. *Baxter Bulletin*, Mountain Home, Arkansas, May 30, 2009.
2. S.A. Murphy *et al.*," *Journal of Traumatic Stress*, **16**(1), pp17-25, 2003.

Chapter 1 - The Phone Call

The thing feared most becomes real...

A phone ringing in the middle of the night seldom portends good news. The king sized bed barely fit the bedroom's alcove, and because there was no room for a bedside table the phone was on a chest of drawers across the room. Half asleep, Rick nearly fell getting to the phone, but he managed to answer after its third ring. It was his daughter, and she was calling from Durant, Oklahoma. *"Dad! Dad!" She wailed, "Faron is dead. He has been shot several times. He's dead, Dad! Dead!!"* The clock on the chest of drawers showed about 2:30 AM, and it was Saturday, December 15, 2007. The shooting victim was Rick's grandson. Faron had turned twenty only two weeks earlier.

Rick stood there in the darkness, stunned. It was the grandson that he had helped to raise from an infant, the one that he had spent a lot of time with and for whom he had high hopes. Rick had been the old eagle that protected Faron, because Faron's biological father refused to be a father. *"What happened?"* The words came out weakly, almost a whisper. With difficulty the daughter told her father the available details.

Faron had gone into a Durant house that night, having learned from friends that his daughter and girlfriend were there with a man the girlfriend had also been dating. Faron had knocked and the door was unlocked and opened slightly. The one we will call Bud was already armed with a .45 caliber semiautomatic pistol. According to the shooter's *first account*, Faron had barged in, struck him with his fist and sent him stumbling backward. The man then began pulling the trigger. He fired five times, and four of those bullets struck Faron, killing him.

And as Rick stood there in the darkness listening to his daughter sobbing, the thought began to form: *"This is the expected killing."* It was sinking in. The possibility of Faron being murdered had already been in the back of his mind for several months. He had learned from a brother-in-law of a previous marriage, during the summer of 2007, that Faron had witnessed a drug-related homicide and had been subpoenaed by the Oklahoma State Bureau of Investigation (OSBI). Faron was to be a prosecution witness. Both men had agreed that Faron was in danger of becoming the next homicide victim, to keep him from testifying, so this was a worst fear become reality. When his daughter hung up Rick told his wife what had happened. Then he called the brother-in-law, who was Faron's great uncle.

The previous news from Durant had been conflicting. One

source claimed that Faron and his girlfriend, Rose, were under protection, but other information originating from Durant suggested that they were not. Both certainly needed protection because Rose was also present at the earlier murder scene. Eventually it was learned that OSBI does not have the resources to protect its witnesses, and that came from an OSBI agent *after* Faron's death.

Anger took hold of Rick after the phone call, and his heart was pounding. He was overdosing on his own adrenaline. He was so thoroughly shaken by his daughter's call that he was not able to sleep again for about thirty hours. Then he collapsed into a miserable, fitful half-sleep. Some days later a doctor offered a sedative, no doubt concerned about the effect such a tragedy might have on a man approaching seventy years, but Rick chose to take the ordeal head-on. Tranquilizers and sedatives can do worse things to you than the conditions they supposedly alleviate, so maybe it was a choice of better judgment even though a doctor disagreed.

Rick never used drugs at any time during his life; certainly he didn't need more trouble at this point. After some weeks he calmed down enough that his sleeping habits became reasonably normal again, but he still gets up during the wee hours on some nights; he reads a book, checks the weather on Dish Network, listens to the news. He tells his friends: *"Sometimes I just sit in the dark, and I think about what happened to Faron and how it might have been different. I usually go to sleep sitting upright at the end of the couch when I do that."* Old people acquire a tendency to sleep sitting up. The sleep disturbance comes from an underlying problem in Rick's case. He has been suffering from a degree of post-traumatic stress, and the symptoms still recur more than two years after the shooting.

The prosecutor at Durant had released Bud on the same day that he killed Faron. Bud was not charged with anything. The way the authorities handled Faron's death was more disturbing and intriguing than the shooting itself, and Rick's anger was almost overwhelming at first. *"Bud killed your prosecution witness, and you turned him loose?!! Are you crazy?"* The anger is no longer a consuming fire, but it still smolders at times. The insurmountable problem, the thing that drove the anger, is the perceived lack of justice; it destroyed confidence in the legal system. Rick wonders how prosecuting attorneys can stomach such decisions.

The death of a grandson -- at least that part -- was eventually accepted, if only because it can't be undone. At length came the realization that the situation would never change and that *anyone* could unwittingly become a castle law victim. That led to a conclusion: the public should be made aware of the fact that the self-defense laws are being applied in situations that might not have anything to do with actual self-defense

Rick wore out an old rocking chair during Faron's beginning years. He'd hold the bottle while Faron fed from it, burp him, rock him to sleep and tuck him in bed. When Faron was a little older he'd tell him stories or read to him from a book. He took Faron to the city parks almost daily. Those are the things that bond a parent to a child, and in Rick's mind Faron seemed more like a son than a grandson. But again, there was that inherent limitation: the real father was missing.

Rick had indeed been the father figure in Faron's life, and the two spent a lot of time together. They were close, yet it was not enough. Grandfathers are important in a boy's life, but there are limits to what a grandfather can be. There is no perfect surrogate father; nothing is better than the *real one* if he lives up to his responsibility, but when he is not there, the children suffer. Even so, Rick and Faron fished, hunted, hiked and generally traveled together. They even flew together, because Rick was a private pilot. And it was like that until Faron was about fifteen years old. That was when the boy began to follow the wrong crowd. He started getting into trouble.

One day Faron told Rick that someone had introduced him to

marijuana at age twelve. There followed warnings and pleadings, but they did not have the desired effect. Faron turned to harder drugs. In November of 2005 Rick tried to get Faron into a methamphetamine rehabilitation program located in another state, hundreds of miles from Durant. The effort failed. Rick remembers telling Faron, "*If you will not ride with me in that seat, the outcome may be fatal.*" Today he wishes he had never said that.

Rick sometimes has dreams about Faron, and they are good dreams, from memories of a better time. But there persists a *nightmare* much worse than the dreamy kind: he still wakes up to the *reality* of what has happened, especially the oppressive feeling of an injustice. It refuses to go away. How does anyone deal with a thing like that? *It helps immeasurably to have faith in God, but even with faith, injuries still hurt.*

We have to protect the innocent

The homicide just described took place in Durant, an Oklahoma town near the Red River. It would not be stretching the truth to say that the local media did little to inform the public of the *details* of the incident. Perhaps the editors were afraid of a lawsuit, because the recently instated Oklahoma castle law vigorously protects those who even *claim* that they had to kill someone in self-defense. Individuals that commit a homicide under those conditions are immune to prosecution and civil lawsuits.

The man who killed Faron was released immediately. During the writing of this book a lawyer's opinion was solicited, and the author was told that because the state's prosecutor has apparently ruled that the one who killed Faron was protected by the state's castle law, he is *legally innocent.* Putting that into simple language, the author could get into far more trouble for using the man's real name than *that man* did for actually killing someone. Thus, he has been given the name "Bud," which is not his real name. On the other hand, Faron was the actual name of the man Bud killed.

Some of the individuals who were close to Faron's homicide were informed that a book was being written, and they were quite apprehensive about having their names in print. Their concerns are valid, because the criminal activity that put two young men in mortal danger -- drug trafficking -- is still afoot in Texas and Oklahoma. Something should be said about those names. First, there is no point in bringing more individuals into this story than is absolutely necessary. The names of juveniles and those more peripherally involved with the two homicides have been withheld. Faron's girlfriend and the mother of his daughter will be known only as Rose, which is not her real name. Addresses and things of that nature have been omitted. It is the essence of the story that matters.

Murderers and public officials don't qualify for anonymous status because they are subject to scrutiny concerning their actions. A writer is protected by the First Amendment as long as genuine malice is not involved and there is a sincere effort to be factual. In this case a castle law incident is being examined in detail to illustrate how a homicide ruled in self-defense *might* be on shaky premises. The rest of the book examines broader issues.

The prosecuting attorney who released Bud was Emily Redman of Oklahoma District 19, and she had three assistants at the time. One of those assistants was Timothy Webster, who was to be closely involved with the upcoming Charles Bussey and Bobby Don Mullinix murder trials. Faron's shooting death was the *second* of two associated homicides; he was a subpoenaed witness for the prosecution in those trials. Faron was indeed a *direct witness* to that *first* homicide, which was the murder of Tristan York, allegedly perpetrated by Bussey and Mullinix, but the authorities denied that there was any possible connection between Faron's shooting death and the first killing.

Most of the residents of Durant and Bryan County apparently accepted Emily's decision, but those who are aware of the actual facts are left with doubts. The public has been kept in the dark about the incident.

In the time frame of Faron's shooting there was a case in Texas where a newspaper covered a similar fatal shooting, described as a castle law example, without revealing the name of the one who did the shooting. Concern for a lawsuit was the suspected reason. If that is the trend, then court officials will be operating in virtual secrecy in some situations, including homicides. Certain kinds of homicides will not involve a regular trial with a judge, counsel and jury deliberating; the decision will be made by the prosecutor, and you will hear little or nothing about the details from that day forward.

Such a situation has much potential for abuse. There is no statute of limitation for a murder, not even in Oklahoma, but because of the way the self-defense laws are written in states like Texas and Oklahoma, so-called self-defense killings are not liable to get much in-depth scrutiny. Since all homicides have a potential for being reconsidered as murders at *any time*, how does one go about tying *those* loose ends together? The public needs to know about this situation because it affects everyone. For example, these laws surely increase the risk to a child that strays onto a stranger's property, and those who read the gas and electric meters are similarly put into more jeopardy. When a prosecution witness is killed less than a week before his court date, one has good cause to doubt a ruling of self-defense. Faron's case is only one example of what the author calls "the darker side of the castle laws."

The reader should realize that the researched information concerning the homicides of Faron and Tristan York (obtained from police reports, court records, open source information, lab tests, what individuals said, etc.), consumed the equivalent of hundreds of pages of paper. Research into the *larger issue*, namely the castle laws across the entire United States, produced a much larger file. A Dell laptop computer was used to manage all of the material; the accumulated resource file contained about 135 megabytes of information, which consisted of text, compressed images, photocopies, etc. Thus, the entire content of this book relies on strong documentation, much of it official.

This book is factual, and it uses real names where possible. Relevant information previously unavailable to the public will be presented, but it is not offered as an absolute proof that a court or a court official was in error. Even with that limitation acknowledged, the research behind this book did not leave the feeling that justice had been done.

Were conclusions drawn too soon?

The situation just portrayed is the basic setting of Faron's homicide and how the first two chapters of the book are being written. It was heard on the day of the funeral, which was on the 19th of December, 2007, that Faron's court date as a prosecution witness had been set for December 20th, 2007, and that would have been only five days after the shooting. But Emily Redman turned Bud loose immediately. The homicide has been attributed to self-defense under Oklahoma's Castle Law. It was a controversial decision if only the fact of Faron's status as a prosecution witness was taken into account, but there are *other serious reasons* for concern. Many impartial individuals have heard the full background of this story, meaning the facts not publicized in Bryan County, and their reactions tilt strongly toward murder, with few exceptions. Here is a sampling of some of the comments:

"That's a transparent murder."

"Well, it was in Oklahoma. Hell, what do you expect?"

"The people who sell drugs will kill you for little or nothing. They're all crazy."

"Sounds like some money was exchanged for a favor."

"That's how the drug cartels do business."

"What was the DA's motive?" etc...

Others disagreed:

"If he barged into someone's house he should have been shot."

"I would have shot him." etc...

Remarks like the latter two sting Rick and his family. *"It's fine to shoot someone on your own turf. I like the new law."* The viewpoints vary, and it appears that there may be more than two sides to the issue. One of those offhand remarks was blurted out by a hearing impaired man, *one of Rick's prior church friends*; he didn't realize that there was a blood relationship between Rick and the one killed. The man apologized later. He had been backing proposed self-defense legislation in another state (where he lives today) and had not considered the possibility that those laws might lead to failures of justice. He probably still doesn't want to believe it.

One needs to know what the different perspectives are. There is more involved here than the shooting death of just one young man. All homicides need careful scrutiny no matter what the first impressions are, and that requires knowing the circumstances behind each case. A characterization of those circumstances requires a thorough investigation. It looks as if the castle laws have created an exception to the quest for detail.

The disturbing indicators in Faron's shooting death intrigued

Rick; he wanted to know *what really happened.* The official explanations have not been adequate to his satisfaction, and the officials obviously didn't treat some of the available information as evidence, as he learned. An independent investigation into Faron's death was thus pursued, and it turned up findings that caused one to think that Faron was actually killed *with premeditation and a purpose* related to the York murder trials, to silence him. Faron witnessed the murder of Tristan York, but *he also witnessed drug trafficking between Texas and Oklahoma.* The latter fact may be more significant than the witnessed murder. Motives were quite visible, but they have apparently been ignored.

There is a second interpretation of what happened, which is that Faron was killed out of jealousy in a love triangle, also with premeditation. This was the kind of speculation raised in the early newspaper accounts. But the first explanation, a homicide to prevent testimony in a criminal case, seems more compelling even though it is not a certainty. The two possibilities are thus still *unsettled* even though the prosecutor has made a decision; however, it is clear that *neither* of the two described motives qualify as self-defense. *It does not seem likely that Faron's shooting death was a simple case of self-defense*, and in what follows, alternatives to the prosecutor's conclusions will be supported with relevant *information.*

The word *information*[a] is being used here rather than *evidence,* but those words are closely related. We may equate evidence with information in most situations, but how a court views *evidence* is not quite the same thing as the evidence of ordinary language; *i.e.,* a chemist would view evidence as "something that furnishes proof" (from Webster's Ninth New Collegiate Dictionary). And a court's evidence is also a type of information -- it furnishes proof. But a court will not necessarily accept information as evidence, even if it seems to be relevant from an ordinary citizen's point of view. The correct legal term is *admissible evidence.* Courts operate (theoretically) under a set of rules that decide if evidence is or is not admissible. With that distinction and limitation established, we also know of cases where the *information* that a court chose not to admit was later shown to be correct! Court errors of that type are well-documented and have led to countless appeals.[1] Then there is the problem of erroneous or inadequate police investigations. The way the Connecticut State Police handled the Barbara Gibbons murder in 1973[2] is a classical example of bad police work. Those kinds of situations undermine the validity of admissible evidence, and they are not uncommon.

Thus, the *information* a district attorney chooses *not to consider* and which was found outside of a police investigation *is not legal evidence.* This point is being made because the Durant Police and the prosecuting attorney certainly did not take into account all of the available *information* related to Faron's death, and by limiting what was considered from all that was actually available, *the conclusion was also restricted.* In any case, being too selective with information (e.g., a court's evidence or scientific data) rather that considering *everything relevant* is a formula for drawing wrong conclusions. At least in science one has to consider *all* of the available experimental evidence, even if some parts seem to disagree with the outcomes of other experiments, and especially if those results continue to be reproducible. In science, *everything* is on the table. It is not like that in a criminal case.

The issue of conflicting evidence brings to mind the analogy of the three blind men and an elephant; each had a different description of the animal because each one touched a different part of the elephant. This mind set of selectivity has been a significant source of legal failures, examples being convicted individuals who were later shown to be innocent on the basis of DNA evidence. It's even worse if politics gets into the process! And having been a scientist, the author can tell you that while science supposedly tries to avoid this kind of thing, it isn't always true. Scientists are not immune to the error. The tendency to jump to a conclusion without reference to *all* of the available information is a human trait.

Faron was the only *direct* witness to the murder of Tristan York, which happened in Durant in May of 2007. Bobby Don Mullinix and Charles Bussey took turns killing Tristan York; Faron was forced to watch the slaying. One semi-retired lawyer in the Mountain Home, Arkansas area suggested that in such cases as Faron's, the *priority* should have been "*the aggravated homicide of a prosecution witness*," which is a capital offense in most states (except perhaps Oklahoma, because he didn't know how Oklahoma viewed it). Bud, who killed Faron, might have been charged with murder in *other* places. A layman's reading of the Oklahoma Statutes indeed seems to indicate that the intentional death of a prosecution witness is counted as a case of "*aggravating circumstances.*" Statute 21-701.12.5. states that aggravating circumstances apply if "*The murder was committed for the purpose of avoiding or <u>preventing</u> a lawful arrest or <u>prosecution</u>*" [underlining was added for emphasis]. At least there should have been an overriding suspicion of that possibility. Do you turn a suspect loose if a reason for suspicion exists? Or should you go slowly until everything is carefully evaluated?

Based on a lifetime of teaching chemistry and conducting funded research projects the author knows enough about lab work to think that a thorough forensic analysis could not happen overnight. Would a month suffice? Probably not. Neither could a background investigation of the associations (meaning connections), prior addresses, prior criminal offenses, etc. That's the thing detectives do. One cannot help having the feeling that something is wrong; *the conclusions could have been premature.*

The question now changes to one of priority; do so-called self-defense shootings take priority over all other kinds of homicides in Oklahoma? If the Oklahoma castle law has a higher priority than aggravated homicides, then the state has created an ingenious way to murder people, including prosecution witnesses, and get away with it! Common sense suggests that the legislators who wrote the law had no such intentions.

Nevertheless, the Durant prosecutor released Bud on the same day that he shot Faron, and on the day of Faron's funeral, December 19, 2007, a police detective, Randall Cheney, told Rick that he believed it was a case of "self-defense." How could these officials come to such conclusions in so little time? *How could the prosecuting attorney describe Faron as a critical witness, enough so to require postponing Charles Bussey's murder trial to a later date, and yet assure the public that his death could not possibly be related to the earlier crime?* The York murder occurred in a drug-use, drug-trafficking situation, and the pre-trial transcripts show it very clearly. Murder is not uncommon among drug criminals. Faron knew who killed Tristan York but he was also aware of *other* criminal activities related to drug trafficking. *There certainly were motives (plural) for silencing him.* So the question thus remains: was Faron's shooting death actually a murder? Information that the Durant prosecutor chose to ignore and even some of the official evidence suggests that it might have been.

Faron's family has not retained an Oklahoma lawyer to pursue possible options, and it might be asked why that has not been done thus far. For one thing Faron's family has no confidence in the Oklahoma system of justice. Emily Redman and the other officials eradicated any vestige of confidence that might have existed. The family learned that such attempts would be a waste of time and money, *because the statute blocks appeals from the family if a homicide has been attributed to self-defense.* And, of course, Rick and the others are hardly wealthy; Rick is fully retired and lives on a fixed income. He has to worry about managing what little he has during what is left of his life. The necessary financial resources just aren't there. Have we reached the point where a questionable killing cannot be further investigated? If we have, then we're all in trouble. That kind of situation alone is a strong justification for a book of this type.

The official reports and their *evidence,* at least the parts that the family had access to,[b] contain what appear to be logical inconsistencies. Additional *information* gleaned from open sources begs to be considered, and *more is known than what is printed here.* What has been heard indirectly from other individuals is hearsay, but there *are* people out there who know a great deal about the one who killed Faron. *Their* accounts only reinforce the uneasy feeling. Some think he'll do it again, and one was surprised that his first victim wasn't a woman.

The following more detailed account of the incident is based mostly on what could be found *in writing* in the documented information sources, *including the official evidence*, to justify conclusions. Rick came to *believe* that *Faron was actually murdered*, but that is just his opinion. Belief is not the same as a proof.

Faron's homicide -- an in-depth account of what happened

First of all, there is a lot more detail here than you will find in a newspaper account of a shooting death. Some critics of the castle laws have voiced concern that apparently justifiable shootings might take on a different character if they were examined more carefully. The following serves as an example of why that might be true. More examples will come up later in this book.

The killing happened only five days before Faron's court date as a critical witness for the prosecution in the trials surrounding the murder of a man named Tristan York. The local news media probably knew that this was the case but portrayed the shooting as a lover's triangle rather than pay much attention to the death of a prosecution witness. The newspapers simply quoted an official statement from the prosecutor's office to the effect that Faron's death was "unrelated" to his status as a prosecution witness. Here is the essence of some of those articles, though the wording had to be modified a little to obscure some names. The word "murder" was used in the original *Durant Democrat* article. Underlining has been added for emphasis:

"*Saturday murder* ...

Early Saturday morning the Durant Police Department

responded to a shooting that resulted in a death.
According to the Police Chief, the shooting took place at
approximately 1 a.m. at a Durant residence. Faron
[surname omitted], 20, was left dead after the shooting.
Police cannot confirm how many times Faron was shot,
but five shell casings were found at the scene."

The article went on to say that the police were investigating
and looking for witnesses. Meanwhile, Bud was already free. A
following article in the *Durant Democrat*, published early-on
during the week following the shooting, noted that Faron had
been a prosecution witness but dismissed any notion that his
death was related to his status as a prosecution witness:

"Witness' death ...

The preliminary hearing for Charles Bussey, accused of
murdering Tristan York, has been postponed due to the
death of a witness. Bussey, along with Bobby Don
Mullinix, has been charged with the murder of York. Linda
Haworth was charged with accessory to murder. Faron,
20, who was shot to death in an unrelated incident early
Saturday morning, was a witness in the Bussey case.
Faron was involved in a 'love triangle' and was shot early

51

Saturday morning by Bud...who claims it was self defense..."

The article reported that the trial would have to be postponed. If Faron's shooting death was unrelated, then why was the trial postponed? The logic seemed absurd. The assistant prosecutor had noted that every witness was important. However, Faron was the *only direct witness* to York's murder, the one person beside the two killers who actually saw the killing. The journalist either didn't know that, or failed to point it out. The article raised the possibility of a love triangle. In some states the existence of a "love triangle" forces the issues of *probable provocations* and *motives other than self-defense,* which can lead to charges of murder. If you shoot someone out of jealousy, that's just plain murder. It's a miscarriage of justice if such crimes are allowed to be passed off as "self-defense."

A rumor went around the town, and neither Rick nor anyone with a bloodline relationship to Faron had started it. In fact, that story was not heard until the day of Faron's funeral, and it came from someone that Rick did not know well. That person had said that the five-day spacing between Faron's death and the trial preliminary "wasn't supposed to be out," that the knowledge was under a "gag order." And *that* was the rumor: *it was being hushed up.*

The rumor was hearsay. In hindsight, it didn't matter if Faron was shot to death one day or two months before his court date. The fact is simply that he was killed *before he could testify,* and putting numbers on the time line is not especially important, although it had a terrible impact on the family at first. You do not kill a prosecution witness with impunity. Many states (probably including Oklahoma) treat it as a capital offense; it's like killing judges, prosecuting attorneys and jurors. And in that news release the prosecutor's assistant, Timothy Webster, had gone on record to say that the trial preliminary had to be rescheduled because of the "death of a witness," meaning Faron, but it was also stated that his death was "*unrelated*" to the previous murder. Some of Durant's citizens probably raised an eyebrow when they read the article.

Rick's daughter was understandably outraged when she heard that Faron had been killed immediately before his court date. Rick was angered, too. Others knew about it and reacted similarly, but what could they do? Anyone who has lived in Durant for a few years has heard this remark: "You can kill someone in Durant or Bryan County and get away with it; just don't write a hot check!" The statement has a basis in fact even if you ignore Faron's death and consider all the *other homicides* that have taken place in that district![c] The natives have lived with this situation for a long time, and most of them are ashamed of the negative image thus created for their region.

In reading the rest of this account, bear in mind that it is hard to remember exactly what happened when a homicide has been witnessed. The military calls it *fog of war*. Ask ten G.I.s to describe the sequence of events of a shooting engagement with enemy forces, and you are likely to get ten different versions of how it went! Everyone is in a different location, and the mind's perception of time often becomes very distorted when violence is afoot.

Faron was not armed. He did not have a gun or a club or a knife when he went to Bud's place. Actually, that doesn't matter because of the wording of the Oklahoma statute. The armed citizen is given a license to shoot even if he *thinks* he's endangered and says so. It's acceptable to kill an unarmed intruder.

The door was opened to Faron. Bud made no effort to depend on locks and a call to 911. But of course, that apparently doesn't matter in Oklahoma because of the wording of their castle law. In another state it might get you prosecuted for causing a confrontation that resulted in a death. You could be charged with murder or perhaps manslaughter at the least. Granted, opening a door to danger is a very stupid thing to do even if you are armed, because it *can* backfire. Even well-trained police officers have been killed with their own guns after felons disarmed them.

Here is Bud's version of what happened. It comes from a police lieutenant's interview with Bud, which was a component of the final police report (it is transcribed verbatim, including typographical errors, etc.; but it uses the pseudonyms "Bud" and "Rose"):

"Bud opened the door. He observed Faron standing on the porch. Faron told him 'come out here and talk to me.' Bud told him no. Faron said 'No come out here and talk to me.' Bud said 'dude no, you need to leave.' Faron then asked 'What, do you have a gun back there or something?' Bud said, 'Yeah I have a gun, you need to leave.' Bud then exposed the gun, and then returned it to a hidden position. Faron then said, 'Where's Rose at?' Bud told him, 'dude she's asleep just leave you can talk to her in the morning.' "

Then, *according to Bud*, he gets knocked back, Faron barges in and Bud shoots Faron while he's trying to regain his footing. Accuracy suffers if you stumble while you are shooting, because your reflexes use your arms and legs to restore balance. His stated disbelief that Faron attacked after the gun was presented ignores the psychology of provocation because he told Faron that Rose (and by inference, his daughter) were present, which was fully provocative if he indeed said that. But with that provocation noted, the notion of someone barging into a house, unarmed, after a clear warning that the person inside was holding a deadly weapon, stretches credibility. It doesn't ring true. And of course, Faron is no longer around to tell us his own version of what happened.

The gun's "hidden position" is of interest. Maybe it was still in his right hand, held behind his back as before, but maybe he kept it closer to a ready position. Either way, that puts the door on Bud's right side, because from Bud's perspective, the door hinges were on his right. The Taurus .45 caliber automatic he used is said to be a double action compact semiautomatic, a little heavy on the first trigger pull, which works against good aim. That's a possible factor, but the distance was short. Faron was almost nose-to-nose with him and supposedly bearing down. An intelligent person would rather not be in that situation -- meaning in either Faron's *or* Bud's shoes. The outcome can go badly one way or the other. Did Bud actually put himself in that much danger, or did something else happen?

This is the part of the Oklahoma castle law that was apparently evoked in Faron's case; the law applies if the person defending fears death or great bodily harm:

"21-1289.25.B. A person [meaning Bud in this case] *is presumed to have held a reasonable fear of imminent peril of death or great bodily harm to himself or herself or another when using defensive force that is intended or likely to cause death or great bodily harm to another if: 1. The person against whom the defensive force was used was in the process of unlawfully and forcefully entering, or had unlawfully and forcibly entered, a dwelling, residence, or occupied vehicle, or if that person had removed or was attempting to remove another against the will of that person from the dwelling, residence, or occupied vehicle..."*.

But going to the door with a loaded gun in hand, *unlocking the door* and confronting an unarmed rival does not convey a convincing picture of a "*...reasonable fear of imminent peril of death or great bodily harm...*" If genuine fear were involved, the door would stay locked and the homeowner would call 911. Then, if the intruder broke in *before* the police arrived, a shooting in self-defense might be justifiable. That would be true even in Arkansas, for example. Arkansas doesn't have a full-fledged castle law, but it does allow a citizen to use deadly force against an armed intruder who breaks in. The existing Arkansas law expressly forbids actions that create a confrontation. There is wisdom in their law.

Faron was shot four times. Five spent .45 ACP cartridge casings were found at the scene; the Medical Examiner's report notes that four bullets actually hit Faron; two of those hits were inherently and rapidly fatal, and those two rounds lodged in Faron's body. Two more bullets struck him, one in his arm and another in his side. Those two were more peripheral; they went through-and-through and were not immediately life-threatening. *Multiple gunshots generally show anger and intent to kill, and Faron might have been shot after he fell to the floor -- there was a bullet in the floor.* Even so, a presumption of innocence prevailed, because the applicable statute requires it. Psychology and common sense are not considerations.

A neighbor, [name withheld], who lived close to the address of the shooting, heard the commotion and went to his window, where he saw the developing situation. Then he heard what he believed to be *"...gunshots fired rapidly."* This is quoted from what a police detective wrote in his case summary/time line report. It is found on page 17 of the final police report. That person's handwritten account of December 15, 2007 simply says

"...*I heard four or five shots fired.*" Presumably the "*fired rapidly*" came from further questioning. But another neighbor, [name withheld], said he heard four shots and then a fifth; the wording implied that the fifth came after a substantial delay. This difference between the accounts of two neighbors sounds like a *fog of war* effect, and it isn't surprising since people were being awakened from sleep by the kind of sounds no one wants to hear.

The story changes and has logical flaws. Bud claimed that Faron shoved the door into his face, bringing blood, but he also claims that he was looking around the edge of the door, so the door should have hit his shoulder -- inconsistent logic. In the original police report the story from Bud was that Faron *might* have hit him with his fist, and he had fired as he fell to the floor. It did not seem to bother the police that Bud's account was not quite the same in their initial and final reports.

The blood on Bud's face could have been Faron's. Bud claimed that he tried CPR on Faron, which brings up a serious conflict with the police and OSBI logic. Since two bullets went through Faron's lungs there was blood coming from Faron's mouth. About a year after the shooting one of the officers said that there were no photos of the blood on Bud's face (Rick's son-in-law had asked to see a photo.), although the initial police report noted that officers observed blood on Bud's face. A buccal swab was taken from Bud, presumably for DNA analysis. Nothing was said about a DNA sample from Faron or the blood on Bud's face, and considering the circumstances, that would have been the logical thing to do. But there is an excuse: Oklahoma is strapped for law enforcement funds; the state doesn't even offer witness protection!

The Medical Examiner did not mention anything about Faron's DNA. Did OSBI analyze his genetic material? How the authorities reached a conclusion that the blood was Bud's and not Faron's was not shared with Faron's family, and the sense was that the officials were hedging the issue and did not have any such evidence. That feeling might not have existed if they had seen all of the reports. Maybe a medical doctor actually confirmed that Bud had a split lip, but nothing of that kind is found in the information that the family was allowed to see.

The Oklahoma Medical Examiner stores biological specimens from all homicide victims, and they are kept for five years. Rick offered to pay to have Faron's preserved biological specimen submitted for *legal* DNA profiling, just to have the information on record for confirmation of paternity and in case the blood on Bud's face was actually sampled (and for any other reason that might come up). Faron's stored specimen was viable, and a certified sample of his DNA is now banked, *legally*, at a secure facility *outside of Oklahoma*. An unofficial paternity test of the child presumed to be his daughter, who was inside the house when the homicide took place, had this result: *"The alleged father* [Faron] *is not excluded as the biological father of the tested child."* The sixteen locus assay found a 99.998% probability of parentage.

A judge in Oklahoma City had ordered DNA testing of Faron's stored specimen. Rick does not believe that a Durant judge would have done that. Why would he go to such trouble and expense? The daughter has Faron's features, and Faron's family never doubted parentage. *Their position is that the test adds scientific validity to their belief that the child clause of Oklahoma's self-defense statute (1289.25) should have been applicable but was ignored*; more will be said about that. Unless OSBI obtained DNA evidence and didn't bother to tell the family, there is no such information for Faron on file other than the banking and profiling that the family paid for.

Rose said she saw blood on Bud's mouth after hearing the loud gunfire, when she came into the living room; she saw Faron dying on the floor and Bud was *backing away*. That might reinforce Bud's account. But was the blood from spatter or direct contact with Faron, or was it actually Bud's blood? The reports indicate that she and her toddler daughter were doing a lot of screaming, which is not hard to believe. Rose had just been caught up in a *second homicide* in less than a year! The mind tends to retreat into a primitive corner when such things happen. Time lines can become very distorted in that situation. It's the *fog of war* effect described earlier. It was recorded that Bud told Rose to call 911. While she's doing that he tries CPR on Faron. When the police arrive he tells them that he thinks he killed his "friend." It seems abundantly clear that Faron and Bud were mutual adversaries, and calling Faron a friend was strange.

It is also recorded in the final police report that one of Rose's cohorts, [a female, name withheld], reported that Rose told her on December 1, 2007, which was Faron's twentieth birthday, that Bud said he would make *her life* [meaning Rose's life] "...*a living hell and that she will want to leave Durant.*" Bud was angry because Rose had gone back to Faron's place "...*so that* [her daughter by Faron, name withheld] *could be close to her father.*" After Faron's birthday Bud dumped Rose's things in the Lowe's parking lot, where Faron later picked them up. There were thus clear indications that Bud was having serious hostility problems, or at least was putting on an act. Given all of this background of hostility, the police nevertheless accepted Bud's version of what happened on December 15, 2007. Killing someone out of jealousy does not qualify as self-defense, but what Bud was doing could also be construed as *manipulation*. It's hard to ignore that he killed a prosecution witness *before* the witness could testify.

There is no evidence that Faron actually hit Bud with his fist. The Medical Examiner's report notes that Faron's hands were bagged at the scene. No fresh contusions were found on either of his hands. Reading from the *external exam* of the ME Report [case number withheld], page 5 near the top: "*The left arm is noted to be intact and atraumatic. The hands also appear intact and atraumatic with exception of a callous overlying the dorsum of the left 2nd finger. In addition, there is some faint gray discoloration or deposit noted at the left thumb.*" It is noted that the door of Bud's residence was painted red at the time of the killing. Perhaps the gray discoloration came from the outward opening storm door or some other source external to that house or even the floor. Or was it a powder burn?

The term "callous" is used in the ME report, which is an adjective (as it might be used in a "callous remark" or a "callous decision"). This spelling appears to be a typographical error. Various medical dictionaries define a *Callus* as a kind of scar tissue, a thickening and hardening of the skin caused by frequent exposure to friction, use of tools, etc. A callus is thus an old scar, which is distinctly different from a fresh injury such as a cut or a contusion.

The essential point is this: if Faron struck Bud with his fist -- hard enough to knock him down -- then there would very likely have been a fresh wound on one of Faron's hands. Hitting someone in the mouth is especially likely to injure the hand that delivered the blow, because teeth are hard and sharp-edged. Faron was left-handed. That would put the door in the way because the door was hinged on the left-hand side as seen by someone entering the house.

There are probably several possible (equivocal) interpretations of the Medical Examiner's evidence, one of which is that Bud shot Faron while both were standing fully erect. The angle of the impacts around the vertical axis of Faron's body varied by perhaps 160 degrees, and only one of the four bullets that struck Faron followed a front-to-back path. Faron was hit four times, but the *order* of the impacts is not entirely clear from the available information. The bullet that involved his heart and aortic arch had a nearly level trajectory but went front to back and left to right; The impact point and the location of Faron's aorta indicates that Faron's left shoulder was turned toward Bud by about 20 to 30 degrees from head-on. Another bullet went through Faron's right flank near his waist, front to back and downward. Because of that path, Faron had to be facing Bud more or less head-on when the gun was fired; it could have been the first round fired because people usually face each other when they are arguing. However, it isn't a certainty. A bullet that entered the upper part of Faron's right arm went into his right lung, caused severe internal hemorrhaging and almost exited from his right back near the spinal column -- its trajectory was mostly right to left and downward. Faron's torso would have to be turned so that his right shoulder approximately faced Bud when that shot was fired. A fourth bullet went completely through Faron's right arm further down (but above the elbow), and it broke the humerus bone. That bullet grazed the right side of Faron's chest after exiting his arm, and it angled away *in front of him*; thus, it was fired with Faron's *back* presented to Bud. The approximate paths of the four impacting bullets are shown in the diagram on the following page.

These findings come from the Medical Examiner's report, and they show the dynamics of the shooting. Faron went down in a hail of gunfire. The apparent angle of fire varied by at least 140 degrees and perhaps as much as 160 degrees around the vertical axis, which assumes, of course, that Faron was not yet on the floor when all of the bullets hit him. Faron was either turning as he took the impacts or Bud was moving around him. Or was it a combination? Witnesses said that the shots were fired rapidly. This looks more like an execution or a fit of rage than a defensive shooting. Contrast this with a situation where a brute

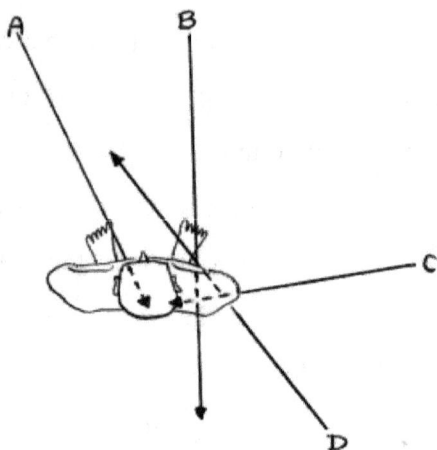

Bullet paths as seen from above Faron's head, looking straight down. This figure assumes that he was standing fully erect when all the bullets struck him, but he probably began to fall as the shots were fired. *The purpose of this figure is to show how much the angle of fire varied.* That angle is defined by a rotation of his body around an axis going from the top of his head to a point between his heels. Figure legends: A - Fatal heart/aorta shot, bullet did not exit; B - Non-fatal flank shot, going through-and-through; C - Fatal lung shot, bullet did not exit; D - Non-fatal backside shot that broke the right humerus and grazed the chest, going through-and-through.

is charging toward the one using the gun. The bullet impacts would be generally front to back in such a case.

The fired round that involved Faron's heart and aorta had a left to right, front to back and slightly downward trajectory. The skin around the bullet's entry point showed indications of a close-up shot. The final police report buys into Bud's claim that he fired as he fell or stumbled backwards. But there are physiological reflexes in such a fall, and it is not known if they were taken into account. The claim doesn't seem to fit the available evidence, because if Faron had been on his feet and Bud was on the floor (or on his way down) the bullet that hit Faron's heart should have had a distinctly upward trajectory through Faron's chest, which does not agree with the Medical Examiner's evidence. Faron was 6' 1" while Bud stands 5' 8" (these were the measurements in the police and medical examiner's reports), and if Bud had held the gun straight out from his right shoulder while standing fully erect, it would have been pointing on a level path to Faron's heart, give or take a little -- consistent with what was observed during the autopsy. In other words, the bullet path could have been slightly downward, level or slightly upward (depending on Bud's exact shoulder height and the bullet's impact point). Slightly downward is consistent with the ME's findings. These conclusions came from measurements using scaled anatomical templates.

It's hard to get a downward bullet trajectory if the one being shot is still standing and the shooter is nearer to the floor. Supposing that Faron was *lunging* toward Bud when the shot was fired (which would tilt his chest toward the gun), then a level or downward bullet path *could* take place, but if that had been the situation, Faron's body would have ended up closer to Bud (who was said to be behind the door), most likely with his head toward that position. That was not what happened. If you stood at the door looking straight into the house, Faron would have been to the right, with his head at the 2-o'clock position (12-o'clock being straight ahead). Faron's head was thus found away from Bud's stated shooting position, and his feet were toward Bud.

The muzzle energy of a .45 caliber bullet is significant, 350 foot-pounds or more, depending on the properties of the cartridge used, but contrary to what a lot of people think, it is *not* able to knock a man over like a bowling pin. While the bullet from a .45 automatic is well known for its *shocking power*, its *shock effect* derives from tissue destruction, bleeding and pain, not an ability to hurl a human body across a room.[d] Thus, if Faron had been lunging toward Bud when he was shot he would have fallen in the direction of motion, head approximately toward 8-o'clock.

The reflexes of Bud's stumble cannot be ignored. First of all, if we stumble backward there are reflex actions to consider, and *they work against shooting accuracy.* It is instructive to watch videos of actual falls. When an adult stumbles the knees and hip joints tend to flex at both ends of the femur. This is also what a barely-walking toddler does when balance is lost in the backward direction; the child usually lands on its butt rather than the back of its head! In the case of older children and adults the arms are more involved; they are moved in appropriate directions (up, down, front, back, right or left -- however is necessary) to regain balance when a tipping point is approached, but the hands tend to go downward to break the fall when balance is fully lost in the backward direction. It's a common way to get a fractured wrist. It takes a great deal of self-control to override the reflexes of a fall. A lot of individuals would be on the floor before shooting with any accuracy could begin. It is suspected that Bud was never on the floor, and if there was a stumble, it was minimal. Four of five shots fired actually hit Faron. Were these realities taken into consideration?

The slightly downward bullet path of the heart shot seems much more likely *if* both Bud and Faron were standing. If Bud had actually aimed the gun the trajectory might have been even more downward, because aligning the sights to the eye-to-target line would require bringing the gun up a little and tilting the barrel downward (e.g., the head is higher than the shoulder). However, at near contact distances handgun shooters simply point and pull the trigger. Also, the room was darkened so that there was probably more light coming through the door from the streetlight than from the house's interior. The ME evidence indicates that the heart shot was fired with the gun's muzzle close to Faron's chest. It could have been the *first shot fired*. But how does that square with the other shots being from a greater distance and the witnessed "shots fired rapidly?" If it was the *last shot fired* it would have followed the impact of a second fatal bullet, one that hit Faron's right shoulder and went into his right lung, causing severe hemorrhaging. The angle of those two fatal shots differed by more than 90 degrees. Both of those bullets remained inside of Faron's body. Faron was apparently found face up on the floor, so it makes you wonder if Bud moved toward Faron as he shot and was standing beside him when he fired the heart shot. If Faron was already on the floor when the heart shot was fired it was an execution. *There is no way to prove or disprove that possibility, because the bullet didn't exit Faron's body and hit a wall or the floor and thus give some indication of its true path.* Neighbors apparently heard a rapid succession of gunshots, but one neighbor heard "...about four gunshots go off...," then a long delay -- long enough for Faron's friends to leave the yard, drive away in their truck and then return -- before he heard what he thought was a fifth shot; this comes from page five of the first police report.

There are several other *equivocal* interpretations. A*ll kinds of trajectories were possible.* Thus, one is justified in wanting to know how the police and OSBI pruned their way through those possibilities. The author's career was highly technical, but he has no *official* capacity to question the police and OSBI reports. It is his belief that an *impartial* forensic scientist would see problems in the way that the evidence was *interpreted.* Perhaps access to *all of the official evidence* would modify the picture. Based on what *is* available, the conclusions stated above are not unreasonable. The discrepancies pointed out are disturbing.

The police were puzzled by a .45 cal round found in the floor. The police did not tell the family where all of the bullets went. Five empty .45 caliber cartridge casings were found on the floor. Two bullets stayed in Faron's body and one was *in* the floor. Where did the other two go? The family was not provided with that information, but it could have been on the censored pages of the final police report, the ones they did not receive. They were curious to know why *any part* of the evidence was withheld from them.

Nothing has been made clear about the destination of the two through-and-through bullets. The *search warrant return* describes the homicide weapon as a Taurus Millennium Pro

71

PT745C. It fires the .45 caliber ACP cartridge, the same cartridge used in the 1911 Army Colt .45 automatic pistol and the Thompson and M-3 submachine guns used by American forces during World War II. On one page the police record simply says that one bullet found in the floor wasn't one that hit Faron, with no justification given. Did forensics check it for tissue and blood? By that description two more bullets remain to be accounted for, and *where* they might have ended up is very significant information that should be taken into account. But the numbers given in the reports are confusing, because another police officer describes *two* recovered projectiles (bullets), five empty .45 caliber shell casings and two unfired .45 caliber cartridges (found in the gun's magazine; Bud didn't empty the magazine).

Do the simple math again: five rounds were fired, four bullets hit Faron. The ME report says two of the bullets stayed inside Faron's body. Thus three of the bullets ended up somewhere outside of Faron's body. Two of those ought to have Faron's tissue on them. If the first account is correct, then only one of those three bullets has been accounted for -- i.e., in the floor. The second account, the *search warrant return*, describes two bullets recovered without saying where they came to rest. Were those the missing two? Or was the one in the floor included in the count? Did one or both of those two through-and-through bullets come close to hitting Rose or her daughter? Did one or both go through a window, or were they found in a wall? If even one bullet ended up "...*in the floor...*" the gun had to be pointing downward when it was fired. And if it didn't go through Faron's body (thereby giving up a significant part of its original muzzle energy) it ought to have penetrated deep into the floor, or even gone through the floor boards and ended up in the soil beneath the house. Why shouldn't the family know those details?

A photo of that house with a red door -- where Faron was killed -- was obtained from Faron's family. The photo was taken from the street, and it shows the west side of the house and especially a portion of the brick foundation wall. A vent is clearly visible in that foundation, and that tells us that the house is a pier and beam structure; it has a wooden floor. The author was moved to try an experiment. Some boards and a small square of carpet material were taken to a shooting range. It would have been better to use a Taurus compact .45 automatic, but the author did not own one, nor did he know someone who would loan one. He used the handgun available to him, a .32 long revolver. Handguns accommodating the .32 Smith and Wesson long cartridge were carried by New York City police during the early part of the 20th century. Premium Remington-

Peters round nosed, bare lead bullets were shot into sandwiches of wood and carpet. A sandwich consisting of a very hard 7/8 inch thick oak board laid over an aged (resinous) plank of 3/4 inch thick yellow pine is comparable to what you might find in a hardwood floor (i.e., a sub-floor of pine overlaid with oak). The lead .32 bullet had more penetrating power than was expected; it almost made it through the sandwich! The bullet's relatively small diameter no doubt enhances penetration. The back side of the pine board was splintered, and the bullet was within a quarter inch of full penetration; but the bullet was thoroughly deformed. With the carpet in place (on top) the bullet went through the carpet and the oak board and gouged into the pine board only about a quarter inch. These shots were fired at a downward angle of about 70 degrees. You have to be careful shooting into hard wood because a bullet can actually ricochet.

What is the point? The ME report indicates that the .45 caliber bullets that hit Faron were metal jacketed (domed "yellow metal," not the gray of lead), thus less likely to deform than bare lead. A bullet that keeps its shape is better at penetrating. The .32 long is certainly not a powerful gun compared with a .45 automatic. An old ballistic table records that the .32 long ought to penetrate four standard boards of 7/8 inch thick *soft* white pine. In comparison, the same table notes that the .45 caliber cartridge that Bud used on Faron will penetrate *six* of those soft white pine boards. Thus, it's possible that the gun that killed Faron might have shot right through a hardwood floor, carpet and all. But according to the lady who owned the home, only a little square of carpet had been cut out. The police report simply noted that a bullet was found *in* the floor. That's different than saying "we removed a bullet from the soil under the crawl space." If it wasn't the latter, then perhaps *something* slowed the bullet down, and one has an idea of what that might have been. The test presumed that Bud's house had a hardwood floor. If the top layer of the flooring was not of hardwood then it is likely that even a .32 Smith and Wesson long bullet would have penetrated it.

The pages of the final police report that were withheld from Faron's family were as follows: page 16 (from the time line), pages 20-30 (the full crime scene investigation), pages 43-49 (shooting incident reconstruction) and pages 85-87 (emergency medical services). Until it is shown otherwise, there is a strong feeling that the forensic evidence is incomplete.

Bud's stalking around Faron's home prior to the shooting (e.g., starting at about the time of Faron's birthday, two weeks earlier) was witnessed by several individuals, and there were multiple stalking events. The officials ignored those facts. Bud allegedly "dreamed" that he killed Faron before he actually killed him. Earlier on the night of the shooting (i.e., on the evening of December 14, 2007), Bud dined with Rose and told her that he'd had a dream that he killed Faron. According to Rose, he told her this about six hours before he actually killed him. Rose wrote it down in a kind of statement, in *her own cursive handwriting.* Rick keeps a photocopy of that document, and its transcript, set in cursive fonts, is as follows:

"Three or four days after Faron's birthday Bud came to Faron's residense in [the location is omitted], demanding to talk to me. I went outside to avoid a confrontation, Faron followed me & I told him to go back inside. Bud yelled an obsenity towards Faron & he just walked in the house, as in Faron. Then Bud asked me questions like are we broke up, why are you going back to Faron & so forth. I asked him to leave, he wouldn't, so I had to force him to his van. And he drove off yelling something at me & Faron at the door. Weeks later he asked me if I knew that he had a gun w/him?! The following morning he came to Lowe's where I work & dropped my T.V., clothes, furniture, etc. in the parking lot. Management made him leave, & Faron came to get it all @ 6:45 that morning."

"Dec 14th, 2007 Bud asked me to go out to dinner w/him. I agreed to talk to *him. Over dinner he told me something very bizarre. He told me about this dream he had, & in this dream he killed Faron. I would also like to add that he was drinking that night.*

Rose ..."

Square brackets show where text was omitted, because it contained a specific location. Rose used several abbreviations when she composed the letter. The letter had originated on April 14, 2008. It was later taken to an Oklahoma notary, where it received the seal and the notary's signature. Rose verified and signed the statement on May 1, 2008. Although a Notary Public witnessed and put her seal on it, the document has no legal value. The statement was apparently not "admissible" in the way lawyers view evidence, because Emily Redman received a copy of it and did nothing. It is offered here only as relevant *information.*

On the other hand, the cursive handwriting points to a specific writer. In another setting -- in an actual murder trial -- a statement of this type might be inculpatory if it could be allowed as evidence. A cross examination might go like this: Q. *"Did you actually write this statement?"* W. *"Yes."* Q. *"Do you say that what you wrote is the truth?"* W. *"Yes."* Q. *"Are you sure that you heard him claim that he was armed with a gun when he went to Faron's home?"* ...and so forth.

But there was no trial in Faron's case; by evoking the castle law the district attorney was able to circumvent a trial! There is no doubt that the hostile incident actually took place, because *others* witnessed it; in fact, there was much talk about it. It was highly relevant, yet the authorities simply ignored Rose's statement.

Perhaps we shouldn't make too much of Bud's alleged dream, and a psychologist might be more curious about Rose's *motive* for making a written record of the incidents than the details. As for the *content* of the record, if Rose's account is true, *then Faron's death was in Bud's mind only a few hours before he actually killed him!* This raises questions about premeditation. The so-called "dream" could have been Bud's fantasy, i.e., not an actual dream while sleeping but something made up, because he indeed displayed (or feigned) jealousy about Rose and her prior relationship with Faron. Either way -- dream or fantasy -- it is not something to casually ignore.

The statement also alleges that Bud claimed that he went to Faron's home with a gun. That happened during the two-week period immediately preceding Faron's shooting death, and his presence at Faron's home *was witnessed by family members,* probably even by neighbors. Faron's grandmother was one of those witnesses -- she owns the home where Faron lived. She wasn't alone in being aware of Bud's presence in her neighborhood; he would drive by slowly, and on one occasion she came home and found him parked in front of her place in a white van. When he saw her coming up behind him he took off. She was there when the heated confrontation between Bud, Rose and Faron happened. So even if Rose recants what she wrote, it still remains that Bud's stalking at Faron's place was observed by *others.* The plurality is emphasized, and Rose and Faron are not in that count of "others."

One consultant asked this question: "Is it possible that the rest of Rose's story is fabricated?" If she did that it raises serious questions about validity of her testimony during the two trials related to Tristan York's murder. Her entanglement in *two* homicides is not an enviable situation. She might even be charged as an accomplice if a court ever reconsiders the presumption of Bud's innocence for Faron's homicide.

Faron's shooting death was not a clear-cut case of self-defense, and it is the kind of powder keg that can go off at any time. Cases that were closed too quickly are not uncommon. For example, a recent shooting spree in Alabama left three university colleagues dead and others injured. This focused attention on the alleged shooter, Amy Bishop, because she had been involved in an earlier incident in Massachusetts. She had shot and killed her own brother in 1986, but the incident had been attributed to an "*accident.*" Now the 1986 tragedy is being re-examined, because a political fix might have been involved (see reference 22 of chapter 10).

Bud's demeanor during those encounters at Faron's home fits the definition of *hostile stalking.* At least that part of Rose's statement agrees with what the *others* witnessed. There were several incidents, and the one described in Rose's statement had been aggressive on the part of Bud (not Faron), with abusive language. Rose also claimed that Bud was drinking on the night that he shot Faron, but Faron was drinking, too, based on the Medical Examiner's findings. In some states intoxication of the shooter would have been taken into consideration. All of these things seem to indicate a situation "...*with malice aforethought...,*" which comes from the Oklahoma Statute defining murder (21-701.7.A).

But the Durant police and the district attorney refused to

consider Rose's statement about the drinking or the witnessed stalking incidents; the response to Rick's daughter was of this type: "It was Faron that stalked Bud." They had it backward. Bud *provoked* Faron. Maybe the written statement was simply *inconvenient* because of decisions already made.

Do we just ignore the things that are not favorable to the shooter? Perhaps that's the presumption of innocence working, although it is nothing more than legalistic nonsense to the ordinary citizen. Why would the DA let this go by? One possibility comes from the simple fact that the disposition of such a case is even easier than plea-bargaining -- if you evoke the castle law. One of the lawyers consulted wondered about Emily's *motive.*

The dream remark reinforced the family's belief that Faron's homicide was a *premeditated* murder. There were other reasons for suspecting murder, not the least being that Faron was killed immediately before his court date, and of course, Bud had been shadowing Faron's home for about two weeks. Faron had been involved with drugs and could have testified against criminals operating in the Texoma region, not just Charles Bussey and Bobby Don Mullinix but *others.*

Bud has a criminal record. On December 19, 2007, the day of Faron's funeral, Rick told Durant detective Randall Cheney

82

that the odds were good that Bud used drugs, because he knew that Rose and Faron had been hanging out with people who were involved with drugs, notably meth and marijuana. The detective replied that he hadn't found a criminal record for Bud, so it wasn't an issue to consider. Rick did not believe the detective, so he went looking through court records in Texas and Oklahoma.

The detective's statement was erroneous, because a search of those records found that Bud had been busted for possession of marijuana, and that happened in Highland Village near Lewisville, a city north of Dallas, Texas. The cause record was located with surprising ease through the Denton County Criminal Court II website, but its file number is withheld because it reveals Bud's real name. The cause record is *public information,* and no access fee is required. The date of birth, physical description, and middle name found in the court record were in agreement with *other open source information* about Bud, along with what was recorded in the Durant police reports. It was the same Bud that killed Faron. Are we to believe that a police detective could not locate a prior criminal offense? The task ought to be easier for a detective than ordinary citizens.

Bud's offense was a misdemeanor -- not a heavy crime, but it certainly shows that he has flirted with drugs. It doesn't prove that he was involved with illegal drugs or drug trafficking in

2007, but it certainly does not prove that he was clean. There may be other information about him out there. For example, if he used methamphetamine or even alcohol excessively and ran into toxic effects, a medical doctor might have ordered a comprehensive metabolic panel. That's highly privileged information, and it might be overlooked unless a police detective were tenacious enough to go looking for it with court orders in hand. It is not the kind of thing that a citizen investigator could find without doing something illegal.

The use of marijuana has been so trivialized in recent years that it is almost accepted as a given. A lawyer thought that prior criminal offenses *should be relevant* to any homicide case but noted that the rules of evidence often excludes them. Rule 404 of the Federal Rules of Evidence places a strong restriction on the use of prior convictions in portraying the character of a defendant while making it easy to impugn the character of a witness. Even if Federal Rule 404 or a closely comparable rule is applicable in Oklahoma, it would most likely be used to *exclude* the character evidence. That's what we've come to. So even though Rick's intuition and his comment to the detective had been correct, it has little value in today's courts.

Bud looks very *protected* in all of this. Of course. That's the presumption of innocence at work. But there could be more here than a mindless application of the Oklahoma castle law. If *you* had shot a prosecution witness under the same conditions, would *you* expect to be turned loose right away? Or would you worry about being prosecuted for murdering a witness? That such a situation could exist at all is yet another example of how we protect homicidal individuals.

Faron had been a drug user, but he stopped using meth after the York killing and actually held a job almost until the time of his death. A photo of Faron taken on his daughter's birthday in the fall of 2007 shows clearly that he had lost the emaciated look of meth abuse. He had been working out again, getting his body back into shape. In Rick's final handwritten letter from his grandson, Faron described his rehab status. Rick responded: "*It's the best news I've heard in a long time.*" But hope for a better future was forever shattered on December 15, 2007.

The word "murder" was used selectively. On the day of Faron's funeral, December 19, 2007, Durant detective Randall Cheney told Rick that Faron's shooting death was probably a case of self-defense; yet on December 21, 2007 -- two days later -- that same detective used the word "*murder*" in his application to the court for a warrant to obtain phone records. Those documents, which requested records for several cell phones, contain this wording: "...*the victim Faron... had contact with*

Rose just prior to his murder using his cell phone..." [underline added for emphasis]. It seems likely that the detective had to portray it as a murder in order to be allowed access to the phone records. If it wasn't the truth the request for a court order was in conflict with the Fourth Amendment: "*...no warrants shall issue, but upon probable cause...*" If you tell a judge "I have probable cause because my evidence points to a murder" while telling others "I don't think it was a murder," then you are being dishonest. Imagine telling the judge: "I don't have reason to believe it was a murder, but I want to see their phone records, anyway."

What the Oklahoma Castle Law says about "children or grandchildren" being present at a shooting scene was simply ignored. Faron's daughter by Rose was *inside* Bud's residence when the shooting took place. In the initial police report Bud acknowledged the child's presence and said that Faron was her father (page five of the initial police report). Rose also acknowledged that the toddler she was holding was Faron's child (page six of the initial police report). Oklahoma's 1289.25 has this wording:

"C. The *presumption* set forth in subsection B of this section does not apply if - 2. *The person or persons sought to be removed are children or grandchildren, or are otherwise in the lawful custody or under the lawful guardianship of, the person against whom the defensive force is used...".* Was that in Faron's mind? Did he intend to remove her? Apparently he did.

Several states with strong self-defense laws have a child clause because a child can be used to lure a parent into a trap, but the probable official response will be that the daughter was in the home with her mother, who wasn't actually married to Faron. Thus, Faron was not recognized *legally* as the father even though he *was* her biological father. The child's presence was considered *irrelevant* to Faron's motive for coming to the home. *But the reality is that they were mutually bonded as father and daughter.* Here is another example of how *legality* and *reality* can follow totally different paths. We live in the 21st century. Biochemists can profile our DNA and determine who belongs to whom. Similarly, a psychologist can observe a child interacting with its parent and tell you if mutual bonding exists. At the same time a court official can disregard all of that; the unwed mother is the only *legal* parent. A trap is nonetheless possible.

Rick received a letter from his daughter, and it contained this: "*I have heard (and not verified) but one of the women I went to school with heard a girl, who was sitting behind her at Faron's funeral talking about that night* [when Faron was killed]. *She says she was there too and that he went to get his baby...this message I relayed to Cheney. He said he'd check it out. Whether he did or not I don't know."* Apparently he didn't. Others seemed to know about Faron's reason for going to Bud's place that night. Someone who signed "Julie" sent this comment to the KXII TV website:

"If they knew Faron was coming over why didn't they just call the police? The girl involved had been seeing both men. Faron has a little girl with the girl [meaning Rose] *and he went to get his kid."*

There were still others who said Faron went to get his child. Emily's decision to ignore C.2. was arbitrary in some minds. Moral intuition says that the parent/child relationship *should be* a strong consideration, and it is *relevant* no matter what a district attorney thinks the law requires or allows. Only a few states have an explicit child restriction in their self-defense laws.

From Faron's perspective, learning that his girlfriend and daughter were at Bud's place must have seemed as if Bud had said to him, *"Look, I have control over them."* That's outright provocation, considering the circumstances; Rose and the child had been staying at Faron's home for *two weeks*, then suddenly, without giving a reason or even notice, she's back with Bud. Any normal man would want to know where the mother and child were. Apparently Faron was asking if anyone knew where they were and someone told him.

Killing a parent in the presence of a child is a diabolical act, and there was no pre-existing condition, certainly not a restraining order, to suggest that Faron shouldn't be with his own daughter. Even Rose thought Faron should have access to his daughter. The writers of Oklahoma's 1289.25 might as well have omitted the child exception. Some of the outrages that happened during World War II are comparable. A case known to the author was a blond-headed Estonian boy who was forced to watch as his parents were executed by a Nazi firing squad. The incident left its mark on him, for life. As it happened, he later immigrated to America, and the author knew him as a friend.

In the letter Rick received from his daughter it was also written that "*Rose said she* [Faron's daughter] *even tried to crawl onto Faron* [after Faron was shot] *and she* [Rose] *had to pull her off him.*" Faron's daughter was more than a year old at the time of the homicide, and she will very likely remember the deafening gunfire and the screaming. Those are the kinds of memories that persist over long stretches of time. More than a year after the shooting a Fourth of July incident witnessed by the family may have been a manifestation of that trauma. The child was utterly terrified by the sound of firecrackers going off. The noise sent her running into the arms of an adult, where she held on tightly and hid her face, trembling.

Were the daughter and Rose the bait that lured Faron to his death? It is a very strong possibility considering that Faron was a subpoenaed prosecution witness, and Rick knew his grandson well enough to think that his grandson's daughter was at least *a reason*, if not his *main reason*, for going into that house; more likely it was *the primary reason.* If it was a trap, it worked. Rose described Faron as a good father, and others agreed. Faron had a tattoo of his daughter's name down the back of his left arm. The tattoo was sketched in the Medical Examiner's report, and Rick has a shallow angle photograph of it. The two, the father and daughter, were close.

Faron and Rose had their daughter out of wedlock, but they were planning to marry and were still together at the time of the York murder. Afterward they broke up, and Rose became involved with Bud, allegedly having met him at Lowe's where they both worked. Faron and Rose were together again from December 1, 2007 until Faron's death two weeks later. Faron was born on December 1, 1987, and Rose brought their daughter to his 20th birthday party. Ostensibly, she came back to Faron because she believed he should have access to his own daughter (that stated reason is found in the final police report), *but was it the beginning of a set-up? Was she threatened into doing it?*

"Do it or else...; you owe us!" She was actually living at Faron's place during those final two weeks. Then the situation changed, abruptly. Why was she at Bud's house on the night of the killing? Were Rose and her daughter the bait, *knowingly or unknowingly,* that lured Faron to Bud's place?

Rose's webpage has a sort of shrine to Faron's memory, and the rear window of her car has this lettering: *"In loving memory of Faron..."*. Such displays suggest that she feels some guilt for his death. Perhaps that was also the motive for the written statement about Bud's stalking, but a fear of ostracism or exposure rather than an ingrained sense of right and wrong could be involved. *Rose and Bud parted on the day Faron was killed.*

Rose was a major factor in Faron's death, on a level comparable to Bud's part in the killing. She followed a wild crowd -- lost friends to reckless driving accidents even before Tristan York's murder. People who are involved with drugs and alcohol certainly do borrow trouble. Rose's use of marijuana and methamphetamine is clearly stated in the sworn testimony of the murder trial preliminary hearings, but Faron abused drugs, too.

Faron is not around to say *why* he went to Bud's house. There is no doubt that he was quite angry after he was told where Rose and his daughter were, and who wouldn't be under the circumstances? Bud had already been taunting him for two weeks. Maybe that was the desired *effect*, because *anger can be a tool for manipulating people.* It certainly got Faron into a totally compromised situation. The situation that existed on the night of the killing looks like a trap. Bud took up a relationship with Rose not long after the York murder, then tried to provoke a confrontation with Faron during the final two and a half weeks before the trial preliminary. There *were* visible motives related to the York murder, and the plausibility of a set-up is thus not easily dismissed by a rational mind.

During those last two weeks of Faron's life, Bud gave at least the appearance of being intensely jealous. At one point he dumped the things that Rose had left at his place. He took them to the Lowe's parking lot and threw them on the pavement. He thus created an ugly scene, and Lowe's management had to send him away. But Bud was no longer working at Lowe's when he did that, having taken up with a carpet cleaning business. Faron drove to Lowe's and retrieved Rose's things, but some of the items were damaged beyond repair. Bud also came to Faron's residence during that two-week period, showing considerable hostility. Later he would tell Rose that he had carried a gun with him during one of those visits. These incidents show a clear pattern of hostility.

Although the events described here actually happened, they

were disregarded by the police and the prosecutor even though the information was brought to their attention. Even the Oklahoma statutes probably would have required charging Bud with manslaughter or murder if it had been established that he bore malice toward Faron and had stalked him before he actually killed him. This shunning of information causes Rick to believe that the prosecutor did not intend to charge Bud from the very beginning. What the prosecutors *didn't do* overshadows the police report discrepancies. But why?

The prosecutorial staff can infer whatever it pleases, and of course, there is that overriding presumption of innocence which supposedly puts the burden of proof upon the prosecutor. Deciding for a homicide in self-defense under Oklahoma's castle law gets an easier disposition than plea-bargaining or a full-blown trial! *"He got himself killed and created a heavier workload for us."* Was it something like that? Someone who commented on the KXII TV website had a similar explanation: *"I am so afraid that because Faron has gotten into some trouble with the law* [previously] *that they automatically assume*[d] *the worst. He DIDN'T deserve to be killed..."*. In other words, his case may have been brushed aside because the police and the court thought he was a nuisance. He had indeed been in trouble but not for the kind of crime that puts someone in a hospital or a casket. He spent time at a juvenile detention center in Manitou, Oklahoma. One of the allegations leveled against him was later shown to be false, although the court refused to reconsider it.

There was yet another possibility. A friend who was familiar with the situation thought that a prosecution of Faron's killer would complicate the district attorney's case against Charles Bussey and Bobby Don Mullinix for the murder of Tristan York. Rose was present at *both* of the homicide scenes, and she had close ties to two of the killers, Charles Bussey and Bud. There were other possible connections, and Rose was the mother of Faron's child. If much attention had been focused on Faron's homicide, Rose's credibility as a witness in the upcoming murder trials would have been seriously challenged. The two homicides *were* entangled, and the statement from an assistant prosecutor describing them as "unrelated" is not believed. His statement could have been an attempt to keep the two homicides well separated. But in the end even the Bussey and Mullinix murder trials were resolved by plea bargaining.

Whatever happened in Faron's case, the decision will always be subject to questions. There are too many loose ends, and in the long run the most damaging may be Bud's stalking and the presence of Faron's daughter at his homicide scene. It looks as if the spirit of a law was disregarded.

Don't be surprised; court decisions like this happen all the time. Maybe you are watching too many TV programs like CSI, Law and Order and NCIS; they are meant for entertainment and are not altogether realistic.

It seems likely that the outcome of the case was decided from day one, because there is no indication that Bud had to make bond before he left Oklahoma. The reason for handling it that way remains unknown, although some possibilities were just cited. To make sense of it, we would have to know the actual motive of the prosecutor (and that's how one lawyer put it), but we are not mind readers. The prosecutor can say, *"The castle law made me do it."* That would sound like a weak excuse to many individuals. Were they obscuring something deeper? It even makes one wonder about drug-related corruption, although there is no proof of it.

A complaint against Emily Redman's actions was sent to the Oklahoma Bar Association (OBA), and it was rejected. The wording of the OBA reply to Rick's letter was as follows:

"We have received your complaint against the above-referenced attorney.

Thank you for bringing this matter to our attention.

However, it is our opinion that we are not in a position to resolve this matter for you.

The Office of the General Counsel addresses grievances alleging attorney conduct which violates the Oklahoma Rules of Professional Conduct. Although the conduct of an attorney may seem inappropriate to you, it may not necessarily constitute a violation of the Rules of Professional Conduct.

We will take no further action in this matter at this time."

The hope and expectation held by Rick and the others (including Faron's mother and his close friends) had been that this case would be re-examined by *impartial investigators* who had no relationships with *any* of the police officials or the prosecuting attorneys in the Durant district. It was stressed that there was a need for an impartial review, because those who investigated this homicide certainly did not take all of the available information into account and also because the shooting was described as a homicide in self-defense, literally from the day of the shooting, without sufficient time for a careful analysis of the facts to be accomplished. In other words, there was a suspicion that a nominal investigation was used to support the prosecutor's original action but that the case had been closed, *de facto*, from the very beginning.

Right after the killing Rick was moved to pay a lawyer to look into possible ways of appealing Faron's case, but that lawyer's efforts came to a dead end. Rick no longer lives in Oklahoma, and the lawyer he paid to look into the possibilities was not licensed to practice in Oklahoma; that was an understanding from the beginning -- it was to be advice and nothing else. The lawyer's efforts were thoroughly stonewalled! The assistant attorney general contacted, Joel-lyn McCormick, did not have the courtesy to answer the lawyer's letters at first, although he kept writing to her for nearly a year. Finally he got a reply, but *that* letter did not acknowledge and address the questions asked! Silence has been the typical response from Oklahoma officials, although there have been a few exceptions.

There is good reason to believe that Bud was not put under much scrutiny. Those who knew where he went claimed that he was in Texas by sundown on December 15, 2007, so the decision to turn him loose must have been made in record time if that had been the actual case! This alone is a good reason for believing that the way Oklahoma is applying its castle law is seriously flawed.

All self-defense laws need safeguards, and a safeguard may be defined as a set of criteria that restricts justifiable shootings to those motivated *only by self-preservation*, where no other possible motives exist. These criteria will be addressed in chapter 3 and again in chapter 10. Some states indeed have safeguarding criteria; Oklahoma's self-defense statute is more vague. Courts play around with poorly written laws. If Faron's death was an actual murder passed off as self-defense, then we may be sure that it will not be the only one in Oklahoma or any other state that has a deficient self-defense law.

Even if the law is well-written there is a problem. There have been recent cases in Texas where the prosecutors failed to follow the wording of the law, and a legislator who drafted the law is now saying that what happened wasn't what was intended. Safeguards are needed to protect innocent citizens *from* the courts, but what do you do if a prosecutor or a judge simply ignores a safeguard? They seem to do it frequently.

A court that overlooks a probable murder fails to protect law-abiding citizens. A murderer turned loose is encouraged to think he is invincible.

The earliest newspaper report called Faron's shooting death a *murder*, then the story changed. We are thus left with many haunting questions. Was Faron shot to prevent his testimony in the Tristan York murder trials? Did a drug syndicate go after him? Or was it because of a love triangle -- a grudge killing? What sort of information was there on those pages kept from the family? Regardless of the official position, which holds that Faron's death was not related to the York murder, there are facts that point in the *other direction*. The circumstances of the York murder will be taken into account in the next chapter. It is very much a part of Faron's story.

END NOTES -- Chapter 1

a. One definition of information from the sciences is that *information causes a removal of uncertainty* when living beings, electronic devices or machines *process it*. Information is a physical phenomenon. The information in DNA determines what the embryonic organism will *become* -- i.e., certainty is introduced. After considering *new* information, perhaps from reading a book or a letter, you will know more than you did before your mind processed it -- *uncertainty will be removed*. Or in that other way of saying it, you are more certain about something. The symbolic information in a tabulation of DNA fragment characteristics that shows a probable maternity relationship between a woman and her daughter is an example of the removal of uncertainty; a person's fingerprints may also be reduced to symbolic information. If they match the prints found at a crime scene the uncertainty of that person's presence or absence is removed.

The entropy of mathematical information theory has a somewhat different interpretation, but you probably aren't enrolled in electronic engineering or a biochemistry course. There is no point in opening that can of worms! In the legal sense, information can indeed become evidence, as long as a court admits it. Proving something is a way of making it certain. But courts also reject a lot of information that looks relevant to the average person, causing us to wonder how lawyers manage to survive with that limitation.

b. It is acknowledged that lack of access to some of the documents creates the same situation associated with inadmissible evidence. The missing information can indeed affect the conclusions. Perhaps those withheld pages contained personal information, and that is what prevented access. However, it is noted that other sources such as the Texas criminal court records actually revealed home addresses, driver's license numbers, etc., and the general public has access to those records. It is amazing what an open source search can turn up. Black ink is cheap, and personal information, photos, etc. can be censored selectively, especially if a Xerox copy is made of the censored document, so that the underlying print cannot be read using an ultraviolet lamp. It does not seem right that information was withheld from Faron's family.

c. Here is a portion of the information posted on Emily Redman's home page in 2008:

Duties of the District Attorney:

The District Attorney's office prosecutes violations of the criminal laws of Oklahoma; institutes proceedings to protect abused and neglected children; prosecutes juvenile offenders; secures care and treatment in mental commitment cases; serves as legal advisor to all county elected officials; appears before the appellate courts of Oklahoma and the federal courts; and provides services to victims and witnesses to ensure their fair treatment in the criminal justice system. [underline added]

[Then there is a link to a huge list of hot checks...]

Mission Statement:

It is the mission of the District Attorney's office... to represent the people of the state of Oklahoma effectively, efficiently, and fairly. Further, the District Attorney's office seeks to protect the innocent, to punish the guilty, and to make our community a safer place for every citizen.

Did Faron receive fair treatment as a witness? There was a newspaper article: "DA's office continues crack down on bogus check writers," carried by a local newspaper, July 2008. Emily Redman's Special Investigator was quoted as saying this in the article: "We have had a good year on collections since the state's fiscal year began on July 1, 2007...The bogus check restitution program has returned over $397,000 to victims of hot check writers since the end of July last year." And that was fine, because the writers of hot checks ought to pay restitution and face appropriate criminal charges. But it looks strange if, at the same time, someone can shoot a prosecution witness in Durant and walk away as if it never mattered. All the while the local drug problems just go on

100

and on. Those drugs are ruining the lives of a lot of young people.

    d. Forget what you see in the movies. The gangster shoots his rival with a .45 automatic, and it knocks the rival completely off his feet; he lands on his head! Does it really work like that? If a bullet strikes someone and *lodges in the body*, all of its forward momentum is conserved, and the body will move in the direction the bullet was traveling, only a lot slower. Momentum is mass multiplied by velocity: m times v. Momentum is *conserved. It's a natural law, and there are no known exceptions.* We may thus equate the momentum of the bullet before impact to the momentum of the body after the impact, and we are assuming that the bullet stays in the body, thus depositing all of its momentum:

$$m_1 v_1 = m_2 v_2$$

where subscript 1 refers to the bullet and subscript 2 refers to the body. The mass of the body after the impact would actually be $m_1 + m_2$, but we'll use the above equation because the bullet's mass is very small compared with the body's mass. We want to know the velocity of the body after the impact, so we solve for v_2:

$$v_2 = m_1 v_1 / m_2$$

The .45 caliber bullet moves at about 850 feet per second, and it weighs 180 grains (that applies to some loads; others are a little heavier). There are 7000 grains in a pound, so it comes out that the .45 bullet weighs 0.026 pounds. Pounds are force units (the force we call weight), but weight is proportional to mass. It doesn't affect the calculation because we are working a ratio. Let's assume that the body that took the hit weighed about 200 pounds (not a little guy, about Faron's size), so according to the equation we get the velocity of the body after impact by multiplying the mass of the bullet by its velocity and then dividing that result by the body mass:

That is: 0.026 times 850 divided by 200 = 0.11 feet per second. Thus, we get only a bit over a tenth of a foot per second. Unimpressive! That's barely moving. The net velocity of the body would be a little faster than one foot every ten seconds after the impact. That, of course, assumes that the whole body is rigid and moves as one piece. A hinged part of the body, like an arm, which weighs perhaps 13 pounds, will move more visibly when a bullet hits it, but even there, not remarkably. Any movements that you see are mostly from involuntary muscle contractions caused by the bullet's trauma.

101

The producers of the Rambo and Dirty Harry movies have been fibbing to us. If a man is running toward you and you shoot him when he's six feet away -- even with a high powered rifle -- his body will probably fall on you! A bullet from a powerful rifle will go completely through a human body and thus give up only *part* of it's energy.

When you fire a gun it gains momentum. Its momentum is *exactly* the amount that the bullet gets, only the gun and the bullet move in *opposite directions*. The gun is quite a bit heavier than a bullet, but you can feel it kicking back at you. If a bullet could knock a man for a flip the same thing would happen to the shooter. Even in the movies the shooter is still standing after he fires the gun. A submachine gun spews out bullets at a prodigious rate, and the author has fired one; it did not upset his balance. He once fired a .375 H&H magnum rifle, which is of the type used in big game hunts, and he was still on his feet after it went off. It did kick him pretty hard!

The shocking effect of a bullet is a result of tissue destruction (caused by cavitation when the bullet passes through flesh), bleeding and pain. It is not about being knocked over like a bowling pin. The reader is referred to a journal article: "On the physics of momentum in ballistics: Can the human body be displaced or knocked down by a small arms projectile?" by B. Karger and B. P. Kneubuehl, *International Journal of Legal Medicine,* Volume 109, Number 3 / September, 1996. Karger and Kneubuehl showed that "...*the alleged backwards hurling of a person shot is nothing but a myth which should be refuted not only because it is incorrect but also because it can result in miscarriages of justice."*

REFERENCES CITED -- Chapter 1

1. In 1997, the Supreme Court ruled that because the FRE [Federal Rules of Evidence] give trial judges reasonable discretion in admitting or disallowing testimony, an appellate court's duty was to determine whether the trial court abused its discretion by *disallowing* testimony on too-stringent reliability/relevance grounds. See: General Electric Company v. Joiner, 522 U.S. 136 (1997) The document may be found through:

http://www.law.cornell.edu/supct/html/96-188.ZS.html

Some states have adopted the FRE standard; others have not, but most American states have similar rules. The U.S. Supreme Court is thus aware of situations where lower courts were too selective with evidence. On the other hand, the rules came about from lack of confidence in jurors and abuses of evidence, and they tilt strongly toward protecting the defendant. A reading of those rules is not a reassuring experience. The reader is left with a strong feeling that criminals have more rights than victims or witnesses. The Cornell University Law School server posts the current FREs. The link to that website is:

http://www.law.cornell.edu/rules/fre/rules.htm

2. In Connecticut the Barbara Gibbons murder investigation and trial was characterized by over-reliance on what can only be described as a forced confession. The police apparently became so focused on the confession that they didn't see the glaring discrepancies, one being their belief that the suspect could almost behead the victim and -- wearing the same clothes -- not be found with a drop of blood on him about twenty minutes later (it was shown later that the actual time allowed to dispose of a weapon and bloody clothes was only a few minutes)! Worse, the prosecutor held back evidence that was inimical to *his case*. See: Joan Barthel, "A Death in Canaan," Dutton Press; 1st edition, 1976. This early account contained 328 *loose leaf* pages. A reviewer had this to say: "*The most powerful part of Ms. Barthel's book is the actual transcripts of the twenty-five hours that Peter Reilly was kept in police custody. It has to be read to be believed.*" Police work can indeed be very sloppy, but that is not a general rule. The quality of forensic investigations also varies. Some prosecutors are dishonest; most are probably objective and honest.

Chapter 2 - The Unrelated Murder

Tristan York's brutal death came not quite eight months before Faron's. Those who are involved with drugs should take a warning from his tragedy because overdosing isn't the only path to a user's destruction; violence takes their lives, too. It came out in the pre-trial testimony that Tristan defied the men who killed him. A bayonet had been thrust into his chest. In the court testimony it was said that he withdrew it and, with the strength that was left in him, hurled it back at his tormentors, injuring one of them.

Events leading to the murder of Tristan York began on May 21, 2007. Tristan had been arrested on a Texas warrant related to drugs, but Texas had not sent someone to get him. Thus, a Durant judge had released him because of the excessive delay, and on the 21st he was picked up at Tuesday's Bail Bond, which is located near the Durant courthouse. Faron and Rose drove him to Linda Haworth's home in Durant, which was across the street from Faron's place. Charles Bussey, Linda's boyfriend, also resided at Linda's home. That home was and still is in a nice neighborhood, *if* you don't count what happened at the Haworth address two days later! Rick used to live in a house right across the street from Linda's place (where Faron was living when he was killed), or more correctly, his garden plot was opposite her place. And of course, he knew Linda. That and his blood relationship to Faron is *his* connection to all of this.

Tristan spent the night at Linda's home, and the next morning a group consisting of Tristan, Linda, Charles, Faron and Rose went to McKinney, Texas in *two cars* to pick up an unspecified amount of methamphetamine. They were in McKinney for about two hours. Charles Bussey was already in trouble for drug trafficking; he had been holding over $30,000 in cash and crystal meth with a street value of about $80,000 when he was busted earlier in 2007.[1] After receiving the drug package at McKinney they drove back into Oklahoma, but instead of returning to Linda's home in Durant, they stopped near one of those Native American gambling casinos. Such places are found in Oklahoma and in other states, and locals view them as a kind of "Little Las Vegas." The group was looking for a vacancy in a motel within half a mile of the casino, but a room was not secured, so they drove from there to Linda's home. If you believe they were attempting to make their own drug drop in what could be called a gambling zone, that's an inference. Read into it whatever you wish, but there is no information that throws any light on that situation. It just looks odd that they stopped there rather than continuing for the remaining few miles to Durant. McKinney is much closer to Dallas than the Texas-Oklahoma Border. The casino, located at the edge of the small town known as Calera, is less than five miles from Durant. This account of the McKinney trip comes from the transcript of sworn testimony from the Charles Bussey murder trial preliminary hearing.

Later on that day (on the 22nd) the group was at Linda's place, and that was when Bobby Don Mullinix was erroneously released from the Durant Jail. Apparently Charles knew him from a time when both were jailed together, and Bobby Don was picked up at Tuesday's Bail Bond and brought to the Haworth residence. The onset of night found the entire group doing methamphetamine. It was said that Charles, Tristan and Bobby Don were "*shooting up meth*;" while the two women and Faron were "*smoking meth.*" They were smoking marijuana, too. At some point Rose couldn't find one of three new cell phones, and she told Charles about it. Here is how that came out in the testimony:

Rose had set up two of three cell phones apparently purchased by Charles Bussey, and the third was missing. She testified: "...*I couldn't find the third one. And I told Shannon* [Charles Bussey's middle name is Shannon], *and Shannon assumed that Tristan had the other one.*" Tristan York was asleep at this point, and Bussey and Mullinix went to wake him up. He didn't respond, and that's when Mullinix took hold of a baseball bat. After that all hell broke loose. It was the beginning of the murder.

There may have been other reasons behind the cell phone issue. The motive for killing Tristan York is not clear -- perhaps those new phones were replacements for the ones used during the McKinney drug deal, and a reading of the trial transcripts seems to indicate that they were purchased by Charles Bussey. The phones were probably going to be used in future drug dealing activities. It is well known that criminals use the pre-paid cell phones (such as the Tracfone) for making a rendezvous, passing information, etc. One thought -- just a guess -- is that if the use is criminal, as in drug trafficking, then the phone should only be used to contact another cell phone dedicated for the purpose and *never* make calls to residential phones (landlines) because that would establish *traceable connections and locations* at the other ends of the calls.

The investigator asked the clerk at the Dollar General store if he had to provide an address if he paid cash for a Tracfone. The clerk said "No." The question was asked because the investigator had bought his own Tracfone with a credit card, and he always used a credit card when he bought a phone card to add minutes. The next question was: "If I buy an add minutes card from you, do I have to provide an address for cash payments?" Again, the answer was "No." Then: "Surely there is a surveillance camera?" "Yes." The clerk grinned. He pointed to the dark bubble on the ceiling about fifteen feet away from the check-out counter. What of it? Disguise a bit. Park in another location and walk to the store because they probably have outside surveillance cameras. You can still get a cell phone without revealing who you are. Such phones are referred to as "burners" if they are used for criminal purposes. There is nothing wrong with the idea of a pre-paid phone, because many individuals have almost no day-to-day need for a cell phone. They are used for travel, emergencies and the occasional high priority call. But some are used in criminal activities.

If a person has such a phone, what remains is the matter of adding minutes. No sweat. The manual says you can activate your minutes card from any telephone. A person could do that anywhere. Legitimate users often add minutes by internet using a personal computer. That would not do if the phone were used for shady purposes. You shouldn't associate the phone to anything that identifies you, and that means that you shouldn't use your home phone to add minutes. The server might get your ISP address or use caller ID to get your phone number. It probably does. Thus far the cheap phones do not have a GPS locator capability, so they do not track your position with precision. But they can still be tracked to the cell-tower in use or maybe to the overlap zone between two towers, and the uncertainty can be further reduced if a surveillance van outfitted with sophisticated intercept-type communications receivers is on your tail! That kind of equipment is not widely available, so the law of averages still works in favor of the criminal.

The man was wary. He crashed a party, and while everyone was good and drunk, he went into a bedroom and used the host's phone to activate four burner cell phones. A certain woman was using a similar method. She was a telephone repairman, and she made money on the side preparing burner phones. She'd open a junction box, select a red and green pair that wasn't active, connect a phone to those wires, then dial through to the cell phone service number. She did a lot of this when she was not assigned to a specific problem -- off duty (out to lunch, etc.). Who would suspect the girl in the hard hat and the truck with a familiar logo on the door? About a month later came the news of a SWAT raid that scared the hell out of a whole neighborhood. It never occurred to her that she had borrowed the phone line to the raided home. A drug user was also a hacker. He was good at using his computer to loop through several servers, and he employed relocating viruses to add cell phone minutes while hiding his trail. These phones found their way into the hands of drug traffickers and terrorists.[a] A lot of the shady customers used the text option, passing information by means of brief, encrypted messages. Text messages rule out voice printing.

Stealing someone's cell phone is not a reliable option for a criminal user, because once the loss is reported to the service provider, service is stopped. A genuine burner phone of the type described is needed. By restricting calls to a small group of burner phones, one creates an isolated communications network which could be easily destroyed after its use in a major crime (e.g., crush the electronics to smithereens, SIM chip and all, using a four-pound hammer and anvil, etc. -- but don't try that on the phone's battery!). This method of communicating requires serious discipline, and the phones should not be used to call a relative or a friend at a landline number. Perhaps Bussey wondered if Tristan had done something like that or used the phone to call a competing drug dealer. *Or were they mostly worried about Tristan having access to those fast-dial phone numbers that Rose had entered?* Who were the intended *users* of the three phones?

This is speculation. We don't *know* what the motive was. It may be that they were not quite that careful with the cellular phones. So the clock's hands moved through midnight and into the early hours of May 23, 2007. Somewhere in that midnight time frame Bobby Don attacked Tristan with a baseball bat after learning that he might have the missing cell phone. Then Charles got into the fray. Thus, Bobby Don was perpetrating a murder within about nine hours of being released from the Durant jail. Some have speculated that he was turned loose to carry out a contract killing; others opt for a perfectly simple explanation: a homicidal inclination fueled by meth. Meth *can* indeed cause wild behavior. But some of the trial testimony suggests that *criminal competition* was involved. We shouldn't ignore that possibility.

It was a grisly murder, and it took place during an extended period. It was a slow, agonizing death. Tristan no doubt suffered, and he did not deserve to die that way. He was clubbed with a bat and a fireplace poker, then stabbed with a bayonet and finally shot in the head several times using a low powered handgun. His body was rolled into a shower curtain and moved into the home's garage, but based on what was found during his autopsy, it is possible that Tristan was still alive -- barely hanging on -- even *after* he had been rolled up in that shower curtain.

At a later time the killers used a borrowed pickup truck to transport Tristan's body to a Lake Texoma inlet, roughly ten miles west of Durant. His body was dumped into the water, and it was found by fishermen several days later. The house was a bloody mess, and an attempt was made to clean it up, discard rugs and furniture, etc. Then Charles, Linda and Bobby Don fled to Mineral Wells, which is west of Fort Worth, where they were later captured.

The testimony of Linda Haworth stated that they lodged near Calera, Oklahoma in one of the motels near the bingo casino after moving out of her home. They had help; friends got them registered under someone else's name. From there they proceeded to McKinney, Texas, and they stayed in a McKinney motel before going on to Mineral Wells. They had reversed their drug trafficking path between Durant and McKinney, Texas. There is a better route between Durant and the group's chosen hideout west of Fort Worth, one that probably encounters fewer surveillance cameras, and it goes west and then south. That option crosses the Red River at a more rural location and stays rural across a region of rolling hills and mesquite trees once controlled by the dreaded Comanche Indians.

Bussey's choice of an urban route (through Dallas) suggests that the individuals in McKinney, who provided drugs on May 22, 2007, also helped them to hide out for a while. Perhaps the three fugitives didn't have a Texas town in mind when they left Durant; maybe they just didn't know where to go at first. McKinney is barely outside the urban sprawl of Dallas, Texas and is thus within Texas' premier hub of drug trafficking activities. The Mexican Gulf Cartel allegedly operates in that area.

One of the obvious drug routes out of Dallas goes northward through Durant toward the large cities further north, Tulsa being among them; other places such as Kansas City, St. Louis and Chicago are beyond the Oklahoma border, in the northern states. These facts might cause the reader to wonder if Durant is a place of intrigue. Having lived there for decades, Rick can tell you that such speculation abounds! And Durant isn't the only place with a reputation for drug problems. Almost everyone living in Oklahoma, Arkansas and Texas knows that marijuana is grown in southeastern Oklahoma. The author remembers a story that a friend told him after a trip to New York City. While the friend was there he had gone into a shop that sold pullover shirts with clever slogans. He noticed one shirt that was imprinted with the likeness of a marijuana plant. There was a caption on that shirt: "Grown in McCurtain County, Oklahoma." That's the county in the southeastern corner of Oklahoma, which borders with Texas and Arkansas. McCurtain County and those adjoining it are well-known for their marijuana crops! Meth has also been produced in the general area, although restricted access to pseudoephedrine has no doubt curtailed some of that activity. Meth is coming from Mexico lately.

The author witnessed drug related purchases firsthand when he was still living in Durant. One time he was in a discount store's check-out line, and he noticed that the woman in front of him was buying the store's entire stock of OTC pseudoephedrine products! That was before the controls went into effect. The probable destination of the purchase was pointed out, but the clerk replied, "*It's none of my business or yours what she does with it.*" There is a prevailing sense that nothing can be done about such things. As in other parts of the nation, the existing drug problem in Oklahoma is unacceptable.

Tristan's decomposed body was found in the lake a few days after his murder, and that started a manhunt. After being found and arrested in Texas, both Charles Bussey and Bobby Don Mullinix were eventually charged with murder and Linda was charged as an accessory after the fact. The scant information available concerning their arrest on the Texas side indicates that it included a drug issue, although the details were not revealed in the newspaper article. Photographs were printed in that article, and after the preliminary hearing transcripts became available Rick thought there was a discrepancy in Linda's testimony. She had testified that she never saw Bobby Don before the night of Tristan's murder, but Rick believes that he saw Bobby Don at Linda's place while he was still living right across the street from her. Considering the time elapsed, that would have been three or four years before Tristan's murder. The young man he saw was sitting on a motorcycle. Rick placed the trial transcript beside the three photos. *"She claims that was the first time he was ever in her home (pointing to the transcript), but I think I saw him there a few years ago (pointing to Bobby Don's photo)."* Rick still has good vision. He also believes Charles was there longer than she claimed. But maybe he just confused the two with other individuals.

Oklahoma's State Bureau of Investigation subpoenaed Faron as a prosecution witness. As it would turn out after Faron's shooting death, Rose and Linda became the witnesses that took his place. Other people were involved indirectly in Tristan's homicide, in the form of loaning trucks and in other ways of aiding the fugitives as they fled the area (e.g., by securing a motel room at Calera under a different name). Perhaps they did those things in ignorance of what had happened, but that assumption stretches credibility! Those involved were probably part of the local drug culture, and they are named in the trial transcripts. The name of one of those individuals, who loaned a pickup truck, was submitted to Oklahoma's *On Demand Court Records* website (ODCR), and the search turned up his substantial record of criminal activities, among them *possession of controlled substance* (two counts) and *fugitive from justice*. Who else would Charles and Bobby Don go to for help? But to Rick's knowledge, none of those additional individuals were ever charged as accomplices or accessories after the fact for helping fugitives from justice in a murder case. They probably never will be. That is how it works in Durant.

Rick sympathizes with Tristan's people. His brutal death amounted to torture -- he didn't die fast, and that haunts them. As it was in Faron's case, Tristan also left a young child behind. Some of the letters to the editor were very callous, pointing out that Tristan probably got what he deserved because of his involvement with drugs. Indeed, the whole group at Linda

Haworth's home during the night starting on May 22, 2007 was involved with drugs. But murder does not have a statute of limitations. The statute for murder makes no distinction between the values of different murder victims. It doesn't matter if the victim was a saint or the worst kind of criminal. The rule of law is supposed to apply, and it did in Tristan's case. The two killers plea bargained for life without parole rather than execution. In many minds justice was not quite complete. Tristan's brutal death was grounds for *two* lethal injections. It remains to be seen if those life sentences will even be permanent. Also, the removal of these drug traffickers scarcely affected the flow of drugs into Durant and the surrounding Texoma region.

From reading the trial preliminary transcripts, i.e., from the separate Bussey and Mullinix trials for the murder of Tristan York, and based on recent news in the Texoma region concerning drug activities, it is possible to discern *motives* and *connections* relevant to Faron's death. Consider the following account of the events leading up to and following the Tristan York murder.

Tristan York's murder in more detail and its relationship to Faron's homicide

The setting of the York murder included drug trafficking. On

May 21, 2007, Tristan York was released from the Durant jail, because Texas officials wouldn't follow up on their warrant for his arrest. On the next day, May 22, *Tristan York, Charles Bussey, Faron, Rose and Linda Haworth drove to McKinney, Texas to pick up a quantity of methamphetamine* (This comes from the sworn testimony of the trial preliminary for one of the two men accused of Tristan York's murder, a man who later received a life without parole sentence.). Also, Rose told Rick's daughter that the dealers in McKinney were *Mexicans*. The amount of methamphetamine was not specified, but the group went in two cars; one can imagine that the lead car was in cell phone contact with the carrying car, perhaps looking for police surveillance, roadblocks, etc. Afterward, they drove the illegal substance to a motel near an Indian casino in Oklahoma, then went on to Durant. *That was interstate drug trafficking*, but the FBI apparently did not investigate it.

Rick had e-mailed the federal office in Muskogee because he thought the FBI (and the DEA) would be interested in a clearly stated example of interstate drug trafficking, especially because the information came from sworn testimony. As a result of his e-mailed letter, a Federal Attorney called his home phone, and during the conversation the attorney said that the FBI wouldn't be involved. It was a state matter. That was puzzling. Does it mean that some level of perceived significance has to exist before federal agents will get involved with an interstate case? The statement came from a Federal Attorney that has been tough on organized crime, corruption, pedophiles and drugs. He is not the kind that you would associate with illicit involvements.

Charles Bussey had already been busted for dealing drugs (in pound quantities) and was out on bond when he and Bobby Don Mullinix killed Tristan York.[b] Everyone associated with the York murder, including York himself, was involved with drugs.

The murder of Tristan York occurred at Linda Haworth's residence during the night starting on May 22, 2007, apparently less than nine hours after Bobby Don was released. The murder actually took place in the small hours of May 23. On the previous day (i.e., on the 22nd, apparently toward evening), Charles, Linda and Tristan had picked up Bobby Don at Tuesday's Bail Bond, and all four went to Linda's home. Tristan had already been staying at Linda's residence for a full day.

The impression from the trial transcripts is that Bobby Don initiated the murder and Charles got involved thereafter. Both were charged with first degree murder; the pair pled "guilty" and were given life without parole sentences. The probable identity of the first perpetrator as Bobby Don was recorded

118

during the Charles Bussey trial preliminary, because Bobby Don gets a baseball bat and is going to "wake" Tristan up. The next thing heard was the sound of a bat impacting and a scream. Bobby Don's criminal records show clearly that he was inclined to violence. He was out of control.

Bobby Don was released <u>illegally</u> just hours before York's murder. This controversy has been in the Durant news and is still an open issue in the minds of a lot of Durant's citizens. Angry and disparaging comments began to appear in letters to the area's news media.[c] The unintentional release of dangerous prisoners is not unheard of, but it is usually associated with holding facilities in very large cities, an example being Riker's Island in the New York City area, where the paperwork associated with its large prisoner population is daunting. The county in which Durant is situated has a population on the order of 40,000, and the City itself is only about 14,000. The jail is thus small (and quite inadequate); some public school teachers have larger class enrollments! A jailer should have no problem knowing the background of *each* prisoner in such a situation.

Bobby Don had been brought before a judge in March of 2007, and his parole was revoked because of new criminal acts and unacceptable behavior. He had been *remanded* to the

Oklahoma Department of Corrections, so that means he was merely waiting for a bed and a bus ride to a correctional institution. Who released him? It is beyond the purview of a Sheriff to release a remanded prisoner, especially one convicted of serious crimes, and if a sheriff conspired with a bail bond agent to transact an illegal bond, it would impart culpability to both. If a jailer simply released a prisoner, then criminal charges against the jailer would be the probable outcome. Maybe a secretary blundered somehow and erroneous information was entered on a form. Or perhaps it was what *wasn't entered.* In most places *that* would have ended her low-paying job! We are left with a judge's involvement, and prosecutors are at the heart of the bond-setting process.

In a case of considerable interest, an assistant prosecutor allowed bond for a man who had abducted a girl, apparently even after a judge recommended "no bond." The one who committed the crime almost immediately repeated the offense against the same girl. This happened in 2007 in Durant, which is the seat of Bryan County, in Oklahoma. The district attorney was severely criticized for allowing such a thing to take place.

The alleged perpetrator was a man named Calvin Sterling. After the girl's first kidnapping, which resulted in Sterling's arrest, Sterling's defense attorney pleaded for a bond. An assistant prosecutor, who was not named, agreed on an $11,000 bond even after Judge Trace Sherill had asked for "*no bond.*" The conditions of the bond required that Sterling have no contact with his victim or even enter Bryan County. However, after securing the bond, Sterling proceeded to nab the girl a *second time*; he took her into Texas and was eventually arrested there. That probably got him into hot water with the federal authorities! Fortunately, the girl came out of the ordeal alive.

There is a law in Oklahoma known as "*Caitlin's Law,*" which resulted from the 2005 kidnapping and murder of a girl named Caitlin Wooten. The law basically frowns on bonds for kidnapping perpetrators, and the prosecutors had arbitrarily ignored the statute. It could be said that the spirit of the law and basic common sense were not heeded. Caitlin's stepmother was furious: "*It's as if Caitlin's death meant nothing to the district attorney's office...*" Prosecutor Emily Redman's response was, "*We believed, on the basis of the information we had at that time, that the safety of the public and specifically the alleged victim could be insured by the condition of that bond and obviously we were wrong about that...*"[2]

The Sterling case was totally unrelated to the deaths of Tristan and Faron. But did something like this happen when

Bobby Don Mullinix was released? One has reasonable cause to ask if Emily Redman or one of her assistants allowed bond for Bobby Don. She certainly released the one that killed her prosecution witness! In the case of Faron's homicide it was claimed that his death was unrelated to the murder he had witnessed, which was a weak excuse when you consider all the things that actually took place. The connectivity diagram on the following page shows the considerable entanglement of the two homicides. The broad lines of the diagram connect homicides; narrow lines link individuals and places that have some degree of known interaction.

We do not *know* the process that allowed Bobby Don Mullinix to run free, but it is obvious that serious wrongdoings have happened in Durant. No one has been charged with creating a situation that allowed a brutal murder to happen. *In all likelihood no one will ever be charged.* The others that *think they know* are also in the dark. Anonymous reader comments found through the web pages of the *Durant Democrat* and TV station *KXII* give us a window into how some people in the area

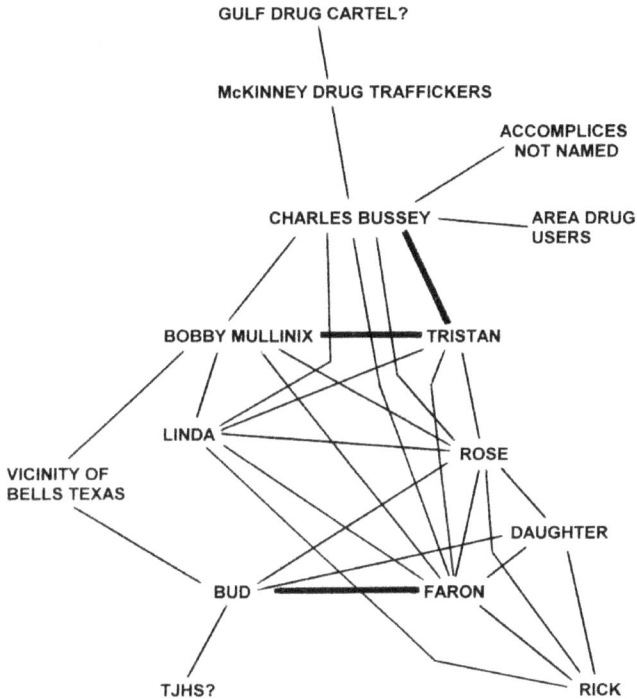

GULF DRUG CARTEL?

McKINNEY DRUG TRAFFICKERS

ACCOMPLICES NOT NAMED

CHARLES BUSSEY

AREA DRUG USERS

BOBBY MULLINIX

TRISTAN

LINDA

ROSE

VICINITY OF BELLS TEXAS

DAUGHTER

BUD

FARON

TJHS?

RICK

The connecting relationships of two homicides: narrow lines show the connectivity of the individuals who were associated with the homicides, or were at least in some degree of contact with those who were directly involved. Broad lines connect the killer-victim relationships. A general location near US highway 82 in Texas is familiar ground for two of the individuals. TJHS is Thomas Jefferson High School in Dallas, Texas. In this diagram the "DAUGHTER" is Faron and Rose's child.

think.[c] Here are some additional quotations, spelling errors and all, but the actual names (or assumed names) of people and locations are obscured:

Case Closed wrote on Sep 24, 2008 8:45 AM:

" Thanks Bill Bob Staggs for the MR Case Closed. I see no reason to do away with Contraband in Jail. There not going any where anyway. Let them have a little fun. Its better in jail than on the streets. What you think??..."

The *"contraband"* referred to is drugs, brought to prisoners by a jailer who was later prosecuted for doing it. *Case Closed* is referring to a *Durant* newspaper article (*"Judge rules sufficient evidence to try Mullinix for murder"*). *Case Closed* is either being sarcastic or actually thinks passing drugs to jail inmates is just fine. It's hard to be certain in a county where drugs have become a serious problem. *Case Closed* also refers to the following comment from another who signed as *"Bill Bob Staggs,"* e.g.:

Bill Bob Staggs wrote on Sep 22, 2008 10:44 AM:

"The DA don't care, all she cares about is Hot-Checks and Plea-Bargans. She has all the documents in the York Murder, she knows that there would have been no murder if the sheriff and his Jail Boss had done their job. She has chose to put all of the

wrong doers in jail except who allowed it to happen. . . .However
she just sent a kid to working at the jail to PRISON for doing the
same thing the sheriff did, allowing a Prisoner to leave the jail,
and allowing Contraband into the jail. Contraband is a Big-
Business in the Durant Jail. and a Contraband Go-Phone is
what started the attack that resulted in the murded [murder] *of*
Mr. York. Maybe, she has a reason to cover up the total truth
about the murder and contraband."

Yes, there have been several cases of prisoners being released illegally over the years, not just in Durant but in other places. But a sheriff cannot casually turn loose a convicted, sentenced and remanded prisoner -- especially one that committed violent felonies. Intuitively, the sheriff theory doesn't fly well. Blaming the sheriff shows superficial thinking, because sheriffs do not have that kind of authority. An action at the level of the court itself was more likely, and an example has already been cited. Mullinix was picked up at a bail bond office, and some kind of paperwork (bogus or real) must have been involved. We really don't know who allowed Bobby Don Mullinix to walk out of the Durant jail and kill Tristan York less than nine hours later.

A lot of people suspect corruption behind the release of Mullinix, and this comes out in a letter submitted by the anonymous writer who signs as *"Case Open."* He, too, is hung up on the sheriff theory.

Case Open wrote on Sep 24, 2008 6:57 PM:

"You are correct they stay in jail until the JA & AJA decides to let one out to murder someone. . . . .However, the jailer Mr. Dobbs was put in prison for bringing Contraband into the jail, and allowing an inmate to leave the jail. So the sheriff and his JA & AJA should be also. They are making Big-Bucks off it. . . . .I am curious of why so much anger comes from the sheriff when the Contraband & York Murder is mentoned??? Could there be a problem if someone besided the sheriff or OSBI investagated the Contraband business. I THINK SO..."

In "Case Open's" comments, the abbreviations "JA" and "AJA" apparently refer to the jail keepers.   OSBI is Oklahoma's version of the FBI.   The controversy isn't limited to drugs; sanitation and sex with female inmates are other issues.

For a while after the York murder, Mullinix was living a charmed life even south of the Red River, because an article found in a central Texas newspaper suggests that he had another opportunity to walk out of a jail.   He was brought before a district judge and advised of his rights. Mullinix was told that if he signed the waiver of extradition, "...the ...County Sheriff's Department would notify Oklahoma authorities and they '...*have 10 days to get you. If after 10 days and you're not picked up, you could be allowed to bond out.'* " As a matter of fact, Bobby Don was *not* back in Durant ten days later! He was a kind of hot potato. Bobby Don remained in Texas, apparently incarcerated (or we hope so), for several months and was finally returned to Durant. The transfer to Durant happened just before his trial. Exactly how the bonding out was avoided is not entirely clear, but it is known that he was in the large Huntsville Texas Penitentiary for drug convictions immediately before being extradited to Durant. No one doubts that he would have fled justice if he had been set free.

Bud certainly was not the first *killer* released by the Durant system (and regardless of the legal description of his act -- *"homicide in self-defense"* -- he did *kill* someone). Neither was Bobby Don Mullinix a first. The old remark often heard in Durant and other Oklahoma towns about the ease of getting away with killing someone may be true. But Bobby Don was finally sentenced to life without parole for the murder of Tristan York. So was Charles Bussey. At least that much was justice.

At this point four motives for killing Faron are visible. <u>One motive</u> is that he knew where the drug drops took place in McKinney, Texas and also in the Durant, Oklahoma area. He may have even known *who* the McKinney drug traffickers were, along with those receiving drugs in the Durant area, although the trial transcripts indicate that Bussey went into that place alone. Faron actually helped Bussey move drugs, and that's stated in the trial transcripts. Faron's knowledge was a threat to the drug traffickers. *Another* related motive is that he was in a rehab situation; the drug dealers (meaning Charles Bussey and *others up the chain* -- probably both north *and* south of the Red River) no longer had *control* over him and no doubt did not trust him. A *third motive* is that Faron knew who actually killed Tristan York. From the Bussey preliminary testimony, Faron at first barricaded himself with the two women in a bedroom when the trouble started, for protection from the violence taking place elsewhere in the home. Later, he was coerced to go into the living room when Tristan was being murdered, and he saw what happened.

A portion of the dialog from Emily Redman's cross examination of Rose puts Faron's status in perspective. She had just asked why Rose and Faron hadn't gone to the police:

Rose: "*It was talked about, but I was really scared at that point. I didn't really know what to do.*"
Redman: "*You were scared that somebody might retaliate against you?*"
Rose: "*Something like that.*"

Redman: "*Did Faron tell you anything about what he had witnessed?*"

Rose: "*Yes.*"

Redman: "*And when was that?*"

Rose: "*When did he tell me?*"

Redman: "*Uh-huh.*"

Rose: "*When we left.*" [Meaning leaving the Haworth Residence on the morning of Tristan's murder, May 23, 2007, and that happened at about sunrise time.]

Further into the testimony this kind of question comes up again, and this was Rose's reply: "*-the most of what happened, that I know, is what Faron witnessed and told me.*" *That* is why Faron was the *critical witness.* The testimony establishes that the two women, Rose and Linda Haworth, were still in the bedroom and only heard the screaming and noises of fighting, things breaking in the living room and gunshots associated with the *actual murder.* They had seen only an early portion of that fight, which spilled briefly into the hallway outside the bedroom's location.

In the transcript of the Mullinix trial preliminary, a defense lawyer asks for *witness contact information* for Rose. Assistant Prosecutor Webster cites Title 22, Section 303, Subpart (A), which allows the court to "*...excuse witness endorsement or some* *part thereof.*" This was about "*...a need for <u>witness protection</u> or preservation of the integrity of the evidence.*" The prosecution allowed the defense lawyer and his staff to have access to Rose's address and phone number, but also asked the court for a Protective Order to restrict the disclosure of Rose's personal information to just the defense lawyer and his private secretary. If Rose needed such protection, then by logic Faron certainly would have. It is thus asked: who could have been a threat to Rose *at the time of the Mullinix preliminary (and by inference, to Faron at an earlier time)*? Of the group present in Linda's home when York was murdered, both Faron and Tristan were dead, and Bobby Don Mullinix and Charles Bussey were in jail. We don't count Rose. She was the one needing protection. That leaves Linda. Rick knows her and does not think she is capable of killing anyone. Linda was even worried about possible "*...threats...*" (see further down). We thus have to look *outside* of the original group, which leaves us with the obvious ones: the drug traffickers at McKinney, Texas, probably others in extreme northern Texas and yet more of the same ilk north of the Red River, near Durant. The general public was not aware of those facts.

There are other indications that Linda, Rose and Faron were worried about their safety. First of all, *Faron told his grandfather that he might not live long*, and something of interest turned up in Faron's room after the shooting. Going through his personal items, the family came across a letter from Linda Haworth, and it was addressed to Faron and Rose. It was dated after York's murder, and the time stamp on the postal envelope shows August 16, 2007. It was handwritten, and Linda was in rehab at the time, in Norman, Oklahoma. The letter contained an unusual question, written as a postscript: *"Have y'all gotten any letters from S.M.? Any threats?"* Rick thinks he knows who "S.M." is. No doubt, Linda and Rose *both* know for sure. This letter was the kind of thing that the Durant police disregarded. They wanted no input from Faron's family. None at all.

It is believed that Rose and Linda are still in some degree of danger because of the situation: the Dallas area drug traffickers, not to mention others more local, are no doubt aware of them and where they are, because as potential witnesses to drug trafficking they might indeed reveal incriminating information. Rick worries that his three-year old great granddaughter might also be at risk, simply because of her proximity to that situation. Oklahoma's witness protection is pathetic -- essentially nonexistent, and it's hard to imagine a program that would work well in small cities like Durant. A criminal could focus on a public bottleneck, such as a Wal-Mart entrance, the courthouse, etc., and look for the desired face, which would likely show up in a day or two, then follow that person to a specific residence. There are numerous other ways to ferret out a targeted person. Extortions, violence, etc., could follow. Relocation of a witness is a better way, but even that measure can be defeated.

Also, from the sworn testimony of Linda Haworth at the Bobby Don Mullinix preliminary hearing we read the following on page 152, from Attorney Webster's cross-examination of Linda Haworth:

Webster: "*During the time after you were called out of the bedroom to help clean up the mess, did you hear Mr. Mullinix say anything about what had taken place?*"
Haworth: "*Mr. Mullinix and Mr. Bussey had told me that it had to be done because Tristan was going to rob them and take all their money and all their drugs.*" [these quotes from the trial transcripts are verbatim; "them" might mean just the men.]

The telling word is "their;" it appears that Charles and Bobby Don were business partners. Haworth's statement points to criminal competition as the motive for Tristan's murder. Would they kill someone over a small cache of money and drugs?

132

Apparently Bussey had more than the $32,000 found in the earlier raid. It would have taken cash to exchange for those drugs picked up in McKinney, Texas on May 22, 2007, and that had happened immediately *before* Mullinix had been released from jail. The Tristan York murder indeed seems to have been mostly about drugs and criminal competition, even though a question of jealousy over Bobby Don's girlfriend had been raised during the trial. York was released *one day* before Bobby Don was turned loose, and *both* were taken to the same home in Durant. This gnaws at the back of one's mind; some think this looks like an intentional setup, and *if* it was, whoever was behind the illegal release of Bobby Don could be involved. From the transcript of the Charles Bussey preliminary hearing the violence apparently started because of the cell phones. Charles and Bobby Don were collecting *all* the phones that night, intent upon stopping further communications. Then came the murder. It looks as if they were preparing for it.

Indeed, why would Charles help Bobby Don murder a man if it was just a love triangle between Bobby Don, York and an underage girl? Charles was *selling* drugs. Those cell phones were involved in drug trafficking. The transcript pictures Bussey as a "...*big-time meth dealer*" (page 101 of the transcript) and that he did his drug dealing in Texas (page 131 of the transcript).

Are we to believe that Charles' drug dealing was done *entirely* in Texas? Bussey's group headed for Oklahoma after obtaining drugs in McKinney Texas. But Charles was probably nearer to the bottom of the drug trafficking chain, perhaps on the second or third rung from the bottom. "Big-time" implies million dollar deals and upward.

There are good reasons for thinking that the official statements made to local newspapers, to the effect that Faron's death was not related to the York murder trials, are *very much in doubt*. The Texas and Oklahoma drug traffickers had motives to kill Faron. Charles and Bobby Don had a mutual motive to stop Faron's testimony. Bud had a motive, too, and it is the _fourth_: Officials of the court hold that Bud's motive was *self-defense*, which is not particularly believable because it ignores quite a lot of available contrary information; *jealousy* is a more plausible motive. *Ostensibly Bud was jealous of Faron's relationship with Rose, but perhaps there was something even more sinister.*

Prisoners do have ways to communicate with criminal cohorts outside, and Faron's death could have been arranged. The connections warrant careful scrutiny. At this point Charles has confessed to the murder of Tristan York, and he has been sentenced to life imprisonment without parole. He had a stake in Faron's death at first, so he had a motive. That leaves Bobby

Don, who also had a clear motive for his death. What the two men did to Tristan, *with Faron watching*, is the basis for the _third motive_, stated earlier.

Just who is this Bobby Don Mullinix? He came from a prominent family. His grandmother was a high level executive, and she retired from that position recently. Bobby Don chose a dangerous lifestyle, and one can imagine how that troubled his people. He, too, was charged for York's murder, and after a plea of "guilty" his sentence was life imprisonment without parole. There are individuals on the Texas side who say that Bobby Don's people frequently used influence to get him out of tight situations, but that's just hearsay based on comments found on a local TV station's website. Actually, his grandmother once turned him in for stealing her car.[d]

Bobby Don's criminal records are available to the general public, and they stand as a warning unheeded. His prior crimes trended to drugs and violence, and it should have been possible to see the inevitable approaching. In Charles Bussey's case the record did not show prior violence; he was a drug trafficker, already awaiting his turn on a court docket when the York murder was committed. It was business as usual even under those circumstances. Both of the killers had ties to the region's drug traffickers, and they could have conveyed a request to have Faron eliminated, or perhaps those same drug traffickers could have made the decision on their own.

It is possible that Bud knew Bobby Don *beforehand*. Information was found indicating that Bud's mother had lived at or near Whitewright, Texas during an earlier time interval, with other relatives nearby, and Bobby Don's hometown was Bells, Texas, *only seven miles away from Whitewright*. However, a prior counselor at the Whitewright High School did not remember a kid named Bud. Bells and Whitewright are small Texas communities with a combined population close to 3,000. Bud's criminal record pointed to a more recent Dallas address, one not far from Love Field. Bud's birth is recorded in extreme Northeastern Texas (the Texarkana area). Bud and Bobby Don are almost the same age; they liked motorcycles. Given the proximity of Bells and Whitewright, the size of the communities and similar ages there is a possibility that Bud and Bobby Don actually knew each other. If so, that could be a significant connection.

In early June of 2009, a wedding couples' registry was brought to Rick's attention. What was found there was not especially surprising: Bud married a girl from the Bells/Whitewright area in 2009. Thus, the suspected connections to Bells and Whitewright had a degree of factual basis. Rick says it would be interesting to hear all the rumors that circulate in the local hot spots like the *Dusty Saddle Club* or *Fat Daddy's*. But as he puts it, *"That's someone else's sleuthing task. I avoid such places."*

The apparent love triangle indeed could have been a set-up for Faron's murder. There could be a connection between Bud and Bobby Don. The authorities have not looked into the possibility, and they probably never will. A good investigator searches for connections, but it appears that the Durant investigators paid scant attention, if any at all, to those aspects of Faron's shooting death. It is likely that most killings believed to be in self-defense will treated that way.

Both Bussey and Mullinix were sentenced to life without parole, which in some ways is worse than a death sentence for a younger man like Mullinix. The York family probably wanted their son's killers to receive lethal injections, and Rick certainly hoped for that outcome. If Mullinix ever gets the chance, he will probably break out of prison. He is the kind that would.

Rick couldn't put his questions aside even though everyone was telling him that he should. *"It's fine with them -- easy advice; but they don't know what it's like. I can't just walk away. Are my friends saying, 'just forget what happened to Faron even if it was a murder?' They would not do that if it had been a natural death. Who would say to a grieving man, 'Forget about that one and move on'?"* He's like a worm on hot ashes at times, mostly because of the perceived miscarriage of justice. His friends should have kept their mouths shut. Rick has to work it out himself.

Other connections

One wonders about the girl Bud married because a previous girlfriend told Rick's daughter that she believed he was dangerous. A relationship had ended, but Bud stalked the earlier girlfriend even after she repeatedly told him that she wanted nothing to do with him. She described a man obsessed with being in control. Allegedly there was a confrontation between Bud, the girl and her fiancé. A violent scuffle between the two men left Bud on the floor, bawling. The prior girlfriend did not know Rick's daughter or Faron, but when she read of Faron's death and *who* had killed him, she immediately believed that it was a murder. Then she told Rick's daughter what she knew.

It posed a question: is Bud's wife at risk, too? Going to Google her name and a town in Texas was typed in, four keywords in all, and her MySpace link came up on the first page.

It was that easy! Her views and comments were not hidden behind a log-in step, and numerous photos were *directly and publicly accessible*: her people, a park scene, at a lake, at a swimming pool, wedding photos, scenes with a sister and girlfriends, etc. Her MySpace profile did not suggest drug use or a lascivious lifestyle. Her parents looked decent. Maybe they didn't even know what their son-in-law had done.

Those photos were examined one-by-one, wondering what they might contain, and it took a while because there were hundreds of images. Eventually there were three images that especially caught the eye, and those were among the beach and swimming pool scenes. Attention became focused on Bud's tattoos. Tattoos can indicate connections. Bud has a large cross on his back, placed high -- up between the shoulder blades. The size, general shape and location of his tattoo is similar to one displayed by members of the Aryan Circle (AC) gang, a gang that originated in Texas, but that might not be what it is. At first glance there are arrow heads at the ends of the arms and at the bottom of the cross, but those arrow heads are decidedly *phallic* on closer inspection! There is also something like a snake wrapped around the vertical part of the cross. The art work looks poor even at the modest resolution of the image, and that tends to indicate a gang tattoo. Legitimate tattoo artists usually will not do a gang tattoo. Thus, gang tattoos tend to be the work of gang members, who are typically not the best artists.

Above the top of Bud's cross is a marking that resembles a "schutzstaffel." The schutzstaffel was the zig-zag rune worn on the collars of Nazi Germany's Waffen SS troops during WWII -- the lightning bolts "SS," but on closer inspection Bud's tat looks more like a cursive numeral four rotated clockwise -- swastika-like -- because one of the line segments is fainter than the others.

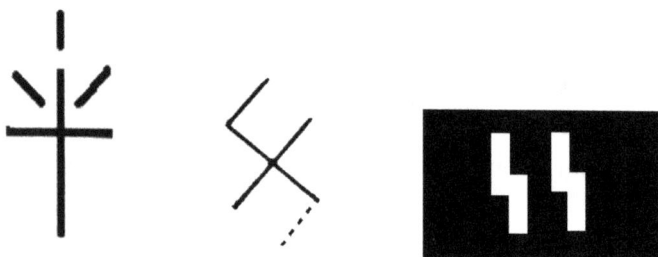

Left -- Sketch of a pachuco cross; **Middle** - Sketch of the tattoo directly above Bud's cross (there are symbols that resemble the letter "w" where those tilted lines are marked above the arms of the pachuco cross). The upper symbol is swastika-like, resembling either a stylized SS or a wolfsangle. If the fainter segment is ignored (the dashed line) it is a cursive numeral four rotated clockwise; **Right** -- The collar insignia of Hitler's Waffen SS troops (i.e., the Schutzstaffel), a zig-zag "SS." The Waffen SS helmet insignia was rotated clockwise, more like the middle figure. Among street gangs and prison inmates the Schutzstaffel tattoo, called "crackerbolts," can mean "I've killed someone."

Numerals are common in gang tattoos, but the meaning of a four is unknown. An example of gang symbols with numerals is the notorious 4-13-9 pyramid. Gang tattoos generally have cryptic meanings.

Bud's tattoo had other symbols *above the arms of the cross*, but the resolution of the image is not good enough to be sure of what those are. They resemble the letter "w," and there is one above each arm; the letter "w" *can* mean white supremacy. But Bud's best man at the wedding had Hispanic features. That seemed to contradict an Aryan connection. Also, those markings above Bud's cross are near the positions of the three extra marks of the Pachuco Cross displayed by Latino gangs. The address given in his Texas court record is within a substantially Hispanic part of North Dallas (including the district of the problematic Thomas Jefferson High School, where the drug "cheese" got started). The reader is reminded that the drug dealers Charles Bussey did business with in McKinney, Texas were said to be Mexicans.

Checking at the Oklahoma DOC website, Bobby Don's tattoos are of skulls and the grim reaper. The Nazi "totenkopf" icon, a skull (the death's head) is well known, but skulls are also seen among Mexican gangs, including the Zetas. The grim reaper -- a hooded skull -- could represent Santa Muerte, the *Saint of the Dead* of Mexican culture, associated with the Day of the Dead event. Both Bud and Bobby Don *might* be involved with a gang (or gangs) and all that goes with such associations,[3] but it was not possible to find a strong connection between the two men on the basis of their tattoos and other information available. There is a feeling that the symbolism points to Aryans and other white supremacists, but Hispanic groups are not ruled out. These are guesses. Some sources claim that in Texas the Aryan and Hispanic gangs maintain a fragile truce, so that their lucrative drug trafficking deals can take place. A law enforcement tattoo expert could tell us more, but police authorities do not publicize detailed information since it amounts to investigative intelligence.

A small tattoo on the front side of Bud's chest, above his left nipple, was more interesting. At first it was believed to be an oriental kanji symbol, but then it was noticed that the marking seemed to have a central spot with five lines radiating and ending in what looked like droplets -- star-like. Thus, a new thought took form: "*Is it a gunshot wound tattoo?*" Does the spot represent a bullet hole, and do the lines radiating outward represent blood oozing out? *It was placed close to the location where one of Bud's bullets hit Faron and penetrated his aorta.* Rick's daughter heard by rumor that Bud got a new tattoo after he'd killed Faron, to boast about what he'd done.

An overlooked photo found later on the same website provided better detail. It showed writing more toward Bud's armpit (and not evident in the first photograph) resembling the "w" markings on Bud's back, from which an arrow pointed to the central spot near the nipple. There may be *another* such tattoo near Bud's right side (just below his waist) in one of his backside photos, also close to the exit point of one of Faron's bullet wounds. It is in a shadow and is much less certain. We are thus left with unresolved questions about Bud's tattoos -- there are limitations to what can be learned from modest resolution digital images. The tattoos may or may not mean anything, although association with a gang is a possible interpretation. Tats are common in 2010. Most are works of art, but some are related to criminal activity.

Is a gunshot wound tattoo a kind of blood trophy? *If so, having one seems rather sick-minded,* but it is fairly typical of gang ethics. The street language for that sort of thing is "juice," which, in a more primitive time, would have been equivalent to a Kiowa Indian striking the lodge-pole with his lance accomplishing some daring deed. Serial killers often keep jewelry and other artifacts that they take from their victims. A tat could be a kind of souvenir.

Among those photos on the MySpace pages were hunting and

paintball scenes. Many Texans and Oklahomans are avid hunters, and even though paintball games evoke a negative in some minds, a lot of people find recreation in that activity. One has to consider the *whole picture*, including the homicide, the tattoos, stalking incidents, dreams, drug use, associations, incident accounts from people who think he's a time bomb, etc., and it makes one ask questions: "What is going on in the man's mind? Will he kill again?" Emily certainly sent him away with a strong impression: "You can kill and get away with it." If he does she will have much to regret.

Faron and Rose came to know Linda Haworth and Charles Bussey because they lived right across the street from them. Bud cohabited with Rose after the York murder. He certainly knew *someone* (Rose) closely associated with Charles Bussey. Rose programmed the cell phones for Charles, which was stated in the sworn testimony of the Bussey trial preliminary. She is very near the middle of the web of connections surrounding *two* homicides, which -- alone -- raises suspicions. Charles knew Bobby Don and was responsible for bringing him to the Haworth residence when someone released him *illegally*. It is interesting that no one paid a bit of attention to the fact that one *known* drug trafficker was picked up by another one at the bail bond office! If the police or the sheriff had bothered to watch that situation, then they might have helped to bust a drug smuggling ring operating out of the Dallas, Texas area and perhaps might have even prevented a murder. Or was the release intentional, as a few Bryan County residents suspect? This kind of thing actually happens in Mexico.[4]

Concluding

It was pointed out in the first chapter that the real names of certain individuals have been intentionally obscured. Otherwise, the details of this story came directly from personal comments, official documents and other written records. The information sources included the sworn testimonies from the York murder trial preliminaries, the police and medical examiner reports and other kinds of written information. Faron's family also discovered relevant information among his personal effects. Transcripts of the Bussey and Mullinix trial preliminaries, police reports, etc., were purchased out of pocket. None of the information was obtained illegally.

Rick said, "*I do not want to benefit financially in a lawsuit over Faron's death.*" He is thus not personally interested in pursuing a civil lawsuit, and statute 1289.25 prevents it even if he were interested. *His only concern is for justice, because he believes that Faron was actually murdered.* His daughter does, too, but she disagrees concerning the lawsuit, thinking that Bud should be accountable for what he did, indirectly, to Faron's daughter. Both think there is a glaring problem in Oklahoma's criminal justice system and that the problem isn't going to go away easily, but this kind of situation exists in *other* states. The general public ought to take notice of these developments.

Others similarly affected by the castle laws of Oklahoma and other castle law states might also be more inclined to seek a civil lawsuit, and that is why the question of constitutionality has been raised. If terrorists -- enemies of the United States -- have the right to legal redress, then why shouldn't innocent family members -- American citizens who have lost someone to a homicide -- have the same right?

In Rick's mind Bud murdered Faron with purpose and premeditation, but that is his personal opinion. Bud indeed bears a *moral accountability* for how his deed will impact Faron's daughter. What he did *could have been avoided.* The prosecutors and the police who dealt with this case will point to a law that says we have to presume his innocence. Others will say, *"Why did you turn him loose so fast? Why did you disregard Bud's stalking of Faron and other relevant information?"* The prosecutor will have to live with those choices. The application of Oklahoma's castle law to Faron's homicide has been disturbing to many who have learned more than what the scant press releases contained. Ordinary folks easily discern the *differences* between *reality, morality* and *legality* even if lawyers and judges can't see them. For example, child-parent bonding *can* exist without a legal marriage. Thus, the reason for a child clause can exist even without marriage.

There is no reason to think that Faron's case will be reopened, given the nature of courts and law enforcement systems. His death should stand as a warning to those who think the self-defense laws are working smoothly. The primary purpose of this book is to *warn* the reader. Other cases of senseless or suspicious shootings are beginning to accumulate, and these detract from the intent of the castle laws. If the trend continues, the Second Amendment to the U.S. Constitution may even be jeopardized. The author would not want that to happen, and many others share his view. There have been and will continue to be clear-cut cases of defensive shootings in private homes, and the public needs to be able to protect itself when it comes down to genuine self-preservation. However, a license to commit murder is another thing. Something is needed to separate *bona fide* self-defense homicides from the unwarranted killings.

Relatives of castle law victims are treated with disrespect and indifference. Attempts to confront various Oklahoma officials with the information being ignored fell on deaf ears. Rick wrote a letter to Emily Redman, but there was no reply even though he had been Faron's legal guardian when Faron was still a minor. Oklahoma State Senator Harry E. Coates, who had backed the Oklahoma castle law legislation, received two letters from him. Senator Coates never replied. On the other hand, two years after the killing a letter was sent to Oklahoma State Senator Susan Paddack, who authored Caitlin's Law. She responded immediately, and did not hesitate to supply the requested information concerning the self-defense bill's numbering and voting record.

Rick had sent two letters to Assistant Oklahoma Attorney General Joel-lyn McCormick. Those letters noted that Emily had released the man who killed *her witness* and that the witness, Faron, had been caught up in a drug related murder. They also pointed out that Faron's daughter was present at the scene of the homicide *when the shooting happened*, which gets into a very touchy area of Oklahoma's castle law. Ms. McCormick never responded. The lawyer that attempted to find options for Rick had also written letters to the same assistant attorney at the Office of the Oklahoma Attorney General. Months later the lawyer finally received a terse response, but Ms. McCormick did not address the questions or acknowledge that Rick had ever leveled a complaint against Emily Redman. Here is how her response was worded:

"This letter is to advise that I have spoken to D.A. Emily Redman. Ms. Redman advised that she would contact this office if she needs our assistance in an investigation or prosecution concerning the referenced matter. At this time no request has been made for our assistance.

Please let me know if we can be of further assistance."

Neither Rick nor the lawyer asked the OAG to help Ms. Redman investigate or prosecute a case! Rick's letters raised the possibility that *Emily* was possibly involved in misconduct, and the lawyer was asking about legal options and pointing out the suspicious nature of the homicide.

The family doubts that Ms. McCormick read much of the material that was sent to her by Rick or the hired attorney. The letters had been directed to her office because she is the one charged with investigating and prosecuting the wrongdoings of district attorneys, What does it take to make the officials look into a suspicious killing and the way the court officials handled it? Joel-lyn McCormick has investigated serious D.A.

corruptions in Cherokee County but apparently has chosen to ignore the death of a prosecution witness in Durant.

In fairness it must also be noted that a different Assistant Oklahoma Attorney General, Sandra Balzer, cooperated with Rick and his daughter in the matter of having Faron's DNA submitted for analysis. Ms. Balzer was both civil and helpful.

Faron's family found OSBI and the local police to be indifferent and even hostile in some cases. It is not the OSBI that author thought he knew. A number of his prior chemistry students have forensic or field agent jobs with OSBI, and what he heard after Faron's death surprised him. Faron was OSBI's subpoenaed witness, and it would have helped his family to see *all* of the available evidence associated with his shooting death, or at least some sincere explanations. Why would evidence be withheld from the family?

There was a time *before* an OSBI office even existed in Durant when investigators sometimes asked university scientists for help with forensic questions, although a forensic science division of OSBI has existed since 1953. Such was the case when police officials and prosecutors solicited the author for help in forensic issues; he willingly advised or performed the necessary chemical tests and never asked for personal compensation. Today the certification process for forensic scientists who *handle* evidence is strict, but collaboration in research projects is not ruled out.

The author lived in Oklahoma for a long time, and during those early years a district attorney and friend used him as a consultant, notably in the monofluoroacetamide poisoning deaths of three local children. There were other consultations with the prosecutor and a police detective, such as assaying a white powder the detective found in a frankfurter; it was suspected of being a poison intended to kill a dog, but it had been placed out in the open, where an unsuspecting child might have picked it up. If so, the perpetrator had endangered human lives. The powder turned out to be deadly strychnine. Strychnine is supertoxic; ten milligrams will kill a child, and the total amount found in the frankfurter was over a gram (A gram equals 1000 milligrams.).

The author never hesitated to share technical resources with law enforcement during his career as a university professor. Younger faculty members at the university still collaborate with OSBI in such things as method development (i.e., forensic research), an example known to the author being one professor's use of state of the art capillary electrophoresis and mass spectroscopy to characterize patterns of impurities of methamphetamine preparations seized during drug busts as possible supporting evidence. The method might be used to identify sources of the illegal drugs based on variations in the "cooking" process. Today OSBI and the police at Durant apparently live in a different world. There are surely decent people in both of those places, but it seems that the official policy is to circle the wagons when you ask how they justify their conclusions.

The U.S. Department of Justice responded to another of Rick's letters, and the Oklahoma Bar Association did, too, although negatively. The Oklahoma Medical Examiner's staff did not ignore *any* requests for information. They let the family have the findings from Faron's autopsy, and the office continues to cooperate. One official at the Oklahoma Attorney General's office helped while another did not. One State Senator helped while another didn't. But beyond those exceptions, it seems that no one did anything where it counted. Even long time friends turned their heads the other way, or would not talk about Faron. Most were still friends, but they didn't know what to say.

The disregarded information and questions were brought to the attention of newspapers in and around Durant, but that did not move anyone to pursue investigative reporting. Contact was also made with TV stations with the same result. The silence was deafening. There was no legal recourse. There were insults to grieving people. Future vindictiveness is possible. Faron's family is left with good reasons to suspect wrongdoing, but no one cares to hear their opinion. They wonder what lies ahead for them.

Those who survived this spate of violence still harbor fears. They aren't just worried about the drug dealers; they don't trust the police or the court officers, either. It caused Rick to ask a question that he had never considered before all of this: *who lives in the craziest world? Is it the lawmaker or the court official, who seems to be more on the side of the criminal than the innocent person, or is it the ordinary citizen, who is compelled to live in that kind of environment?*

We are left with uneasy feelings and questions about guilt and innocence, but let God sort all of that out. The story just told serves to illustrate some of the factors that bear upon, lead to or derive from homicides claimed to have been a result of someone's self-preservation. The focus is on the so-called castle laws along with everything directly related to them and how well -- or poorly -- they serve their intended purpose. That's what this book is about.

END NOTES -- Chapter 2

a.   Drug   traffickers   and   terrorists   probably   use   similar communications methods. These groups certainly haven't ignored the technological possibilities. See the following book: Richard M. Pearlstein, "Fatal Future? Transnational Terrorism and the New Global Disorder," University of Texas Press, 2004, especially pages 23, 33 and 98.

b. Before the York murder, when Charles Bussey was arrested for drug trafficking in Oklahoma, Linda Haworth's home was searched, and drugs were found. Bussey was caught with $32,000 in cash during the bust, and that figure comes from Linda Haworth's sworn testimony on page 132 of the Bobby Don Mullinix murder trial preliminary hearing. Linda had also been jailed during that drug bust, because it happened in her own home. During the direct examination the defense lawyer asked her: "*Would you describe him* [Bussey] *as sort of a big-time meth dealer?*" Linda Haworth answered: "*Yes.*" Realistically, the figure pegs Bussey as being a mid-level drug dealer in the world of drug trafficking. We don't know if $32,000 was all of the cash, and the purchase of meth in McKinney, Texas on May 22, 2007 suggests it wasn't. The amount of money points to pound quantities of meth. It did involve interstate drug trafficking. Bussey probably interacted with dealers at a more serious level in Northern Texas, and that connection is probably relevant to Faron's shooting death; Faron was in McKinney when those deals were made. Bussey was allowed to bond out in March of 2007, and that was his status when Tristan York was murdered at the Haworth residence. There is a feeling that something deeper was going on here, such as a planned murder. Aggressiveness caused by the psychotropic effects of methamphetamine certainly was a factor.

c. Here are some choice comments from the public. Only the names of people and places have been changed a bit, and the spelling and grammatical errors found in the source were not corrected. The comments reflect public anger at what has happened, but they also show the degree of confusion that exists in many minds:

Posted by: Overwhelmed Location: Texas on Jun 6, 2007 at 01:38 PM
"...there is no justification for allowing Bobby Don Mullinix---or the others involved in this case---to bond out of jail. His criminal history is easily available to the public, yet the law enforcement OFFICIALS didn't know enough to check? Give me a break. Mullinix is a punk who enjoys inflicting pain on others. I am well acquainted with one of his victims. He has been given TOO MANY second chances. He has escalated from assalt and rape to murder. Will he get what he deserves now?"

Posted by: Anonymous Location: Durant on Jun 6, 2007 at 10:19 AM
"This makes me so ashamed to live in Durant, my own home town. I can't understand why someone from the Federal Government hasn't stepped in and taken over the jail situation since we have been in the news so long. I agree that there should be a civil suit, although my taxes will go to settle it. The York family deserves compensation to help raise his child and this county needs to pay it, both with money and with the jobs of everyone who was ignorant, careless or just didn't care. Fire the jailer, the sheriff, the judge, DA and clean this city up. I'm tired of being the butt of jokes and weary from worrying about escaped prisoners walking our streets. It's time to stop this disregard for our citizens and have someone take over before more are murdered."

Posted by: Battie Location: Doonesbury on Jun 5, 2007 at 08:27 AM
"Does this really surprise any one that the Durant police department dose not know how come Mullinix was "accidentally released" come on people. Lets see how many jail breaks has the county had? You know I'am not even going to comment to this any more. Durant says it all!"

Posted by: Slim Location: Thackerville on Jun 5, 2007 at 01:14 AM
" 'Authorities say 24-year-old Bobby Don Mullinix was released accidentally from the Jail last week.' So now the Jail's blunders, consistant blunders we should say, have led to a murder."

Posted by: Jacob Location: Durant, OK on Jun 5, 2007 at 07:12 PM
"In case no one remembers ... in Durant the Sheriff DOES NOT run the jail. The former county commissioner created the famous Jail Trust Authority several years ago which effectivaly removed control of the jail from the Sheriff and thats when all the problems started. Get rid of the jail trust authority and return control of the jails to the Sheriff where they belong and the way it is in nearly every other county. DO NOT blame the sheriff for something he has NO CONTROL over."

      d. This was found in the records of the United States District Court, Eastern District of Texas, Sherman Division. A portion of the text of that document gives you some insight into the nature of Bobby Don Mullinix. There is no point in naming the victimized girl.

From Case 4:03-cr-00128-RAS-DDB Document 34 Filed 04/11/2006, Pages 3 and 4 of 5 pages total:

"Officer Jones testified that in May or June of 2005, Defendant's grandmother had asked him to locate Defendant because Defendant was driving her car without permission. On June 2, 2005, Officer Jones saw Defendant driving his grandmother's car and attempted to apprehend Defendant. When Officer Jones turned on his overhead lights, Defendant threw a pink bag out the window of the car and then fled on foot. Officer Jones did not catch Defendant, but he retrieved the bag, which he discovered to contain methamphetamine and drug paraphernalia. Officer Dennis Roberson of the Whitewright Police Department testified that [a girl, name withheld] accused Defendant of taking her money, breaking her finger, and bruising her arm on or about June 6, 2005. [the girl] also accused Defendant of brandishing a firearm and threatening to kill her and her family. Officer Susan Armstrong of the Whitewright police department testified that [the girl] complained that Defendant had assaulted her, choked her, and taken her purse. Officer Shea Rhoades of the Sherman Police Department testified that [the girl] had complained that Defendant had pulled her hair and threatened to kill himself and her. Officer Rhoades also corroborated testimony that Defendant was brandishing a firearm on the occasion at issue."

REFERENCES CITED -- Chapter 2

1. Kristi Branam, "Bryan County Drug Bust," *KTEN News*, March 25, 2007.

2. Emi FitzGerald, "Family wonders why 'Caitlin's Law' wasn't enforced," *KXII TV 12 News*, October 18, 2007.

3. CNN Wire Staff, "Feds hit biker gang leaders in 7 states," *CNN Justice*, June 16, 2010. Involvement with criminal gang activity can include "...robbery, extortion, witness intimidation, drug dealing, illegal gambling and weapons violations." Sometimes gangs go beyond mere witness intimidation and carry out contract murders.

4. Mark Stevenson, "Mexico: Prison guards let killers out, lent guns," *Associated Press*, July 25, 2010. About a decade earlier the Caribbean drug lord Jose' Figueroa Agosto used a *forged release order* to literally walk out of prison! He had been sentenced to 209 years for murder. Take no comfort from so-called "life without parole" sentences.

Chapter 3 - What the castle laws allow

"If a thief is caught breaking in and is struck so that he dies, the defender is not guilty of bloodshed; but if it happens after sunrise, he is guilty of bloodshed."
- From the Holy Bible, Exodus 22:2

"And the law of England has so particular and tender a regard to the immunity of a man's house, that it stiles it his castle, and will never suffer it to be violated with immunity: agreeing herein with the sentiments of ancient Rome..."
- From William Blackstone's Commentaries on the Laws of England, Book 4, chapter 16.

Self-defense laws have always existed in human civilizations

If, after reading the previous two chapters, the reader is puzzled and perhaps a little disturbed from learning that someone could kill a prosecution witness and yet be turned loose by the very prosecutor that was going to *use* that witness, who called it self-defense, then it should be said that even worse things have happened. People have been killed for merely straying onto someone's property, unintentionally, and the one doing the shooting was not charged. Those living in places like New York City will be shocked by such incidents, but in Indiana, Alabama and Texas, few are likely to be surprised. To understand the phenomenon, we have to examine the self-defense laws across the land.

Self-defense is thought of as a given right, but the range of options granted to a citizen varies from place to place. The law in Texas supports an individual's right to protect his or her life, with deadly force if necessary, and not be prosecuted or faced with a lawsuit, whereas in Chicago or Washington DC there is much less permissiveness. Given this situation, it is thus necessary to have reference points for comparisons, and one question worth asking is this: just how *repressive* can statutes be regarding the ownership and use of weapons for self-defense when one's personal domain is being intruded upon? For contrast we also ask, just how *permissive* can the situation be? Both questions focus on the use of force -- even deadly force -- and a *variety* of defensive weapon, because the possibilities include not only guns but also things like pepper spray, stun guns, tasers, batons and knives.

A professor at the author's university -- a colleague -- gained some insight into the *extent* of differences one fall morning when two Oklahoma students came into his classroom *wearing camouflage clothing*. The students had been on a bow hunt, and no one brought up in Oklahoma, Arkansas or Texas would attach any significance to a pair of hunters returning from a hunt. Of course, they were not carrying their equipment -- certainly not the weapons; it was just the hunter's clothing visible to all. But university classrooms are *international*, and an African student became very agitated and pointed to the hunters. The student told a chilling story. In *his* province the government held sway by military force, and it was a capital offense for subjects to be caught with weapons. *It was even a capital offence to wear camouflage if you were not a government soldier*, because *that* was proof of your affiliation with the rebels! As the student put it, "*You must not wear those clothes. They will take you out and kill you.*" The statement came out of the mouth of a good student, not some ignoramus. It was what he had accepted as the norm.

In Cuba men were executed for merely saying the wrong thing or being found with a gun. Castro's vision of utopia led to decaying cities, where people to this day worry about where their next meal will come from. Dissidents still pine away in the Cuban prisons. Marxist governments have historically controlled citizen access to weapons, and in Nazi Germany during WWII, even possession of a shortwave radio (let alone an unauthorized gun) could be grounds for an execution. From a military point of view a radio is indeed a weapon, or at least part of a weapon system. The Germans went into Holland with a prepared list of amateur radio operators, and many of those targeted were rounded up and shot dead as a preemptory measure, thinking that they might take up with a resistance. The Germans probably created a situation that might not have existed, because some of those Dutch radio operators who escaped indeed *did* work with the resistance. You have no right to self-defense if you live in such a place.

England used to recognize the right to self-defense, but in 1920 the Firearms Act required certification of gun owners. One had to have a good reason to own a gun, and the definition of "good reason" changed over the years. By about 1970 the Home Office took the view: "*...it should never be necessary for anyone to possess a firearm for the protection of his house or person.*" The Prevention of Crime act (1953) had already made it illegal to carry defensive devices, and if you were caught with one you were prosecuted. When attempts were made to get an amendment the government response was: "*It would be a great pity if anything were done explicitly by statute to condone actions which imply the inability of the forces of law and order to maintain the Queen's peace.*"

Meanwhile, crime increased in England. Criminals *were* armed while the public wasn't. Street gangs carried guns, and they killed people. Burglars entered homes with impunity. If you killed a burglar -- God forbid -- you went to prison, and you were at risk of being killed or beaten senseless by the intruder if you didn't defend yourself. The official justifications continued, and one journalist noted that: "Government lawyers say burglars need protection." Lord Salton took umbrage at that mentality. He said: "Unless there is not only a right but also a fundamental willingness amongst the people to defend themselves, no police force, however large, can do it." This situation in England is documented in a book by Joyce Malcom.[1] Attempts to restore the original self-defense law in England continue but without success thus far.

So it is that in cities like London and Washington D.C., citizens have cause to worry about armed thugs breaking in and doing whatever they please. Some of those criminals carry more firepower than police officers do. In Washington D.C. you can keep certain kinds of guns at home, but the gun must be unloaded, a trigger lock must be installed, etc., even if there are no children in the household. Forget self-defense with such a limitation imposed, but some will load the gun and have it ready, anyway. You can't blame a citizen for wanting to stay alive, but when it comes to an actual showdown it's too bad for the burglar *and* the one who shot him. The imposition of such rules in Washington D.C. has been deemed unconstitutional, but nothing favoring the innocent citizen has happened so far.

The best way to understand the self-defense statutes of the United States is by reading them and comparing them state-by-state. Some states do not even have a self-defense law. The detailed wording of the statutes of three states -- New York, Arkansas and Oklahoma -- will be examined in depth because they show a progression from laws that merely recognize a citizen's right to defend against arson and burglaries, to laws *intended to protect individuals* from criminal prosecution or civil litigation if they have to resort to deadly force to defend themselves.

Self-Defense in America: a minimal self-defense law

Statutes are not exactly fun reading, but this chapter contains some select examples that represent the extent to which the self-defense laws vary across the land. The laws do vary quite a bit. What the author experienced in reading through the self-defense laws of almost *every* state in the nation was his punishment for making life miserable for the students who had to take general chemistry as a degree requirement for a major other than chemistry but dreaded and loathed every minute of it! It was like eating tortilla chips without salsa. The legal literature put him to sleep numerous times, but it has to be understood to appreciate how the laws are *supposed* to work.

Consider the applicable New York Statute, which is fairly weak. The points of interest are underlined for emphasis:

"New York Penal Law Section §35.20 - Justification; Use Of Physical Force In Defense Of Premises And In Defense Of A Person In The Course Of Burglary:

1. Any person may use physical force upon another person when he or she reasonably believes such to be necessary to prevent or terminate what he or she reasonably believes to be the commission or attempted commission by such other person of a crime involving damage to premises. Such person may use any degree of physical force, other than deadly physical force, which he or she reasonably believes to be necessary for such purpose, and may use deadly physical force if he or she reasonably believes such to be necessary to prevent or terminate the commission or attempted commission of arson.

2. A person in possession or control of any premises, or a person licensed or privileged to be thereon or therein, may use physical force upon another person when he or she reasonably believes such to be necessary to prevent or terminate what he or she reasonably believes to be the commission or attempted commission by such other person of a criminal trespass upon such premises. Such person may use any degree of physical force, other than deadly physical force, which he or she reasonably believes to be necessary for such purpose, and may use deadly physical force in order to prevent or terminate the commission or attempted commission of arson, as prescribed in subdivision one, or in the course of a burglary or attempted burglary, as prescribed in subdivision three.

3. A person in possession or control of, or licensed or privileged to be in, a dwelling or an occupied building, <u>who reasonably believes that another person is committing or attempting to commit a burglary of such dwelling or building, may use deadly physical force upon such other person when he or she reasonably believes such to be necessary to prevent or terminate the commission or attempted commission of such burglary.</u>

4. As used in this section, the following terms have the following meanings: (a) The terms 'premises,' 'building' and 'dwelling' have the meanings prescribed in section 140.00; (b) Persons 'licensed or privileged' to be in buildings or upon other premises include, but are not limited to: (i) police officers or peace officers acting in the performance of their duties; and (ii) security personnel or employees of nuclear powered electric generating facilities located within the state who are employed as part of any security plan approved by the federal operating license agencies acting in the performance of their duties at such generating facilities. For purposes of this subparagraph, the term 'nuclear powered electric generating facility' shall mean a facility that generates electricity using nuclear power for sale, directly or indirectly, to the public, including the land upon which the facility is located and the safety and security zones as defined under federal regulations."

This statute places emphasis on situations involving arson, which is probably a reasonable consideration in view of the state's urban areas. The statute allows New York State residents to use deadly force on arsonists and burglars, but watch out for that "...*reasonably believes*..." part. If you use deadly force it had better be in a bona-fide *you or them* situation, *nothing less.* A court will decide if what you did was reasonable! Even if the criminal court lets you go, you may have to face a follow-on civil lawsuit.

Also, everywhere in New York State handguns have to be registered. Possession of long guns (shotguns and rifles) is legal in most areas of the state, but all guns have to be registered in New York City. Getting a gun registered in that city is a hassle, and it works against the average citizen even having a gun for self-defense. Does that keep guns out of the wrong hands? It's time for reality assessment. Violent criminals never worry about such things, and they never will. The situation in New York is nevertheless more favorable to the law-abiding citizen than the one in the United Kingdom, at least on paper.

A stronger self-defense law

Arkansas was not counted as a castle law state when this book was being written. However, the state has liberal gun laws, and many of the citizens of Arkansas own guns. If Arkansans are willing to pay instructional and background check fees of less than $300 they may obtain a concealed handgun carry license (CHCL) by completing a course of instruction, which includes a live firing session for evaluating proficiency and safety; in addition they must pass an FBI background evaluation. It is thus instructive to compare the Arkansas statutes with those of the more restrictive states like New York and also with those of states which have the most permissive "castle laws."

The applicable Arkansas statutes fall under *Title 5: Criminal Offenses*. First, 5-1-102 is a lengthy glossary of terms, such as "deadly weapon," "knowingly," "reasonably believes," etc, and parts 5-2-606, 5-2-607, 5-2-608, 5-2-620 and 5-2-621 go into the provisions for the use of defensive force by the citizens of Arkansas. Points of interest have been underlined for emphasis. The Arkansas law is a lot more detailed than its New York State counterpart.

"5-2-606. Use of physical force in defense of a person.

(a) A person is justified in using physical force upon another person to defend himself or a third person from what he reasonably believes to be the use or imminent use of unlawful physical force by that other person, and he may use a degree of force that he reasonably believes to be necessary. However, he may not use deadly physical force except as provided in § 5-2-607.
(b) A person is not justified in using physical force upon another person if:
(1) With purpose to cause physical injury or death to the other person, he provokes the use of unlawful physical force by the

166

other person; or

(2) He is the initial aggressor; but his use of physical force upon another person is justifiable if he in good faith withdraws from the encounter and effectively communicates to the other person his purpose to do so, and the latter continues or threatens to continue the use of unlawful physical force; or

(3) The physical force involved is the product of a combat by agreement not authorized by law.

5-2-607. Use of deadly physical force in defense of a person.

(a) A person is justified in using deadly physical force upon another person if he reasonably believes that the other person is:

(1) Committing or about to commit a felony involving force or violence;

(2) Using or about to use unlawful deadly physical force; or

(3) Imminently endangering his or her life or imminently about to victimize the person as described in § 9-15-103(a)(2), from the continuation of a pattern of domestic abuse. For the purposes of this section 'domestic abuse' shall be that described in § 9-15-103(a).

(b) A person may not use deadly physical force in self-defense if he knows that he can avoid the necessity of using that force with complete safety:

(1) By retreating, except that a person is not required to retreat if he is in his dwelling and was not the original aggressor, or if he is a law enforcement officer or a person assisting at the direction of a law enforcement officer; or

(2) By surrendering possession of property to a person claiming a lawful right thereto.

5-2-608. Use of physical force in defense of premises.

(a) A person in lawful possession or control of premises or a

vehicle is justified in using non-deadly physical force upon another person when and to the extent that he reasonably believes it necessary to prevent or terminate the commission or attempted commission of a criminal trespass by the other person in or upon the premises or vehicle.

(b) A person may use deadly physical force under the circumstances set forth in subsection (a) of this section when:
(1) Use of such force is authorized by § 5-2-607; or
(2) He reasonably believes the use of such force is necessary to prevent the commission of arson or burglary by a trespasser.

5-2-609. Use of physical force in defense of property.

A person is justified in using non-deadly physical force upon another person when and to the extent that he or she reasonably believes it necessary to prevent or terminate the person's commission or attempted commission of theft or criminal mischief, or subsequent flight therefrom.

5-2-620. Use of force to defend persons and property within home.

(a) The right of an individual to defend himself and the lives of persons or property in his home against harm, injury, or loss by persons unlawfully entering or attempting to enter or intrude thereupon is reaffirmed as a fundamental right to be preserved and promoted as a public policy in this state.
(b) There shall be a legal presumption that any force or means used to accomplish such purpose was exercised in a lawful and necessary manner, unless that presumption is overcome by clear and convincing evidence to the contrary.
(c) The above-stated public policy shall be strictly complied with by the courts, and appropriate instructions thereof shall be given to juries sitting in trial of criminal charges brought in

connection therewith.

5-2-621. Attempting to protect persons during commission of a felony.

No persons shall be civilly liable for actions or omissions intended to protect themselves or others from personal injuries during the commission of a felony."

Arkansas law requires a retreat from a hostile confrontation, if at all possible, with the exception of hostile encounters in one's own home, where further retreat is not required. This is where the Arkansas statute diverges from strict castle doctrine, which holds that one does not have to retreat from any place where he or she has a right to be. In Arkansas, if a healthy young man is caught outdoors in an assault and if he can sprint forty feet to a door and barricade himself behind it rather than use a legally carried weapon or even an improvised weapon, he is required to retreat. But if the assailant then breaks the door down and thus corners the defender, he is allowed to use the weapon. The court might have to deal with a very similar situation, where an 80-year old man with arthritis was forty feet from that same door. The older man might be well advised to stand his ground and use his weapon, because a sprint to the door is probably physically impossible in his case. A resort to deadly force should happen *only* if an assailant is about to take a life -- pointing a gun, bearing down with a dagger in hand, etc. (this criterion of eligibility for statutory protection does not depend on age or handicaps). But the court would almost certainly take a physical limitation into consideration as evidence that an individual was unable to retreat any further, although the wording of the law does not guarantee it.

The Arkansas law certainly treats home defense as a special situation [5-2-620 (a)], and that ought to be the case. When you are inside your own home you have already retreated to the maximum extent possible -- it is your domain, and you have a right to be there. You are in your castle. Thus, there is a presumption [5-2-620 (b)] that you may use deadly force ("...*any force or means...*") in that situation. But watch out for the "...*unless that presumption is overcome by...*" Your defense will not fly well if you have been provoking the intruder, messing with his wife, fighting him, etc. In Arkansas, If you kill someone in self-defense you probably *will* be taken to court, not released immediately! The circumstances behind the shooting will be brought into careful consideration. But the courts have a record of favoring the defender if nothing detracts from a clear case of self-defense.

While the Arkansas and New York statutes both allow the use of deadly force against an intruder, and there is no requirement to retreat if the hostile intrusion happens in the defender's own home, there is an exception. The Arkansas statute is very specific in disallowing cases where the one defending has been provocative toward the one injured or killed [5-2-606 (b) (1); 5-2-606 (b) (2); 5-2-607 (b)]. The reason for this should be obvious; the intent of the law is corrupted if it allows someone to provoke an intended victim to the point that the victim comes to the aggressor's property and is murdered there. The one perpetrating the murder might claim self-defense, hoping to escape justice, and he might actually succeed. These provisions and others within the Arkansas Statutes ought to *filter out* at least some of the cases where a homicide is not entirely one of self-preservation, and they thus reduce the likelihood of murders passed off as self-defense. However, there are other ways to lure a victim into a trap, and unless each homicide is carefully investigated even the Arkansas law might be defeated. As we will see, some of the castle law states have not clearly stated an exception to incidents where there had been hostility between the shooter and his victim. Those states have opened a door to trouble.

Finally, [5-2-621] protects Arkansas citizens from civil litigation if they have killed or injured an aggressor in the process of defending themselves *or others*. The latter is a distinctly castle doctrine provision. The presumption of a right to defend your own home and not have to retreat in that case is also very similar to castle doctrine, but in Arkansas it is subject to scrutiny. The requirement to retreat if at all possible when you are caught away from your home is where the Arkansas statute deviates significantly from castle doctrine. All considered, the Arkansas self-defense statutes are more favorable to the home defender than what is found in the New York State statutes.

The Arkansas self-defense laws are well written, or at least that's the author's opinion after a careful reading. The laws contain safeguards for weeding out shootings that are not entirely about self-preservation. Also, Arkansas law enforcement officers recognize the statutes. An incident in July of 2009 illustrates the prevailing attitude of the law officers.[2] Two men robbed a farm produce stand in Norfork, Arkansas and took about $250 from a cash box. One of the men maneuvered behind a woman who was operating the stand, and he struck her across the back with a metal baseball bat. She actually had a gun squirreled away for self-defense but "...*her weapon was out of reach at the time*." Access to a defensive weapon during a hostile intrusion is a fairly common problem, and only a few strong hearts are able to mount a resistance after a beating. This violent act -- clubbing a woman to get a mere $250 -- triggered a significant manhunt, and Police Chief Carry Manuel offered this advice to business owners:[2] *"You can protect yourself and the law backs you up -- you can act in self defense."* Sgt. Tim Phillips, Chief of Security for the County Court System, offered a set of recommendations for business owners, and they are presented in a condensed form in chapter 10.

Enter now the castle doctrine

The castle doctrine, upon which the various state castle laws are based, allows an individual to use force -- even deadly force -- if he or she is confronted by an aggressor, and the defender is further protected from criminal prosecution or civil lawsuit for injuring or killing an aggressor. We may compare the Arkansas laws with what is found in the statutes of states that follow a concept known as the *castle doctrine*. Here is what one of the National Rifle Association publications has to say about that doctrine:[3]

"Castle Doctrine, in essence, simply places into law what is a fundamental right: self-defense. If a person is in a place he or she has a right to be—in the front yard, on the road, working in their office, strolling in the park—and is confronted by an armed predator, he or she can respond in force in defense of their life.

Castle Doctrine also protects the law-abiding from criminal and civil charges for defending themselves against an attacker whereby, after enduring the trauma of a violent attack, they aren't again tied to the tracks of a drawn-out, nightmarish legal battle that could derail their financial future."

The doctrine also broadens the kinds of locations where self-defense is allowed, notably not just in your own home but also anywhere on your premises, in a nearby park, at the workplace (assuming that guns are permitted there) or in your car while traveling. It surely doesn't mean in a public school or a bank or a court room, where personal weapons are forbidden -- and for good reason. The concept itself is not illogical, but a weakness arises when someone is killed under circumstances where a claim of self-defense looks reasonable, but in fact, it was *not* self-defense. So how do you know that it really was motivated by self-preservation (and nothing else) as opposed to *malice aforethought, purposeful, vengeful, culpable...etc.?* After all, purposeful killers often try to claim self-defense (another familiar chorus is of this type: "*It was an accident*"). In cases where the castle doctrine is applicable, *one can die for an offense that would not carry a death penalty in a court of law*, and that is simply not acceptable![a] These are the potential weaknesses of the doctrine, because most statutes based on the concept presume innocence unless a prosecuting attorney chooses to carry out a thorough investigation.

Those states that are lately being called "castle doctrine states" actually go beyond the original concept. *Our houses are our castles; they are where we actually live.* It might be a mobile home or maybe even a tent, or in the author's case, a sturdy old wood frame house beside a street. Some houses have rock veneer; some even look like the castles of old. The castle is what's *inside* the house's walls. Property outside is defined by fences and streets. The property not inside a person's home but out on his lot should not be a kill zone. If there is an obnoxious disturbance outside, if rocks are thrown through the windows, etc. (as in a riot), then a 911 call by cell phone is the smartest move, just in case someone cut the regular phone line. If someone shoots into your home, you should take cover while making that call, and if you keep a gun, be ready with it. Don't open your door; stand back from it. Then if someone batters their way inside, the gun becomes an *immediate option*. If the one who barges in is holding a knife or a club rather than a firearm, then you ought to warn before using your own weapon. But if the intruder has a gun in his hand and shows an intent to use it rather than flee, you will have good reason to shoot. If he's a uniformed law enforcement officer outside knocking or calling by means of a loudspeaker, there should be no contest; ground your weapon! In no case should *anyone* intentionally open a door to trouble. That's the author's opinion; others see it differently.

Going beyond the castle is another matter. States that subscribe to the "stand your ground" concept regarding vehicles and workplaces generally apply the same eligibility considerations used for incidents involving home defense. States like Arkansas have more constraining rules about what you can or can't do *out there*, but self-defense beyond the home is nevertheless allowed. The need for self-defense outside the castle is not disputed, but calling that part of a self-defense statute "castle doctrine" is a poor choice of words.

The criteria for validity

What is not stated clearly in the above NRA description is that presumption of innocence found in the self-defense statutes of some states; if a shooter claims self-defense in a setting that looks like self-defense, then the district attorney has to presume innocence, but if he or she suspects otherwise, then the burden of proof is upon the one that makes the decision to prosecute or let it go. The one deciding is the district attorney, not a judge. Actually, that sounds stretched out of proportion, because prosecuting attorneys always have to prove their case even if a trial is involved. It comes down to the reality of the prosecutor's available resources of time and funds, court schedules and how all of that affects case *dispositions*; the prosecutor tries the hard core cases and plea bargains the milder ones (or maybe the politically easier ones). Plea bargains are even used in exchange for testimonies against more serious offenders. Apparent killings in self-defense are easier to deal with than other kinds of homicide. One can rubber stamp them as protected by castle doctrine -- just let it go at that and be done with it. The castle laws have made that temptation possible. This view is not meant to characterize prosecutors as being lazy; resources of time, jail space, courtroom capacity and other considerations are indeed strapped in most locations, but a prosecutor does not square well with public confidence if offenders are getting away with murder.

Thus, what the laws *allow* is only *half of the issue*, and justice is not likely to be served if the statute does not contain *safeguards* for weeding out cases where self-defense was not the motive. Going beyond the NRA's statement of the castle doctrine, there are at least eight criteria for deciding if a killing or serious injury should actually be protected by a castle law. Failure to meet *any one* of the following eight criteria *removes eligibility for protection,* or at least it *ought to* even if a self-defense law doesn't expressly state the safeguard; failing a criterion, the prosecutor *could* pursue a charge of assault and battery if it's an injury, or manslaughter or murder if it's a homicide.[b] (A castle doctrine situation *does not even exist if the home is vacant.* That puts the case under another statute, perhaps an intrusion for burglary or arson). Here are the criteria:

1. The intruder must not be a law officer acting in the line of duty, and the one defending has been made aware of that.

2. The intruder must be acting illegally -- attempting to enter forcibly.

3. The defender must *reasonably fear* serious injury or death.

4. If the defender has *provoked* the intruder, was the initial aggressor, invited an intrusion, set up a trap, etc., there should be no protection.

5. The defender must reasonably believe that the intruder intends to commit a felony, such as an arson or a burglary. The intruder's criminal record regarding arson or burglaries (or lack of a record) should be taken into account. If the defender also has a criminal record, it should not be ignored, either.

6. The defender must be the legal occupant of the home he was

defending.

7. The defender must not be a fugitive from justice.

8. The defender must not be acting conspiratorially to use a self-defense provision to aid and abet a fugitive from justice.

Criterion 8 is entirely about disallowing purposeful murders (for example, killing a witness to help a felon evade prosecution for a capital offense). These details of eligibility come from a broad examination of the various self-defense statutes. But individual states typically do not embody all of them in the wording of their self-defense laws even though they are often found elsewhere, i.e., in other statutes. Their existence is thus implied, but it would be better to have all of them stated clearly, or specifically *cross-referenced to*. Failure to meet one or more of the criteria removes eligibility for consideration; it was not self-defense, and the one who tried to claim self-defense will be charged with assault and battery, manslaughter or murder, depending on the motives and extent of injuries.

This brings up yet another question, namely that of the prioritization of statutes. We are asking this question: if two or more statutes apply to a given situation, which one takes priority? In Faron's case there was a question about *death of a prosecution witness* versus *homicide in self-defense*. Does the aggravated homicide statute take precedence over the self-defense statute, or is it the other way around? Only a lawyer licensed to practice in a given state could answer such a question concerning *that state's* system of statutes. Also, what is true for one state might not be the case for another. The ordinary citizen is in near total darkness concerning the ranking of statutes. Attorneys and judges probably argue a lot about statute priorities, including the castle doctrine statutes. This sort of thing is inferred from reading appeal cases, which frequently point out illegal procedures, misapplication of statutes, etc.; if such problems did not exist, why do we even have appellate courts? Lawyers make mistakes; so do scientists, medical doctors, cooks and carpenters.

The characteristics of the self-defense laws that exist in America are shown in the large table at the end of this chapter. On examining the table one immediately notices that nearly all of the states do not require retreat from an intruder in one's own home. Some of those states justify the use of deadly force when certain conditions exist and one's life is clearly threatened; others require that the defender only *believe* that he is in danger. A true castle law, as defined by NRA, exists if there is no duty to retreat in one's own home or anywhere else (i.e., in your car or at work, or maybe in a city park), and defenders are also protected from civil litigation if they injure or kill someone while defending themselves. This seems to go *beyond* the original meaning of a man's castle, but it has become the language in use. These characteristics are found in columns one through three, and in a state that fully accepts the castle doctrine the respective entries in the table will be N, N and Y (see the definitions in the table's footnotes). Those first three columns show the protections afforded to *individuals who have to use force*, including deadly force, as a matter of *genuine self-preservation*, but the fourth column separates states according to their emphasis on filtering out situations involving grudges, lovers' quarrels and so forth, where the use of force was not about self-preservation. If we don't apply those criteria for eligibility, murderers could escape justice.

Column four thus tells us if the state's self-defense law also specifies acceptable safeguards for *protecting the general public*. Does the statute have a *statement* about prior provocations? Does it at least explicitly cross-reference to other statutes that weed out such wrong motives? If so, the entry to column four will be "Y." An additional entry in column four is "C" *if* the state has a *child present* clause. An individual with malice has created the ultimate kind of provocation if someone else's child is in his or her home, thereby causing the parent to come for the child and walk into a trap. But even in the absence of manifest malice, the use of force with the child present should not be permitted. The overriding concern should be for the child-parent relationship.

Killing a parent in the presence of their child causes revulsion in most minds. In some states this is recognized; in most states it is not, but again, those cases may be covered elsewhere in a state's system of laws. If we can presume that an intruder is a threat to life merely because of his or her presence on someone's property, then we can make a much better assumption that the *presence* of a child in a hostile person's home is a strong provocation to that child's parent. Whether or not the child exception is considered or ignored is another matter, and that seems to be a developing problem. District attorneys apparently disregarded the safeguards in the ways they have handled recent killings in Texas and Oklahoma. An example was presented in chapter 1, and others will come up in chapters 8 and 10.

If there is *any* evidence to show that the one claiming self-defense harbored hostility toward the shooting victim, provoked him or her in any way or gave any indication of intent to create a trap, then the motive was probably not about self-defense, and the statute should not protect the individual using force. The other seven criteria just stated are also equally relevant; perhaps additional columns should be added to the table (requiring a fold-out page -- but *forget that!*). For example, you don't shoot a law officer, although many states require that he be on official duty and clearly indicates who he is before entering. Neither do you have justification for self-defense if the one injured has a right to be in the home; this separates the domestic disputes. The criteria for validity are entirely reasonable. Most of the published literature on castle doctrine has focused on the rights of the one defending while little or no attention is being paid to those safeguarding criteria. The two halves of the statute are equally important.

State officials, at least some of them, are aware of the need for balance. Governor Freudenthal of Wyoming was worried about problems that might arise by making his state's statute too broad or too vague when he signed Wyoming's castle doctrine legislation into law. Quoting his original reaction: "*I was troubled as it came out of the House because it went outside the castle...Inadvertently, I think some of the language went a little broad and I think the Senate brought it back into what is really much more consistent with our traditional jury instructions...*".
After all, the English common law, on which self-defense statutes are based, holds that a man's *home* is his castle. A park six blocks down the street is a public place and does not qualify as a man's castle, and it is not unreasonable to ask someone to

retreat from an aggressor in a city park, if indeed retreat is possible (thus, for Wyoming, the column two entry is "R" -- one must try to retreat before resorting to force).

But even the Wyoming law does not clearly address prior provocations in a way comprehensible to ordinary citizens (the column four entry is "--"), although the restriction is probably implicit in the wording if the person claiming self-defense is engaged in "...*an unlawful activity*..." Only a practicing Wyoming lawyer could tell us if that is true or not. If mere citizens do not understand the limitations of a statute, trouble is soon to come.

Examining Oklahoma's castle law

Here is the wording of Oklahoma's so-called castle law:

"Oklahoma Statutes Citationized
Title 21. Crimes and Punishments
Chapter 53 - Manufacture, Sale, and Wearing of Weapons
Oklahoma Firearms Act of 1971
Section 1289.25 - Physical or Deadly Force Against Intruder

A. The Legislature hereby recognizes that the citizens of the State of Oklahoma have a right to expect absolute safety within their own homes.

B. A person is presumed to have held a reasonable fear of

184

imminent peril of death or great bodily harm to himself or herself or another when using defensive force that is intended or likely to cause death or great bodily harm to another if:

1. The person against whom the defensive force was used was in the process of unlawfully and forcefully entering, or had unlawfully and forcibly entered, a dwelling, residence, or occupied vehicle, or if that person had removed or was attempting to remove another against the will of that person from the dwelling, residence, or occupied vehicle; and

2. The person who uses defensive force knew or had reason to believe that an unlawful and forcible entry or unlawful and forcible act was occurring or had occurred.

C. The presumption set forth in subsection B of this section does not apply if:

1. The person against whom the defensive force is used has the right to be in or is a lawful resident of the dwelling, residence, or vehicle, such as an owner, lessee, or titleholder, and there is not a protective order from domestic violence in effect or a written pretrial supervision order of no contact against that person;

2. The person or persons sought to be removed are children or grandchildren, or are otherwise in the lawful custody or under the lawful guardianship of, the person against whom the defensive force is used; or

3. The person who uses defensive force is engaged in an unlawful activity or is using the dwelling, residence, or occupied vehicle to further an unlawful activity.

D. A person who is not engaged in an unlawful activity and who is attacked in any other place where he or she has a right to be has no duty to retreat and has the right to stand his or her ground and meet force with force, including deadly force, if he or she reasonably believes it is necessary to do so to prevent death or great bodily harm to himself or herself or another or to prevent the commission of a forcible felony.

E. *A person who unlawfully and by force enters or attempts to enter the dwelling, residence, or occupied vehicle of another person is presumed to be doing so with the intent to commit an unlawful act involving force or violence.*

F. *A person who uses force, as permitted pursuant to the provisions of subsections B and D of this section, is justified in using such force and is immune from criminal prosecution and civil action for the use of such force. As used in this subsection, the term 'criminal prosecution' includes charging or prosecuting the defendant.*

G. *A law enforcement agency may use standard procedures for investigating the use of force, but the law enforcement agency may not arrest the person for using force unless it determines that there is probable cause that the force that was used was unlawful.*

H. *The court shall award reasonable attorney fees, court costs, compensation for loss of income, and all expenses incurred by the defendant in defense of any civil action brought by a plaintiff if the court finds that the defendant is immune from prosecution as provided in subsection F of this section.*

I. *The provisions of this section and the provisions of the Oklahoma Self-Defense Act, Sections 1290.1 through 1290.26 of this title, shall not be construed to require any person using a pistol pursuant to the provisions of this section to be licensed in any manner.*

J. As used in this section:

1. 'Dwelling' means a building or conveyance of any kind, including any attached porch, whether the building or conveyance is temporary or permanent, mobile or immobile, which has a roof over it, including a tent, and is designed to be occupied by people;

2. 'Residence' means a dwelling in which a person resides either temporarily or permanently or is visiting as an invited guest; and

3. 'Vehicle' means a conveyance of any kind, whether or not motorized, which is designed to transport people or property."

Nowhere in this statute do we find a meaningful filter for separating questionable shootings from genuine self-defense. The law does not specifically cite other Oklahoma statutes that address murders, provocations and entrapments, although 1289.25.B.3 and 1289.25.G seem to be where the Oklahoma law interfaces with other statutes that do set restrictions; maybe a provision actually exists elsewhere. The wording ought to be contained within 1289.25, or else 1289.25 should refer to an appropriate statute. This is perceived as a weakness of Oklahoma's law, and the law does not appear to be well-written; it will tend to accommodate cases that are not actual self-defenses. The Oklahoma statute does, however, include the "...*reasonably believes...*" wording, and there is a strong restriction concerning children or grandchildren present. Unfortunately, the child restriction doesn't appear to work in practice!

Oklahoma State Senator Susan Paddack, who voted for the state's castle law, was contacted for information concerning HB 2615 (which became statute 1289.25), especially the Senate's final vote on the bill. She was very helpful, and she complied fully with the request. The Senate Record showed a minority voice of five who opposed the bill after the third reading, among them State Senator James Wilson of Tahlequah. A certified letter was sent to Senator Wilson expecting a reply in some depth as to why the bill was opposed and why a child clause was put in the bill, and it was suggested that if he didn't have time to pursue the request, perhaps an assistant might research it. That's exactly what happened, and here is how his assistant, Amy Schroeder, responded: "*Thank you for your recent email and letter. I believe that guns are a poor way to handle any dispute.*"

That was *the entire response*! One is tempted to conclude that Ms. Schroeder's terse response was the actual thinking behind the Senator's vote, but if so, it is awfully weak. The castle law is about defending one's self from a dangerous intruder, not settling disputes! Killing someone simply because he or she has a dispute with you has a distinct description: *murder*.

Others who voted against the bill were contacted by e-mail, but they never responded. The actual *motives* behind the child clause and other kinds of exceptions, along with the reasons why some of the lawmakers did not support the bill are highly relevant to the issues of this book. It is unfortunate that those who opposed the Oklahoma castle law either didn't know much about what they were voting against, or didn't care to tell the public why their vote was "nay". Finding an answer required looking outside of Oklahoma.

Stonewalling has been typical of the majority of Oklahoma officials contacted (meaning the police, court officials, OSBI, legislators, etc.). The general attitude seems to be "don't bother us," and the exceptions (such as Senator Paddack's) have been few and far between. The reality of Oklahoma's criminal justice system appears to be frequent errors and arbitrariness, and no one seems to be willing to face that problem. Others in Oklahoma will eventually experience the frustration of people like Rick and his family, because the ill advised shootings are not going to go away.

Alabama's statute has a similar wording concerning children

present, but a case that involved it was not found. The other criteria apparently do not work well in Alabama because a man who had no criminal intent was shot to death for accidentally walking into another person's apartment, one that was structurally equivalent to his own apartment (which was nearby), yet his death was attributed to a homicide in self-defense. This was a mindless application of the castle law because the one doing the shooting allegedly had a criminal record and showed indications of psychological unbalance. That case will be given more attention in Chapter 10.

In other states that follow the castle doctrine, the exceptions are more clearly spelled out. As an example, the Texas castle law is very clear in disallowing shootings with motives other than self-defense:

"A person who has a right to be present at the location where the deadly force is used, who has not provoked the person against whom the deadly force is used, and who is not engaged in criminal activity at the time the deadly force is used is not

required to retreat before using deadly force as described by this section."

Even so, some of the most senseless shootings have happened in Texas. Many other states put the exception to provocation in their self-defense laws. For example, West Virginia's 55-7-22

(e) has this to say about provocation:

"The full and complete civil defense created by the provisions of this section is not available to a person who: (1) Is attempting to commit, committing or escaping from the commission of a felony; (2) Initially provokes the use of force against himself, herself or another with the intent to use such force as an excuse to inflict bodily harm upon the assailant; or (3) Otherwise initially provokes the use of force against himself, herself or another, unless he or she withdraws from physical contact with the assailant and indicates clearly to the assailant that he or she desires to withdraw and terminate the use of force, but the assailant continues or resumes the use of force."

Alabama's law has been applied rigidly even in cases that were suspicious (see chapter 10), but it does recognize restrictions:

"a person is not justified in using deadly physical force upon another person if it reasonably appears or he knows that he can avoid the necessity of using such force with complete safety."

and:

"With intent to cause physical injury or death to another person, he provoked the use of unlawful physical force by such other person; or...He was the initial aggressor"

The Oklahoma law is very different from the one in New York because a defender does not have to be licensed to own a handgun in order to use one in self-defense (1289.25.I). The main restriction on handguns in Arkansas and Oklahoma is that they may not be carried concealed beyond one's home without a valid carry permit. Even in that case there are numerous restrictions on where a concealed weapon may go. Understandably, concealed handguns are not allowed in schools, banks, courthouses, etc.

A defender who has injured or killed an intruder is protected from a civil lawsuit (1289.25.F). There is no requirement to retreat if the individual is located where he has a right to be, including in his vehicle (1289.25.B, 1289.25.D and 1289.25.J.3), which stands in contrast to the equivalent Arkansas statute. The presumption of innocence is stated in 1289.25.B.

Maybe Oklahoma and other states with castle doctrine laws should revert to the manner of territorial days -- allow the wearing of holstered handguns on a proper gun belt rather than concealed. At least bystanders would be forewarned. But that was intended to be a cynical comment! The trend to allow a deadly combat other than at home is not a good idea for most people who lack professional training, and it is something that a lot of law officers would rather avoid, e.g., "*A person who is not engaged in an unlawful activity and who is attacked in any other place where he or she has a right to be has no duty to retreat and has the right to stand his or her ground and meet force with force, including deadly force."* If you want to re-live the frontier days, talk with your legislators, but a lot of people would rather not be in that situation. Have we so soon forgotten the realities of the wild west era?

Other States That Have Castle Laws

By one accounting these are the states that follow the castle doctrine: *Alabama, Alaska, Arizona, Connecticut, Florida, Georgia, Hawaii, Idaho, Illinois, Indiana, Kentucky, Louisiana, Maine, Massachusetts, Michigan, Minnesota, Mississippi, Missouri, Montana, North Carolina, Ohio, Oklahoma, Pennsylvania, Rhode Island, South Carolina, Tennessee and Texas.* This list was valid near the end of 2008 based on documents researched, but since other states have pending legislation, the table will probably be incomplete by the time this book appears in print. Bear in mind that there are also differences in the wording of the various self-defense statutes. The table (below) attempts to compare the statutes of all 50 states, at least those for which information could be found, and it notes four characteristics for comparison rather than tell us which states have a castle law and which do not.

SELF-DEFENSE LAWS BY STATE
CHARACTERISTICS OF SELF DEFENSE LAWS$^{\alpha}$

STATE	RETREAT REQUIRED		CRITERIA FOR PROTECTION		
	HOME	ANYWHERE	LAWSUIT	PROVOCATION$^{\beta}$	
Alabama (3)	N	R	Y	Y	C
Alaska (3)	N	R	Y	Y	C
Arizona (3)	N	N	Y	-	C
Arkansas (3)	N	R	Y	Y	
California	N	R	-	Y	
Colorado	N	-	Y	Y	
Connecticut	N	R	-	Y	
Delaware	N	R	Y	Y	
D.C. (1)	The district's strict gun laws have been ruled unconstitutional				
Florida (3)	N	N	Y	Y	C
Georgia (3)	N	N	Y$^{\chi}$	Y	
Hawaii	N	R	-	Y	
Idaho (2)	R	N	-	-	
Illinois (2)	R	R	Y	Y	
Indiana (3)	N	N	-	Y	
Iowa (1)	R	R	-	Y	
Kansas (3)	N	N	-	Y	
Kentucky (3)	N	N	-	-	C
Louisiana (3)	N	N	-	-	
Maine	N	R	-	Y	
Maryland	N	R$^{\chi}$	-	-	
Massachusetts	N	R	-	-	
Michigan (3)	N	N	-	-	C
Minnesota	N	R	-	Y	
Mississippi (3)	N	R	Y	Y	
Missouri (3)	N	R	Y	Y	
Montana (3)	N	R	-	-	
Nebraska	N	R	-	Y	
Nevada+	N	R	Y	Y	
New Hampshire (1)	Governor vetoed recent self defense legislation				

New Jersey$^{\varepsilon}$	N	R	Y	Y	
New Mexico (1)	A law of 1907 is not given broad interpretation				
New York (2)	N$^{\phi}$	-	-	-	
North Carolina	N	R	-	Y	
North Dakota (3)	N	R	Y	Y	C
Ohio (3)	N	R	Y	-	
Oklahoma (3)	N	N	Y	-	C
Oregon	N$^{\gamma}$	R	-	Y	
Penn. (2)$^{\varepsilon?}$	N	R	Y	Y	C
Rhode Island	N	R	-	-	
S. Carolina(3)	N	N	Y	-	C
S. Dakota (3)	N	N	-	-	
Tennessee (3)	N	N	Y	Y	C
Texas (3)	N	N	Y	Y	
Utah	N	R	-	Y	
Vermont$^{\eta}$	-	-	-	-	
Virginia (1)	R	R	-	-	
Washington	N	R	-	-	
West Virginia	N	R	Y	Y	
Wisconsin	N$^{\delta}$	R	-	Y	
Wyoming	N	R	Y	-	C

$^{\alpha}$This table attempts to compare the main properties of the self-defense laws of the United States and the District of Columbia. Entry abbreviations for columns one and two are: retreat is *not required* (N) and retreat is *required* (R). If the entry for column three is *yes* (Y), then the law protects the defender from civil liability if his or her actions are ruled justifiable. A dash (-) indicates that *no positive statement granting civil immunity was found*, or that civil immunity is explicitly *not granted*. In column four a *yes* (Y) means that the statute includes a statement disallowing the use of force or deadly force if the one claiming to do so in self-defense has provoked the one injured *beforehand*. If the entry is (-), an exception to provocations was either *not stated* or *not referenced to* in the examined parts of the statutes. Distinguishing keywords for columns one and two include *retreat, withdraw, avoid*, etc., and column two will indicate *stand ground* or *no retreat required* if the law is granting an innocent citizen maximum protection in self-defense situations. For column three the keywords include *liable, civilly liable, civil action, lawsuit,* etc.; and for column four they include *provoke, initial aggressor, child* or *grandchild,* etc. The one defending is frequently called the "*actor.*"

$^\beta$Unlike the first three columns, the fourth column gives an indication of a state's safeguards against *unwarranted* injuries and death. Prior provocations on the part of the one that caused serious injury or death usually *removes justification* for a homicide in self-defense. If the column entry is a dash (-) it does not mean that an appropriate statute does not exist somewhere else in the system of laws, but that the self-defense statute itself does not make an explicit statement of the criterion or provide a cross-reference to one that exists elsewhere. If the entry in column four is not a Y, then confusion *could* exist in the mind of an ordinary citizen, whereas a lawyer would likely cite a different statute (e.g., "Because the one defending was acting illegally..."). One shouldn't think that prior hostilities between the one purported to be defending and the one injured have no bearing on the incident. Even a hint of hostility is a warning that says: look deeper. Also, if there is a C to the right in column four, the state's self-defense statute takes exception to the legitimacy of an incident if the intruder's child or grandchild was present on the premises when the incident occurred and if the intruder came there for the child, which is likely to the exact motive in most such cases. A parent's worry for the safety of a child can become the ultimate provocation, a means for luring the parent into a trap. There are other criteria for deciding if a homicide is not justifiable, and they will be considered in chapter 9. It is inattention to these criteria that creates the darker side of the castle laws.

$^\chi$conditional provision.

$^\delta$The statute says nothing about a duty to retreat, but case law holds that if a retreat is possible it must be pursued. In 2007 the Wisconsin House passed a castle law bill, but it died in the Senate.

$^\epsilon$Pending legislation cited. Existing Nevada law is tersely written and allows self-defense when life is threatened, with no civil liability protection or safeguarding criteria specified explicitly.

$^\phi$One can defend against arsons and burglaries, but nothing is specified about assaults with other motives.

$^\gamma$The law itself doesn't address retreat/withdrawal, but the state's supreme court has acknowledged that retreat is not practical in some cases, which has created a controversy.

$^\eta$In Vermont anyone of legal age who is able to pass the FBI instant check can buy a handgun and carry it concealed and loaded -- *without* a permit. *Where* it can be carried is restricted (not in schools, courthouses, federal buildings, etc.). The Vermont self-defense statute is very brief, says nothing about retreat or civil liability, and states that an individual may use lethal force for the "*...just and necessary defense of his own life...*" or lives of others threatened. The crime rate in Vermont is quite low.

Special cases for states: A state is tagged as (1) if no meaningful castle doctrine law exists. States tagged with a (2) have fairly weak self-defense laws. States that are said to have castle doctrine laws are tagged with a (3). Changes in statutes are taking place continually, so keep that in mind.

[end of table]

END NOTES -- Chapter 3

a. The author is not at odds with the NRA. A great deal has been blamed on the organization, but the NRA leadership does not endorse questionable shootings. The NRA leaders cringe every time another senseless shooting is in the news. Even gun enthusiasts draw the line when things get out of hand.

b. It should work that way *in theory*, but adherence to the criteria assumes that the court will take all of the facts into account. In practice it rarely happens that way, and chapters 8, 9 and 10 ought to convince the reader that our courts are not being careful with self-defense issues. Selectivity with evidential information is what weakens the safeguards. The stated criteria amount to a *filter* for rooting out attempts to pass off murders as self-defense.

REFERENCES CITED -- Chapter 3

1. Joyce L. Malcolm, "Guns and Violence: the English experience," Harvard University Press; new edition, October 19, 2004.

2. Staff writer, "Businesses can take precautions," *The Baxter Bulletin*, July 28, 2009.

3. Staff writer, " 'This Train Keeps A Rollin': Castle Doctrine Sweeps America," National Rifle Association Document, July 28, 2007.

Chapter 4 - The actual impact
on burglaries and intrusions

"It has been an unqualified success. Since the Make My Day Law came into force, burglary has declined by almost half in Oklahoma. In 1987, there were 58,333 cases; in 2000, just 31,661."

An Oklahoma State Senate press release in 2004[1] reached that conclusion regarding 1289.25, referred to commonly in Oklahoma as the "Make My Day Law" rather than a castle law, and it may be true.

Use of these statistics to establish cause and effect is open to scrutiny even though it seems reasonable to attribute the decline in burglaries (a 45.7 percent drop) to fear of being shot. But be careful with the statistics. This could be like weighing something with your finger pushing down on the balance pan *if more than one cause variable is working*. There may be other cause variables. For example, the same Oklahoma State Senate press release noted that crime rates in other states also fell during the 1990s, which was true, and that included states *without* a strong self-defense law.

"While crime rates throughout America fell in the 1990s,

Make My Day supporters point to a second statistic in Oklahoma they say proves the impact of the new [1987] law: while burglary rates plunged, other forms of theft stayed constant. In 1988, there were 96,418 cases, in 2000, 96,111."

There were two stages in the development of Oklahoma's current self-defense law. This part of the Senate press release refers to a law that went into effect in 1987 and the decline in burglaries that followed; the 1987 law protected a home-defender from civil lawsuits. A "Make My Day" law with real teeth came into effect on May 12, 2006, when Gov. Brad Henry signed HB 2615 into law. The latter retained the immunity from civil lawsuits and granted home defenders more sweeping protections from criminal prosecution.

The level rate of those "other forms of theft" was not compared with anything else.[1] Also, some intrusion crimes are not burglaries. Intuitively, the enhanced prospect of being shot dead for breaking into someone's home ought to deter a lot of prospective burglars, but it is not reasonable to claim that a fear of being killed by a homeowner is the *only* cause variable at work or that burglaries will be stopped entirely. The decline from *58,333* to 31,661 burglaries after the Oklahoma castle law went into effect is a rather large change. Even so, the law did not bring the crime of burglary to a screeching halt.

A contention of this book is that the *details* of individual intrusion incidents that resulted in *defensive* shootings can modify conclusions drawn from the gross statistics. A tabulation of home-defense cases in a certain region might have 75 entries, and there will be a temptation to conclude that *Seventy-five gallant homeowners defended their lives and property.* Realistically, *some* of those 75 will be well-justified, but others might be more questionable. For example, the shooting of a seventeen year old intruder in Durant, Oklahoma during the winter of 2010 happened during a burglary attempt.[2] From the very beginning the officials "*expected*" that no charges would be filed against the shooter, and here is how that was worded: "*No charges are <u>expected</u> against the homeowner due to the state's 'Make my Day' law that gives homeowners the right to use deadly force if they <u>feel</u> in danger.*" [underlining added] The local newspaper reported that the youth admitted that he had broken into the home and was shot, and if so, he should be held accountable for the crime. In fact, the early news reports indicated that he would be charged as an adult. The homeowner was awakened by the sounds of a break-in and took action. With just that much information it is easy to conclude that the shooting was entirely warranted. However, *there is more detail to consider.*

On reading three consecutive articles about the incident -- from the same newspaper[2] -- one learns that the youth was *shot in the back!* That seems to indicate that he was *leaving,* certainly not charging at the home owner; at first you get the feeling that the intruder saw the homeowner holding a gun and ran! The homeowner claimed that he shot because the boy was reaching into his pocket, but how did it come about that he shot the youth in the back? The illumination was probably good enough to distinguish front from back if the homeowner could see the intruder reaching for his pocket. Was this an example of a trigger-happy shooter? The court evidently followed the *applicable* part of 1289.25 (part B) even though the bullet's impact point raises a serious question about the *necessity* of a shooting: "A person is *presumed* to have held a *reasonable fear of imminent peril of death or great bodily harm to himself or herself* ..." [if the intruder] "...*had unlawfully and forcibly entered.*" [underlining added for emphasis] One is inclined to believe that the Oklahoma law actually encourages unwarranted shootings. It is possible to "presume" situations that are not actually real.

A better statistical tabulation would divide shootings into "absolutely necessary for survival" and "questionable." This example looks questionable, but perhaps the intruder was standing with his side toward the shooter and the bullet happened to hit his back (with side or front impacts also possible). More information is needed than could be found through the media.

The youth was flown to a Plano, Texas hospital, and as it turned out, the .45 caliber bullet that hit him missed his vital organs. He was lucky. A reading of those newspaper articles causes one to wonder about the overall accuracy of the journalism. One account said that the homeowner was sleeping when the intruder came in; the other had him preparing for a shower bath. It's the kind of thing that makes Faron's grandfather skeptical of journalistic writing. Also, the same Oklahoma court that releases home defenders who kill or injure intruders under questionable circumstances cannot award the death penalty for an uncomplicated burglary. Thus, we should not ignore the details of the individual incidents because the statistics alone can be deceptive. Some intrusions endanger the homeowner; others do not. Some of the gunplay can and should be avoided. The amount of force used should be *equitable*.

Several other *cause variables* need to be considered, one

being the influence of the economic environment. The young intruder in the Durant shooting incident[2] claimed he was trying to obtain money to help his uncle pay the rent, which, of course, did not justify a burglary. During the early 1980s the stock market *earnings per share curve (S&P 500)* was a roller coaster ride averaging level, but other than the dip around 1991, the earnings per share ballooned up between 1987 and 2000, generally continuing upward until the crash of 2008. The period between 1987 and the end of the century was a better time. On the other hand, bad times create desperate people, and some of them will turn to criminal activities. That certainly doesn't rationalize what they choose to do, but it is a *reality*. The effect of the serious economic downturn of 2008-2009 may result in an increase in intrusion crimes. We thus acknowledge *economic pressure* as a possible *cause variable*.

We may be seeing such an effect because in Mountain Home, Arkansas, which is a fairly affluent area with a population above 10,000, the number of criminal investigations assigned for the first half of 2009 (286) was up 42.2 percent from what it had been in 2008 (201). This increase was due mostly to drug activity, burglaries, general thefts, etc. Fortunately, violent crimes did not increase. These may just be local fluctuations, and it is too soon to draw conclusions. A comprehensive state-by-state assessment would be necessary to decide what is really happening. Is it possible that at least part of Oklahoma's decrease in burglaries during 1987 - 2000 came about because of the more favorable economic situation that existed during those years? Other cause factors to consider include the extent of illicit drug use, changes of morality, the rate of unemployment and population migrations. Oklahoma witnessed population migrations during the Great Depression, and the state's employment rules are currently causing many illegal immigrants to leave the state.[3]

Armed intruders can be very brazen, as the example of a recent Ohio case shows.[4] The possibility of an armed homeowner is not always a deterrent. A man armed with a twelve-inch knife broke into a woman's home and demanded money. The woman's 68-year old brother retrieved a gun, came into the scene and shot at the intruder, who fled. But less than two hours later the same intruder came back for a second attempt. The scene repeated, and the woman's brother shot again, causing serious injury to the intruder that time. Perhaps stupid is a better choice of words for describing the nature of the intruder/robber. This happened after Ohio passed a castle law, so we can't say that the castle laws are entirely effective in deterring intrusion crimes. The war on drugs didn't stop drug trafficking, either. Should we be surprised?

Since the castle laws are about self-defense, most often within the person's own home, the effect on burglary rates is only one indicator for evaluating the castle laws. The criterion is, in fact, *off-track*, because the untrained citizen should not be expected to work law enforcement miracles. We should focus on the following two criteria, more to the point:

1. Did the rate of violent intrusion crimes actually decrease -- *especially in private homes*? Note that this criterion considers only the intrusions that threaten lives, not burglaries generally.
2. Did the rate of unwarranted shootings *increase*, encouraged by the existence of the laws?

The author could not find a study that focused on just those two criteria, and in the case of the first criterion it is probably too soon for a meaningful assessment of that type of information. The Oklahoma statistics apparently counted *all* burglaries, even those that happened when the residents were not home. But other studies have reached similar conclusions, and the supposition that private gun ownership reduces the overall crime rate is supported by facts.⁽⁵⁾

There is no doubt that burglars felt pressure because of the new laws, but how much? An evaluation of hostile intrusions would have to include the workplace and the car for the "anywhere you have a right to be" states. Shootings in such situations are more open to question than the ones in the home setting and are more liable to jeopardize innocent lives.

The answer to the second criterion is *yes* because there is now an accumulating record of senseless shootings where individuals went beyond the intended limits of an applicable castle law, thinking that what they did was right. In those cases we have good reason to believe that the mere existence of a liberal castle law actually encouraged erroneous thinking. Those who shoot without knowing the rules usually try to claim castle law protection. Some of those examples will be treated in chapters 8 and 10.

Prowlers seeking money for drugs are persistent and very bold, and burglars who are sexual predators are the most dangerous kind of intruders.⁽⁶⁾ This phenomenon has been studied in some depth. Many burglars find their activities *thrilling.* One well-known factor in intrusion crimes is their relationship to drug abuse, and that will be examined in chapter

5, which follows. *And again, this should not be overlooked: some intrusion incidents happen with no intent of committing a burglary; some are the result of mutual arguments, and sometimes individuals simply walk through the wrong open door and pay for the innocent mistake with their life.* Nevertheless, shootings arising from the latter cases are often attributed to self-defense, whether or not they should be.

By some accounts justifiable homicides have been increasing in recent years, both nationally and in castle law states. We may compare Texas, a castle law state, with the whole nation.[7] In attempting such a comparison of the available data, uncertainties arise. For one thing, not all homicides tabulated as justifiable took place in the domestic setting. Another is that a careful reading of the self-defense incidents of recent years finds that some of the shootings are questionable even though they were categorized as self-defense. The Durant incident during the winter of 2010 was an example,[2] although it did not involve a death. Other examples will come up in chapters 8 and 10. One is thus not completely sure about the meaning of the various data tabulations. Keeping that limitation in mind, the tabulation on the following page compares justified civilian homicides in Texas with the entire United States for the years 2003-2007:[7]

TEXAS HOMICIDES		NATIONAL HOMICIDES	
Year	Justifiable	Year	Justifiable
2003	32	2003	247
2004	31	2004	222
2005	24	2005	196
2006	34	2006	238
2007	45	2007	254

Justifiable homicides were at a minimum in 2005, both nationally and in Texas. With 2005 as a reference point, the national increase was about 30%, while in Texas the increase was close to 88%. Texas is the second most populated state, and the 2008 estimate of 24 million is approximately 7.8% of the national figure tabulated for February, 2009, which was 306 million. In comparison, the 45 justifiable homicides in Texas in 2007 is about 18% of the national figure of 254 justifiable homicides. Texans are more likely to defend themselves, but that is no surprise. The figure of 196 justifiable homicides needs to be put into proper perspective because according to FBI statistics, there were 10,100 murders by firearms in 2005 (these figures came from the FBI website -- see reference 7). Criminal violence *far outweighs* the defensive use of firearms. Even so, the castle laws do have a darker side, and *that* problem needs to be addressed.

The darker side of the castle laws is a reality. *"There may be occasions where criminals may possibly benefit from bizarre interpretations of the law, but the system works,"* said Jim Dark, past executive director of the Texas State Rifle Association (the pun was not intended). Jim Dark is optimistic about the value of the castle laws, but he has acknowledged something that a lot of people wish would go away. Should we accommodate a few murders just to protect the law itself? There is a problem here. One is not entirely convinced that the castle laws work well *either way.*

REFERENCES CITED -- Chapter 4

1. It is not hard to believe that a significant part of the decline in burglaries in Oklahoma came from a fear of being shot. The complete Oklahoma Senate press release is printed below, and its title is: *"How the 'Make My Day' law cut epidemic of violent burglary."* But it is noted that the adjective "violent" in that title may be misleading, because only an unspecified fraction of those 58,333 cases of burglary in 1987 involved violent confrontations. Burglars generally try to strike when the owners are away, so those cases -- the majority -- did not involve actual violence. Also, those "other forms of theft" are not compared with national data. The release was written by politicians to justify the validity of their "Make My Day" law, and what they presented to the public is not complete in the scientific sense. Perhaps there is a more thorough document behind this document, but it has not been offered.

The following was a key statement: *"We considered it outrageous that someone who protects his home and family should suffer,"* and the author agrees. If it was a do or die situation, then the concept is valid. However, it is also outrageous if the law is allowed to cover a murder. The full public release is printed here, by permission:

For Immediate Release: November 3, 2004

At 3.30am on January 6, 1987, Dr. Frank Sommer, a dentist in Tulsa, Oklahoma, woke to the sound of his garage door opening. He looked at the clock, mentally scolded his son, then 18, or his daughter 20, for getting home so late, and waited for the sound of their footsteps downstairs.

"After a few minutes, I thought that it was odd that I had heard nothing more. I took the gun from my nightstand, left my wife fast asleep and went downstairs to make sure everything was OK," he recalled yesterday.

What happened next was an experience of pure terror. As he looked through the peep-hole from the kitchen into the garage, he saw two strange men. One was pilfering from his wife's car: the other was standing at the opened door, by the tool racks.

Just as he stepped through the door to challenge the intruders, the lights went out. "It was total darkness and suddenly I was very, very scared. I fired one shot and yelled a warning. I saw one figure run off and as I went towards the driveway I saw a body in the doorway. 'Oh no!' I thought. 'He's dead.'"

In those few seconds Dr. Sommer, 66, had been plunged into a case that changed the law in Oklahoma and may yet influence a change in the law in Britain. Within weeks of the incident, the Oklahoma state government passed legislation that became known as the Make My Day Law, named for the celebrated scene in the Clint Eastwood Dirty Harry film.

The law was pushed through by Sen. Charles Ford, a Republican, the opposition party in the state.

"The purpose of the law is to protect the victim of crime who defends his home and his family against unlawful intrusion from any criminal prosecution or civil action," Sen. Ford said last week.

"We considered it outrageous that someone who protects his home and family should suffer. Our law says you can use any force, including deadly force, to defend your home."

It has been an unqualified success. Since the Make My Day Law came into force, burglary has declined by almost half in Oklahoma. In 1987, there were

58,333 cases; in 2000, just 31,661.

While crime rates throughout America fell in the 1990s, Make My Day supporters point to a second statistic in Oklahoma they say proves the impact of the new law: while burglary rates plunged, other forms of theft stayed constant. In 1988, there were 96,418 cases, in 2000, 96,111.

Similar anti-burglar laws have now been adopted in Colorado and Arizona. The reason, said Sen. Ford, was simple: "The law works. We were in the grip of a violent burglary epidemic when Dr. Sommer's home was invaded."

"Over that Christmas, we had six people in their 70s and 80s killed, bludgeoned to death by burglars in their bedrooms. How were they meant to defend themselves if they could not legally resort to lethal force?" he said.

Giving householders immunity from criminal and civil action was also inspired by Dr. Sommer's experience. Although he was taken to the police station and interrogated, the District Attorney read the public mood over the series of deadly burglaries and decided against charging him with the killing of the burglar, Russell Bryant, 19. [underlining added]

An "ambulance chaser" lawyer contacted Bryant's family and sought damages for a lifetime of lost earnings on the grounds that the killing was unlawful.

"This was outrageous and focused attention on the vague state of the law which left the victim of burglary vulnerable," said Sen. Ford, 73.

Prior to the Make My Day legislation, the law, as it remains in most American states, sanctioned force in self-defense and the defense of property, but only on the basis of "reasonable" response to the violence offered by the criminal. This allows a baseball bat against a baseball bat, a knife against a knife, and a gun against a gun -- although in theory the householder should allow the burglar to shoot first.

There have now been at least 11 cases where intruders have been shot dead in Oklahoma and the householders who pulled the trigger have escaped any sanction under the Make My Day law.

While Dr. Sommer is a fervent supporter of the law protecting householders, he said that killing Bryant had left him into overwhelming feelings of guilt and that for years he was tormented by the thought that he had committed the "ultimate sin".

"Every time I go into that garage I think about it," he explained. "But I do not regret it. My wife and children were in our home. I am sorry that young man was in the wrong place at the wrong time. But that was of his choosing."

Oklahoma State Senate
Communications Division
State Capitol
Oklahoma City, Oklahoma 73105

For more information contact:
Senate Communications Office - (405) 521-5774

2. The *Durant Daily Democrat* carried a sequence of accounts following an intrusion incident and shooting that led to a youth being charged with burglary of a residence on January 7, 2010. The article titles are: "Shot juvenile burglar suspect released from hospital, may be charged as adult;" "Police: Juvenile shot in burglary attempt charged as adult;" and "Teen shot by homeowner enters plea to burglary charge." These titles can be found through http://www.durantdemocrat.com/

3. Emily Bazar, "Illegal Immigrants Moving Out," *USA Today*, September 27, 2007; Ron Jackson, "Illegal immigrant living in Oklahoma City decides to leave the American dream," *Oklahoman*, May 30, 2010.

4. Christopher Bobby, "Man cleared of wrongdoing: Police say shooting was self-defense," *Tribune Chronicle*, February 20, 2009; Ed Runyan, "Another area crime victim fights back," *Vindy.com*, February 21, 2009.

5. John R. Lott, Jr., "More Guns, Less Crime: Understanding Crime and Gun Control Laws," Second Edition, University of Chicago Press, 2000.

6. Michael G Vaughn, et al., "Toward a Quantitative Typology of Burglars: A Latent Profile of Career Offenders," *Journal of Forensic Science*, Vol. 53(6), pp1387-1392, 2000.

7. Sourcing documents are these: *2007 Crime in the United States*, U.S. Department of Justice -- Federal Bureau of Investigation; and *The Texas*

213

Crime Report, Texas Department of Public Safety. Current official reports can be found through http://www.fbi.gov/ and http://www.txdps/state.tx.us/).

Chapter 5 - Drugs and crimes, including intrusions

"Now you gushin, ambulance rushin you to the hospital with a bad concussion
Plus ya hit 4 times bullet hit ya spine paralyzed waist down now ya wheel chair bound
Never mind that now you lucky to be alive,
Just think it all started you fussin with 3 guys..."
- Lyrics from "Dead and Gone" by rapper T.I.

This chapter is about America's worst problem -- drugs. It is a problem in other nations, too, but the United States seems to be the leading nation in the matter of drug abuse. Illicit drugs have become the major driving force behind many other ills. Involvement with illegal drugs is often the cause of home intrusion incidents. Users have to support an expensive habit, so they resort to theft, burglary and robbery to obtain the necessary assets. Those who abuse drugs and alcohol are likely to do things that a sober person wouldn't do. We can't say it is always the motive behind such crimes, but it is clear that gangs, burglars, carjackers, etc. tend to be involved with drugs. Those are the kinds of criminals that put innocent citizens in life-threatening situations and for which the castle laws were intended.

The extent of the drug problem

There is a drug war in progress in Mexico, and the bad guys seem to be winning it. The number of homicides in the city of Juarez was 186 in 2003. The rate trended upwards a bit, so that in 2005 it had reached 227. Then, in 2006, President Calderon began an offensive against the drug cartels. In Juarez alone, between January of 2008 and January of 2010, there were more than 4,400 homicides! Counting all of Mexico the toll in January of 2010 had exceeded 15,000. This dramatic increase in violence is almost entirely about drugs, primarily the work of drug cartels fighting over turf. The residents of El Paso are understandably worried, and the rest of us should be, too.

A fairly large segment of the global civilization uses illicit drugs. To focus some light on the *local* extent of the problem, one recent international study found that about 16 percent of Americans had tried cocaine at least once, while approximately 42 percent had used marijuana.[1] The figures are even worse for American minority groups, and in fact, America leads the world in drug abuse. The accuracy of such studies may be open to question, but even with a one percent involvement, millions would be impacted. It is a national disgrace. A lot of homicides would vanish if the problem ceased to exist.

The FBI maintains a genetic data base of criminal cases.[2] which includes DNA profiles from an existing 6.7 million individuals. There were approximately 80,000 genetic samples from unsolved crimes as of 2004. The data base is growing rapidly, and is expected to increase by 1.2 million profiles by the year 2012. Many of those crimes were drug related in one way or another. An individual who uses drugs is inherently involved with illegal activities and violent people. The burglar who breaks into a home while those who dwell there are present is creating the classical castle law situation; the intruder is often an addict looking for a means to support his habit. It is also likely that criminals will attempt to *use* the castle laws to cover both drug related murders and murders with other motives. That is the rationale for including this chapter. *If the drug abuse problem went away, an abatement of other criminal activities would be quite visible.*

Those who pursue the risky lifestyle of the drug culture often have a viewpoint that could be described this way: *you can choose your own version of reality and of what is right or wrong.* That concept rationalizes the behavior. This way of thinking is especially disturbing, because it is at odds with what others hold to be true, especially those involved with science. We live in a world where certain kinds of absolute truths *do exist*, and for those who spend many hours in research laboratories, such conclusions are inevitable. An ill-conceived idea will fall apart when it is put to the test of an experiment; nature doesn't care how we think things should be. Light passing through a diffraction grating is spread out into a rainbow of colors, and that phenomenon obeys an *exact mathematical law*. It is reproducible, and it survives even the most accurate measurements. The motion of a falling rock is like that, too, although a different equation applies. If we drop a piece of copper wire into concentrated nitric acid, brown fumes bubble off the wire. The chemical reaction of nitric acid with copper is always the same; it never fails to happen. And risky behavior has consequences.

Here is where science and religion stand on the same ground. The *"anything goes"* concept seems to originate *well before* the college years, because even beginning freshmen espouse it, and it seems to be having a negative impact upon our nation. How does a scientist fit what he *believes* into the concept? Someone might argue that the scientist is talking about material things like molecules and light, while the issue is *behavior*. However, behavior is a property of living beings, and living beings are chemical entities. *We are thus rooted into those physical laws.* Convince a scientist that behavior is *not* a natural phenomenon or that *all* choices of behavior are *acceptable*! There are consequences to every choice we make; that is, cause and effect is imposed, which resembles the cause and effect of the physical laws. Someone once said that it's fine to have an open mind but that the mind should not be like a house without walls, where any vagrant breeze could blow through. But of course, if a person wants to rationalize a behavior, an excuse can always be found, valid or not.

In the year 2010 most of our population from age ten upward *is not* involved with illicit drugs, *but that a drug culture even exists is unacceptable.* Use of the so-called recreational drugs is a behavioral choice, an acceptable reality to many people, and it isn't just youths who are using drugs. In chapter 2, two of those involved in the York murder were age 40+. Use of the so-called recreational drugs is not an innocent activity because those substances are highly addictive. They are harmful; they cause serious medical problems, premature aging and early deaths. Alcoholics -- another group of substance abusers -- pay the price in the form of traffic accidents, medical problems and domestic strife.

Who promoted the idea that *anything goes*? Did certain

liberated intellectuals introduce it? Or was it just a peer pressure thing? Do we simply blame the drug pushers, who increase their trade by ensnaring gullible thrill-seekers by means of a dependency? That's how they operate. Everyone knows that drug use has serious consequences, and most users are aware of the hazards. Yet this blight continues to exist here in America and elsewhere.

The abuse drugs are designed to cause dependence. Those who produce and traffic the materials are often killed in squabbles over territory. You don't even have to be a drug user or an alcoholic to suffer from the effects of substance abuse if a user runs over you or involves your child in a drive-by shooting. It is not hard to find strong connections between violence, thefts and burglaries, drive-by shootings and drug or alcohol use. A lot of gun violence would not happen in the absence of our thriving drug culture. So why does drug abuse continue to take place? There was supposed to be a war on drugs. Why is there is no indication that anything has come of that war?

Teenagers and young adults on drugs

A suspicious shooting death focused the author's attention on the current drug problems in our land, and he became aware of many disturbing facts. Those of us who do not have drug or alcohol habits tend to ignore the existing trouble until the problem affects us in a very personal way. If you find yourself suddenly in such a position it will hit you very hard. You will wonder, "*How did we ever get into this mess?*"

In searching for the connections surrounding Faron's shooting death, all legal means *accessible* were used, which *included* official documents, letters, phone calls, personal comments, library materials and the *internet*. The situation in Southern Oklahoma and Northern Texas received most of the author's attention. For someone with no access to restricted material (such as NCIC information, CODIS, etc.), the internet proved to be surprisingly productive. Blog sites are very revealing, but they aren't the only useful information sources on the web. You do have to critically evaluate what you find on the internet.

On one such blog page originating in the Red River region of Oklahoma and Texas (known as "Texomaland"), getting high was discussed openly. There were numerous photos of groups and individuals "hanging out" at a party. One such image showed a girl, apparently a teenager, with long, blond hair. She was cute, had a nice grin and was the all-American girl as far as appearances go. She wore a chain necklace...*but... what was that pendant on the chain?* Looking closer it turned out to be a likeness of a handgun, perhaps a 1911 .45 caliber semiautomatic pistol. It was about the size of a quarter. This was an example of "gangsta" identity. They listen to rap music, which is full of profanity, references to criminal activity and violence. Some play a computer game known as "Mobsters." The promotional literature of one mobster game says this: "*You want to be a real Mobster like Al Capone and have everybody at your feet? You want to have fun? You want to make money? ...Enter the Mobster world and you will become the boss of a crime gang...*" A question was posed to a younger friend "*Has Al Capone become a role model?*" The response was "*Oh, it's just a game that kids like to play.*" Young people who become involved that sort of thing probably do it as a passing fantasy. Most will survive the experience, but danger is certainly there because others take it seriously enough to act things out. They carry a gun or a knife with bad intentions, and they risk the possibility that they will either find trouble or trouble will find them. These kids and young adults are teasing around at the edges of a *death culture.* It's not an acceptable behavior.

The first blog page linked to others. Going into another link one could read an account of a boy who was killed in a road accident. It was a needless death due to irresponsible behavior -- driving too fast. Substance abuse may have been involved. In yet another link a blogger writes, "*I'm so gangsta my grilles are gum rappers.*" In case you don't know what a grille is, it's a kind of shiny metal bridgework that inserts over your teeth. It makes you look like that diabolical character with steel teeth in some of the James Bond movies. The blogger's catchy statement was sort of humorous, but you had to weigh the strange humor with everything else on her web site, especially those *other* websites that it linked to. The author received quite a shock when it dawned on him that the blogger was one of his young cousins! She lived within a few block of his home when he was still in Oklahoma. He'd hate to lose her the way Rick lost a grandson.

Yet another blog was entered, one originating in Durant. It was not linked to the previous ones, and chilling things were found there. There were "*RIP Faron*" comments from several individuals. Faron knew those individuals, and Rick had met some of them about a decade earlier when they came over to skateboard as a group. Sometimes Rick would drive them to a skateboard park across the Red River, in Sherman, Texas. They seemed to be good kids at the time. What was especially troubling was the fact that some of those "*rest in peace*" statements appeared to date to times well *before* Faron's death! There was another comment on the page: "*Love will get you killed*" (future tense noted). What was that about? No attempt was made to contact any of them, because those bloggers were clearly members of Durant's drug culture. One could not expect them to communicate with an outsider, nor would an outsider be inclined to trust anything heard from them. They live here on Earth, and the rest of us might as well be aliens from a planet half-way across the galaxy.

This kind of problem is found *everywhere*; Oklahoma is just one place where youths have easy access to drugs. In north Dallas, Texas beginning in 2005 a drug known as "cheese" was being sold in *dime bags* to high school students (The actual price was substantially more than a dime; in case you don't know, terms like "dime bag" or "bindle" are just street lingo for dosing amounts of a drug.). Students could get a small bindle of cheese -- one dose, a "bump" -- for $2. Cheese is a mixture of acetaminophen (Tylenol), Benadryl (an antihistamine that makes you sleepy) and *heroin*. It is addictive because of the third ingredient. Cheese was first noticed at Thomas Jefferson High School, which is located northeast of Dallas Love Field, and the nationwide news media reported it.[3] In view of the home address given in Bud's criminal record, he may have attended *that* school. He certainly has connections to the neighborhood. Law enforcement officers zeroed in on this problem and attempted to track down the pushers as use of the drug spread to other schools in the area. Their job is often like fighting a grass fire in a high wind. The drug problem at Thomas Jefferson was behind other crimes, *property intrusions included.*

It is worthwhile to look at the shooting incidents that happen in *any* large American city within a one-month period. The following article titles were gleaned from an Indianapolis, Indiana TV station's webpage[4] using the keyword "shot", and they are numbered chronologically from May 1, 2009 at the top to April 10, 2009 at the bottom. It is too small to be a scientific sampling:

1. *Woman shot at Westside apartment complex*
2. *Victim shot multiple times on Indianapolis North Side*
3. *Two teenagers shot on the Southside of Indianapolis*
4. *Woman shot in face*
5. *Man shot in the head on Northwest side*
6. *Drug suspect fatally shot by officer in Wal-Mart parking lot*

Seven individuals were shot during a period of about twenty days. Briefly summarizing what was in each of the articles, incident 1 was an attempted robbery. Two assailants tried to rob a woman who was moving from her car to her apartment, and she was shot in the back, apparently as she fled. She lived. In incident 2 the victim was shot three times, but the wounds were not fatal. Incident 3 resembles 2, because two teenage youths were shot, one in the arm and the other in the leg. In incident 4 several people were in an apartment when two men forced their way in, pulled guns and began shooting. A woman in her twenties was hit in the face. She did not die. A possible motive for the shooting was not stated in the article. In incident 5 a woman heard a man on her porch, and she thought it was a prowler trying to get in, so she shot him. It was her boyfriend. As one commenter put it *"Maybe she shot him for hanging out with another girl!"* That could have been the case, and unless some background investigation is carried out, who can be sure about what actually happened? Any prior arguments between the two involved ought to be taken into consideration. Positive control is absent when someone shoots blindly. The nature of that porch has some bearing, i.e., whether it was enclosed (screened) and had a locking outer door or was completely open. In incident 6 Jose' Sanchez, an armed drug trafficker, was shot to death near a Wal-Mart store when a narcotics sting operation got out of control.

Only one of these incidents, number 6, was clearly drug related. It was also the deadly incident. But a lot of robberies are drug related, so incident 1 could have been caused by individuals seeking cash to support a drug habit. Incidents 2, 3 and 4 look like gang violence, with 2 and 3 apparently being street shootings, and if so, drugs are also *implied*, though not proven. Drug use among street gangs approaches 100 percent. In incident 6 the shooter may have been a good example of someone who might start shooting at you if you were found between the street and their front or back door (see chapter 10)! So out of these separate incidents, the drug relevance could be as low as 1 of 6 (17%) or as high as 5 of 6 (83%). Incident 5 was potentially a castle law situation and would have been in some states, while incident 4 could have been (meaning in Indiana, where it happened; Indiana has a castle law), even though no one defended, so that's 2 of 6 (33%). Draw your own conclusions. If you live in a large city you might try keeping a running record of this type, to see where it goes. It takes a much larger sample than the one presented here to characterize trends.

Dirty law officers, crooked court officials and slippery drug lords

It is estimated that ten billion dollars worth of illegal drugs enter the Unites States across the Mexican border every year. Much of it comes across into Arizona, but Texas gets tons of the stuff, too. Dallas is a hub of drug activity. A very serious law enforcement problem took place north of the Dallas metroplex in the community of Van Alstyne, Texas, where deputy constable Robert Benavidez was charged with passing police intelligence information to major drug movers in the area. As stated in a July 14, 2008 article in the *Dallas Morning News*, "He is accused of helping his cousin, Sergio Maldonado, who was believed to have been the North Texas 'cell leader' for the *Zetas*, the ruthless enforcement arm of Mexico's Gulf Cartel drug smuggling operation." Many Zetas have prior military training, and they use *all* technologies available. Some of them are into the *Dia de los Muertos* thing (Day of the Dead) and may have a grim reaper tattoo, or simply the letter "Z." The "help" referred to consisted of Benavidez sending restricted police information to the cousin, notably information related to new warrants being posted for arrests. By doing so, as alleged, the criminals were made aware of any pending actions against them and thus had the option of fleeing before being captured.

US Highway 75 runs from downtown Dallas, Texas through Richardson, Plano and McKinney, on through the smaller towns of Van Alstyne and Howe to the Sherman-Denison area. On the south side of Dension it merges with US 69, and the combined highway, US 69/75, continues generally northeastward across the

Red River, passing close to Cartwright and Colbert and through Calera, Durant, and Atoka to McAlester, Oklahoma, where the highways split. There are other important routes, such as I-30 going to the northeast toward Texarkana, and I-35, which heads almost straight north. These corridors are the preferred paths from Dallas to places like Oklahoma City and Tulsa, and to several large northern cities, such as Kansas City, St. Louis and Chicago. Parts of the US 69/75 route coincide with the old Butterfield overland stage trail. We may be sure that the highways are well traveled by drug trafficking criminals. The Gulf Cartel operating in the Dallas area could very well have been the source of the methamphetamine described in the York murder trial testimony (chapter 2) because Rose told Rick's daughter that the dealers in McKinney were *Mexicans*. McKinney was barely outside of the Dallas urban zone in 2009. Perhaps a forensic analysis of the impurity chemicals present in the meth picked up at McKinney by Charles Bussey could tell us something about its origin, but that isn't public information.

Now that access to pseudoephedrine is more controlled in the United States, a source of raw materials for domestic methamphetamine production has been considerably diminished, and the popular drug is now coming across the Mexican border in record amounts. Meth certainly isn't the only illegal drug being trafficked out of Mexico. As was noted in a July 15, 2008 issue of *Reuters*, "The increasing use of bribes by Mexican drug cartels to corrupt U.S. agents comes as Washington is sending $400 million to help Mexico's army-led war on the trafficking gangs, whose brutal murders have surged to unprecedented levels." This looks like a war on *many* fronts, and we had better be fully aware of what *all* of those fronts are. You just can't win a war if the enemy has crossed into your operating perimeter and is occupying positions of authority! Who can be trusted when that happens?

The situation is made worse when the officials fail to use the technology available to them. Those who have studied the processes of criminal investigations have found that police often shun the use of forensic science in their investigations. This conclusion seems incredible given the scientific methods available in 2010, but the author believes that it was the case in Faron's shooting death (chapter 1), because the available technology apparently was not used to compare Faron's DNA with the blood on Bud's mouth. An investigative article appearing in the *Chicago Tribune*[5] found it troubling that there are even "...*cases where DNA* [evidence] *clears a defendant of a conviction, but law-enforcement officials refuse to consider him innocent or to pursue new suspects through* [FBI] *database matching.*" The impressions we receive from watching TV programs such as NCIS or CSI are *not representative* of the reality of most police investigations, and those cases where forensic technology was not used when it should have been are simply unprofessional and not acceptable. A whole range of technologies is applicable to the drug trafficking problem; they should not be held back.

Those who stray into such a mentality are no doubt driven by a strong desire to close a case, sometimes because they honestly believe the suspect is guilty and sometimes because they feel compelled to bring the matter to completion, in good conscience or not, to avoid the appearance of incompetence. If wrong leads are pursued early-on in an investigation, the likelihood of bringing the actual perpetrators to justice is greatly diminished, and when that happens the conviction of an innocent person is likely to be the result. Some problems simply take longer to solve, and that ought to be admitted.

Cutting corners isn't unique to law enforcement. It happens in every walk of life. Some building contractors ignore the specifications of the materials lists and install cheaper and inferior materials to increase profits. Even in pure science there are some who cheat; a book by Robert Bell, "*Impure Science:*

Fraud, Compromise and Political Influence in Scientific Research" (John Wiley and Sons, Inc.) is an eye opener for researchers and laymen alike. The "global warming" controversy, for example, is beginning to look like corrupted science.

There are other kinds of problems. Police officers are underpaid, and the man or woman with a badge and a gun is subjected to temptations that the ordinary citizen never encounters. Some yield to the temptation. Most officers probably walk the straight and narrow path. Others take bribes and use their badge and uniform in unscrupulous acts. News came in 2008 that a Durant, Oklahoma police lieutenant had been caught on a surveillance tape and charged with stealing drugs from a Durant pharmacy. He was nearing retirement. Why did he take such a chance with the end of an otherwise clean career in sight? Apparently, the lieutenant stole the drug for his own use, perhaps because of chronic pain (which was a stated opinion). It was a relatively minor drug infraction, considering what actually happens on a daily basis in the United States, where marijuana is moved in ton quantities while cocaine, heroin and meth cross our borders with little resistance. But someone like that cannot be relied upon to enforce laws.

Neither can a previous sheriff of Custer County, Oklahoma.

He resigned in 2008 when it was discovered that he was conducting sex-slave activities in his jail. Oklahoma State Bureau of Investigation leveled 35 charges against Michael Burgess, and the charges included kidnapping, forcible oral sodomy, rape (14 counts), bribery of a public official and perjury. Wet T-shirt contests were held in the county jail.[6] Prosecution was handed over to the adjoining Texas County District Attorney when a Washita-Custer County drug court program participant told detectives that Burgess gave her a choice between having sex with him or going to prison. Would a man with such low morals overlook an opportunity to benefit from the thriving illicit drug trade in Texas and Oklahoma? The news reports did not mention a drug involvement, but the possibility makes you wonder.

Corrupted officials such as the three just described and *those who might have colluded with them* have planted many seeds of distrust in the public mind. The question of *others involved* is raised because additional officers *probably were participants* in at least one of those crimes. Nevertheless, there are *many* decent police officers that would not stoop to the kinds of things described in the previous paragraphs, and some of the author's friends wear a badge.

The drug situation often gives the legal profession a black eye, and it ought to be as troubling to lawyers and judges as it is to the concerned public. Court officials are not immune to temptation any more than police officers are. In 2006 Joel-Lyn McCormick, Unit Chief of the Multicounty Grand Jury Unit, which is a component of the Oklahoma Attorney General's Office (OAG), reported this on the OAG website: "Three people, including District Attorney Richard Gray, were indicted by the Multicounty Grand Jury after an investigation of the Cherokee County District Attorney's Office. Richard Gray was indicted on one count of embezzling money seized as evidence in drug investigations. He is accused of taking almost $9,000 in seized money from a drug task force safe. Former assistant district attorney Janel Bickel and office administrator Vyrl Keeter were also indicted after the investigation discovered drug possession, tampering with evidence and a cover-up scheme. Bickel and Keeter pleaded guilty to the charges against them. The case against Gray is ongoing." In contrast, McCormick eventually wrote a terse letter in response to questions raised concerning Faron's shooting death (chapters 1 and 2); she did not address *any* of the questions raised in the several letters submitted to her. It would seem that the homicide of a prosecution witness ought to get more attention than a mere theft of drugs.

In the preface it was pointed out that court officials can have corrupt motives, and the case cited in the last paragraph is a specific example. Would someone who was willing to steal money from an evidence vault also be willing to take a bribe from a drug trafficker? Could that willingness include accepting a bribe to pass off a drug-related murder as a case of self-defense? Over the years the common talk in southeastern Oklahoma included rumor after rumor about corrupted court officials. And it wasn't just a rumor every time. In Durant (District 19) there were cases where judges were removed as being unfit for the office, a notable example being that of County Judge Glenn J Sharpe.[7] A description of the offense is found in the cited appeal document, and it was not about drugs: "*The record in this case reflects that Sharpe received and retained a sum in excess of $13,000.00 for issuing waiver orders dispensing with the blood test documents required..., the three day waiting period required..., and the age requirements...[of applicable Oklahoma statutes]. Sharpe contended that he was accepting gratuities for extra services rather than charging fees. The trial division rejected this contention and found that Sharpe collected and received monies for waiver orders not authorized by law and that this activity constituted corruption in office.*" The issue was about what could be called a "*marriage mill*" that used to operate at Durant, and it caused a considerable uproar among parents, especially those living on the Texas side of the Red River. A reference to the easy marriage problem in Durant comes up in the award winning movie, "*The Last Picture Show*," which was very realistic according to people who actually lived in north Texas when and where the scenes were set.

That was the kind of corruption that happened before drug abuse skyrocketed. Is drug-related corruption the lucrative thing in 2009? Mexican workers, many of them "undocumented," come to the United States in desperation because of the economic misery in Mexico, seeking employment in American agricultural jobs. They tend the vineyards and the large vegetable farms in California, pick oranges in Texas and Florida and work in the chicken processing plants in Arkansas. The Oklahoma marijuana growers apparently need a few low-wage laborers to help them cultivate their marijuana farms.[8] They have to keep the costs down for those $20,000,000 marijuana crops! That happened in 2009 in southeastern Oklahoma, where there are regular farms for growing the weed. It was not obvious from reading the newspaper accounts that any landowners, especially Americans, were hauled into court, and it makes you wonder.

Oklahoma certainly isn't the only place on Earth where questions of corruption have come up. This kind of thing continues to happen everywhere. In the year 1965 there was a judge from Izard County who was a notoriously big spender in northern Arkansas and southern Missouri, and he always used cash to pay for the things he bought. On one occasion a Batesville store owner -- a prior mayor of the city -- had been handed a $500 bill at the check-out counter to cover merchandise purchased, and he had to send his assistant to a bank because he couldn't make change from the till. He quipped sarcastically after the judge walked out of his store: "*Hah! I know they don't pay judges much up there, but you have to count all the bribes they take and the gold they can steal!*" The author was a direct witness to the cash purchase because *he* was the sales assistant that took the $500 bill to the bank! Such an inference concerning the improprieties of an Izard County judge may have been entirely false, but the judge's insistence on cash purchases certainly *looked bad*. Most customers paid by check even in 1965, and the $500 note was already rare in that time frame (it was last printed in 1945 and removed from circulation in 1969). The old proverb probably applies: where there's smoke, there's fire.

Near Durant, Oklahoma, in 1973, a vicious fight that had happened in Cartwright dominated the news for a week or so. Cartwright is south of Durant at the north end of the Lake Texoma Dam, right on the Texas-Oklahoma border. At the time the place was a strip of night spots and bars, said to be rife with all kinds of illegal drugs and prostitution. Two cowboys had gotten into a fight, and one killed the other with a baseball bat! The remark some voiced on hearing of the incident was, "*I thought cowboys did that stuff with guns.*" Such killings were a regular occurrence in those days. Cartwright and a nearby community named Colbert were notorious. Not much was being done about the drug situation and violence. Those activities *looked* protected, so it made people wonder about what was going on along the Red River. A friend in a position of authority, who knew a lot more about the situation in Cartwright than the average person did, pointed out privately that a considerable amount of corruption and drug money was involved. He was a state auditor, and as he put it, he dreaded going into Cartwright.

Not many years after the baseball bat slaying there was a murder of two men at nearby Platter Flats, which is a fishing camp on Lake Texoma not far from Cartwright and southwest of Durant. A Texan named Pete Kay was charged along with others in this killing, which was nothing less than a drug-related assassination. The two men that were murdered, Junior Metcalf and Ernest Fielder, were said to be involved in the shenanigans at Cartwright. There was much fanfare before that trial. After jury selection the judge failed to sequester the jury, and there was a compromise when the jurors went home for a meal! The jury selection process had to be repeated before the trial could resume. One who was involved as a prospective juror claimed that he witnessed the mistake firsthand. He was there during the screening process but was never called to the stand, so his opinion did not affect the trial's outcome. His personal reaction after the trial was over and the dust settled was "*show trial!*" No one involved seemed to have a good feeling about any of it. The man said: "*I hope I am never called for jury duty again, and if I am I will tell the court that I'm already prejudiced about the trial; who wants to spend hours and hours for nothing?*"

Those were just personal opinions, but the prospective juror certainly was not the only one who came to that conclusion. Kay was acquitted, and Silas Jones, another defendant, took the fall.[9] Others who were accomplices in the murders got light treatment because they bargained to be witnesses. It was alleged by some (but not officially) that Kay was too high up in organized crime to fall. If he was, *in fact*, that far up the hierarchy, what could have motivated him to *personally* settle his alleged part in the murder at Platter Flats?

It was also alleged that Kay worked for Jack Ruby at the time President John F. Kennedy was assassinated in Dallas. That allegation was made informally *after* a Kiwanis Club meeting, and it came from the very attorney that had prosecuted Kay and the others for the Platter Flats murders. He had been a staff judge advocate at Carswell Air Force Base (near Ft. Worth) at the time of the Kennedy assassination, so he might have possessed some insight into the Dallas situation. This strange monologue took place not long before the prior Bryan County prosecutor passed away from a long term health problem. The author was present and heard the prosecutor's comments.

But just as it turned out in Bud's case, Kay is *legally innocent*. We have to acknowledge that. What was told amounted to a rumor, nothing more.

Kay's cohort at the time of JFK's death was said to be Charles Harrelson, father of none other than Woody Harrelson, and both were thought to be drug runners for Jack Ruby. Those were some of the *other* rumors floating around. Charles Harrelson was considered as a possible shooter from the grassy knoll in the Kennedy assassination; this belief is held by some of those who do not believe Lee Harvey Oswald acted alone. Jack Anderson, the Pulitzer Prize winning investigative journalist, promoted the notion of a team of assassins, but he also dabbled in UFOs and aliens. There is no absolute proof of the claim, and this book is certainly not about JFK conspiracy theories. Later on Charles Harrelson was convicted of killing Federal Judge John H. Wood in San Antonio, Texas, and that earned him two life sentences in federal prisons, where he eventually died. Killing a federal judge is not far from murdering a senator or even the president. Judge Wood's death was a contract mafia-type hit, said to net Harrelson $250,000. The judge was very tough with drug traffickers and was going after a shadowy Las Vegas figure, Jimmy Chagra, when he was gunned down. This story suggests how the web of Dallas criminal activities, mostly drug related, reaches out into the Texoma countryside.

There were also relatively minor things in that general time frame, but outsiders might find them at least humorous, if not substantially troubling. In Oklahoma, Bryan County Sheriff Gene Hampton allegedly shot a juke box to death! Apparently he went into a bar that was still open after legal hours and told the manager to close shop. One version of the story was that the manager challenged the order, so Gene drew his gun and shot several holes through the blaring juke box!

Gene Hampton followed the path of his father, who had also been a sheriff, and Gene is best remembered for having won re-election as sheriff but not being able to take office because of criminal charges against him. He had been indicted for offenses that are still confusing in many minds. Hampton was tried, convicted and sentenced. He served time. It can't be ignored that Gene was convicted for "...*corruptions, conspiracy and racketeering activities affecting interstate commerce in violation of the Racketeer Influence and Corrupt Organizations Act (RICO)...conspiracy to and obstructing, delaying and affecting interstate commerce by means of extortion under color of official right as Sheriff of Bryan County, Oklahoma in violation of the Hobbs Act...and use of intimidation and physical force with intent to influence the testimony of witnesses...*" Altogether, there were ten counts against him.[10] But Gene was hard to dislike; he did not seem heavy-handed to those who knew him, and lot of people in Oklahoma still wonder if Gene was removed from office for being a nuisance to organized crime figures in the area, like Judge Wood had been in San Antonio (though not by a fatal means). Some actually believe that organized crime used the court to get rid of him! Those rumors of a court influenced by the "Little Dixie Mafia" will never go away. Aside from

Gene's demise, it was evident to all that those nightclubs near the Red River were dens of iniquity, where illicit drugs were moving freely.

Perhaps the most unusual incident that ever happened in the Southeastern Oklahoma area involved a Mexican drug trafficker known as Jose' Contreras-Subias, who was said to be among the top ten of Mexico at the time. In 1985, in Guadalajara, Mexico, U.S. drug agent Enrique Camerena was kidnapped and murdered. Mexican lawmen were also killed by drug criminals in that general time frame. The Mexican drug baron Rafael Caro Quintero was thought to be behind the killings, and Contreras-Subias was considered to be Quintero's action man. Contreras-Subias, a fugitive from justice, was thus targeted for questioning concerning the murders, but he hid out. Many assumed that he was roaming around somewhere between the Rio Grande and the southern tip of Argentina, but Jose' was brazen and clever. Much of his roaming happened *north of the Rio Grande*! It turned out that he and his proxies were laundering drug money by buying ranch land in Texas and Oklahoma, including land in Atoka County, Oklahoma, which is under the Bryan County District Court's jurisdiction and along the US 69/75 corridor.

The 2,800 acre Contreras-Subias ranch in Atoka County was about forty miles from where the author once lived. More specifically, it was near Stringtown,[a] which is a village not far north of the small town of Atoka, and he had purchased it from a local rancher in 1985 for approximately $1 million. Some stories claimed that he bribed his neighbors along with certain Atoka County officials and even had money in a Durant Bank, but those may just be rumors, not substantiated with hard facts. He was eventually captured in California, where he jumped bail and was captured again in Salt Lake City, Utah. Those who investigated Jose' Contreras-Subias' activities discovered that he owned Oklahoma and Texas cattle ranches and had more than $3.5 million in three Oklahoma Banks (the names of those banks were not given); he had also been living in northern Utah from time to time.

Jose' was *indeed* staying in Atoka County during some of those *other* time-to-time periods.[11] He was known to the Oklahoma locals as Jose' Guillen, and one individual in Atoka has been quoted as saying that "...*Contreras-Subias often invited local residents to parties at the ranch.*"[11] Contreras-Subias played a strange game of hide-and-seek *in plain view* on a grand scale, going to places where you'd least expect to find him!

Jose' was clever, but he does not deserve to be glamorized. He was a hard man and was suspected of murders. He helped to get cocaine and marijuana into the hands of American drug abusers. Since the number of individuals affected thereby was quite large, many overdose deaths and long range medical problems were *inevitable* among the users. Some of those with addictions were surely involved in thefts and burglaries. His sentence should have been hanging and probably would have been in another time and place, but it was relatively light considering all the harm done. [12]

One is thus caused to wonder what court dockets would look like if all of the drug-related crimes disappeared overnight. Would there be street scenes of new homeless people, their ranks swelled by the arrival of starving lawyers? Would the populations of prisons dwindle as inmates completed their terms or died? The court would have to focus on things like child neglect and abuse, but with drugs out of the picture, there would probably be fewer neglected and abused children, because their parents might be more sober and responsible. That, too, would impact the courts. When a defense lawyer represents a drug trafficker in a homicide charge, where do you think the money for his fee come from? Possibly drug money? It isn't hard to see that any downsizing of the drug problem would upset the cart in our courts. These problems would exist even if our courts were totally devoid of corruption. Illicit drug activities keep a lot of lawyers employed, and it leads to an indifference and an acceptance of the *status quo*, while the nation decays from a problem that begs for a solution.

The amateur chemists who produce illicit drugs

Drug abuse gives chemistry a bad name. This weighs down on the author, because he *is* a chemist, and he conducted chemical research projects with funding from the National Institutes of Health for almost 40 years (The time span includes work at more than one institution.). Much of that research attempted to find better therapies for coping with human disease. What does it mean when a small army of scientists tries to find cures for diseases like cancer an heart disease while an even larger one is hell-bent on making profits through illegal drugs? What the drug movers do ruins lives and sometimes leads to the kind of homicides described in the first two chapters. We gain ground in one area and lose it in another.

There are enough problems with well-intentioned pharmaceuticals because of serious side effects that were not found during a drug's development period. At least the pharmaceutical industry prepares drugs under carefully controlled conditions and ensures that its products are purified and labeled properly before being passed on to consumers.

The ones who process or make the illicit drugs do so under very crude conditions, perhaps in a barn or in a run-down mobile home tucked away off the beaten trail. The criminals involved in these activities attempt to camouflage their sites as much as possible. That is why aircraft equipped with thermal infrared sensors are often used to look for drug labs, because the "cooking" processes generate a lot of heat.

Illicit drug users ought to have a good look at the so-called labs where meth is synthesized or where cocaine is processed. They are usually messy places, and the products are often seriously impure. Photos of the people who do the cooking are even more disturbing. One photograph of an arrested methamphetamine cooker showed a man in a filthy T-shirt drenched with sweat. He had very bad teeth, said to have been caused by meth use -- it's called "meth mouth." But the man evidently chewed tobacco, too, evidenced by brown stains drooled from his mouth. The tobacco probably contributed to those terrible teeth! He would have looked somewhat better wearing grilles (maybe that's why the gangsta folks wear them!). Meth damages the heart, brain, liver and other organs *irreversibly*. A meth user becomes gaunt and has prematurely aged skin, dental problems, and poor memory. How could such an image inspire confidence among those who buy drugs on the street?

The man or woman who stirs the pot is not likely to be well-versed in chemistry, and the motive is to make a fast buck. A small paper envelope containing a small amount of meth might cost $25 on the street, but the one who makes the drug invests only a few dollars per dose. Profits in the illicit drug trade are huge, but so are the risks of being blown up, or burned to death, or shot dead in a turf war! The cooker's product will be full of impurities, and some of those impurities are probably cancer-causing agents. The solvents used in the process are poisonous, but so is the drug itself. What happens to the user is of no concern to the people who make and traffic illicit drugs. Many of them are also users. They are oblivious to their own uncertain future.

Legalizing drugs - a chemist's reluctance

A brief tutorial on "how drugs work" is appended at the end of this chapter for the reader who wants to know a little more about the subject,[b] and reading it should provide insight into the subject of drugs generally (both the legal ones and those sold illicitly). A book by Nicolas Rasmussen[13] is also recommended if the reader is even more curious about a specific group of drugs, the amphetamines, and what they do. The latter reference goes into the history, properties, medical uses and non-medical abuses of the amphetamines. The amphetamines have been around for a long time.

Methamphetamine, which went under the pharmaceutical name "Pervitin," was used by Germany's stormtroopers during World War II to treat combat fatigue. The Allies used it, too, but both sides quickly became aware of the limitations and undesirable properties of the drug. Abuses were taking place even in that time frame. In 2010 methamphetamine is still a major abuse drug.

With regard to the castle law issues, it is clear that the abuse drugs *and alcohol* are behind a lot of criminal activities, including those leading to home intrusion situations. A White House Paper on drug-related crime[14] noted that drug related offenses fell into three categories: 1. violent behavior resulting from the psychotropic *effects* of the drugs, 2. violence resulting from competition between rival drug dealers and 3. *stealing to get money to buy drugs*. The statistics for the year 1997 were appalling. The percentages of state prison inmates who committed the kinds of crimes that can cause an innocent citizen to fight back (or die) and who were under the influence of drugs at the time of their offense are tabulated here:

Crime	Percentage using drugs
Murder	26.8
Assault	24.2
Sexual assault	21.5
Robbery	39.9
Burglary	38.4
Auto theft	39.0

If the status of the drug war and the sharp upturn in violence in Mexico are reliable indicators of the flow of drugs to American addicts, the situation in our land has not changed for the better.

Several medical doctors known to the author believe that all the illicit drugs should be legalized and dispensed to drug addicts on the cheap, and their logic is that the act would remove any economic reason for drug trafficking. Others outside the medical profession share that point of view. Those same medical doctors are very reputable and held in respect, so it isn't easy to dismiss *their* way of looking at the current drug abuse situation in the United States. The logic in legalizing drugs parallels that of the aftermath of America's prohibition days, which had brought about a black market in moonshine whiskey and many related crimes. Prohibition of ethyl alcohol products simply didn't work. Neither has the so-called war on drugs, which seems to be a total failure, in fact. Thus, a legalization of the abuse drugs (or perhaps alternatives that are not quite so damaging) might be the answer. But the proposed "fix" is too simplistic.

Legalization may do away with the market for illegal drugs and criminal competition, but the psychotropic effects will not go away. Alcohol may be legal, but wives and children continue to be stabbed, shot or beaten to death because of a husband's alcoholic rage. An alcoholic woman, perhaps someone you knew, died from cirrhosis of the liver. Fatal accidents caused by intoxicated drivers and those other tragedies just cited happen on a daily basis. And it will be like that with the other abuse drugs. We are saying, "*They are hopeless; give them the palliative and let them destroy themselves.*" But we should consider what happens to the family and others affected. They are victims, too, even if they are not users.

Criminals being what they are, very likely the illicit drug dealers would shift to a different kind of criminal activity, causing *new problems.* It is also not a given that addicts will be so easily removed from their social world into the sterile environment of medical science. From a chemist's point of view, we should be careful in trying to compare the abuse drugs with ordinary ethyl alcohol, the active stuff in beer, wine and whiskey. Alcohol is a *kind of drug*, but it is a relatively tame one compared with a highly addictive substance like cocaine. Some who start using alcohol become alcoholics, but most alcohol users do so in moderation. Apparently the alcohol and associated substances in wines even have health promoting properties *if used in moderation.* Used in excess the result of alcoholism can be cirrhosis of the liver, pancreatitis, cardiomyopathy and a number of other problems. Most of the abuse drugs are far more health threatening than alcohol products, if only because of their very strong addictive properties. If one uses heroin at all the risk of addiction is high; going to a second and third dosing causes the risk to approach 100 percent. Encouraging the use of such a substance is like handing a loaded gun to a depressed person and saying, *"Here, shoot yourself."*

Methamphetamine, for example, is believed to be more addictive than heroin, and it causes irreversible damage to the brain's blood vessels. One of the possible outcomes is a stroke. Excessive consumption of alcohol can cause a stroke. Cocaine can do the same thing, and the heart becomes pathological with continued cocaine abuse. The brain is irreversibly damaged by heroin use, and users eventually overdose if the habit isn't broken. Overdosing with heroin and its chemical relatives such as codeine, morphine and fentanyl leads to death by respiratory arrest (heroin metabolizes to morphine). Lives can be ruined or lost before adulthood, and the effects on those near the ones with an addiction, who never had a drug problem at any time, have to be included in the accounting. The collateral effects of drug addictions are devastating to innocent people, the bystanders. The anguish is hard to imagine by a person who has not been thus affected.

For these reasons the author simply can't go along with the concept of legalization of the abuse drugs. What is really needed is better insight into why some people have a strong inclination to addictions while others do not. The Department of Health and Human Services, National Institutes of Health (NIH), including its specialized compartments, the National Institute on Drug Abuse (NIDA), and the National Institute of Mental Health (NIMH), have an interest in those tendencies, and as an example, a fairly recent request for research proposals had the title, *"Molecular genetics of drug addiction and related co-morbidities..." (the grant type is R01).* Odds are good that a genetic basis can be mapped out, but it's probably a complex of genes rather than something simple, and biochemists, molecular biologists and medicinal chemists are the ones who could pin the problem down (if it really can be) and find a way to deal with it. There may be more rational ways to control those urges beyond the use of drugs like *methadone*, and the scientists who continue to investigate the genetic aspect of addictions may yet come up with a much better approach to the treatment of addictions.

The other consideration noted earlier in this chapter is that we live in a period wherein traditional morals have been discarded and *almost anything goes*. For the moment it is not politically correct to dispute that fashionable concept of permissiveness, but it is a fact that the same period of moral decline and crime more or less coincides with a period of blossoming drug abuse. The drug problem certainly promotes the kinds of crimes that lead to home intrusions and self-defense situations. Maybe with enough pain we'll re-learn why a more rigid moral code existed in the first place.

END NOTES -- Chapter 5

a. Oklahoma's very talented country and western singer, Reba McEntire, grew up near Stringtown, Oklahoma. She was not involved in any of the Contreras-Subias shenanigans.

b. To understand how drugs work, one needs to acquire minimal insight into a subject called biochemistry. It isn't necessary to go into much detail to understand the basic concept. First of all, the material of life -- the protoplasm inside a living cell -- can be thought of as molecular machinery. This machinery causes purposeful things to happen. But how does a molecular machine work?

Molecules are very small and are assemblies of atoms. The way those atoms are joined together determines what a substance is. For example, very pure water is made up of countless tiny molecules, and every one of those molecules consists of just one atom of oxygen bridging between two atoms of hydrogen in a V-shape. When atoms are rearranged or groups of atoms move from one molecule to another one, a new substance (or new substances) is the result, and we call that a *chemical reaction*.

Molecules move around continually at room temperature. This leads us to the thing we are looking for, the way molecular machinery works, and it will be found in what is summarized here:

Case 1. In moving about, molecules bump into each other and rebound. Nothing happens. There is no chemical reaction. It is like people moving around in a crowd.

Case 2. Some molecules have an *affinity* for each other, and when they bump, they stick. It is a temporary sticking, and after a brief period of bumping around with other molecules, they turn loose and go separate ways. Nothing changes. There is no chemical reaction.

Case 3. There is a third possibility: two molecules have an affinity for each other, and when they bump, they stick, only this time the nature of that sticking process causes one of the molecules to undergo a chemical reaction. When they turn loose, one of the molecules has not changed but the other is now a new substance. One (sometimes both) of the molecules in 2. and 3. is typically a protein.

And that's all you need to know for a basic understanding of drug action. Most of the molecular machinery is based on case 2 or 3 above (or a combination of 2 and 3). These "sticking" properties have a variety of descriptions, such as *simple binding interactions, lock and key effects, active sites* (where chemical reactions occur), *hormone receptors*, etc. Also, there are many different types of purposeful molecules inside a living cell, *literally tens of thousands*, all with *different* chemical structures, and each has at least one *kind* of sticking affinity. DNA is the blueprint substance that determines the molecular structure of the different proteins. In turn, proteins make things happen; they are the gears of the machinery. *Proteins are not just food.* This microcosm of binding affinities, collectively, carries out all of the necessary processes that keep living things alive and able to reproduce. In what follows we'll examine some cases that show how natural biological processes work and how drugs and poisons get into the act:

There is a fairly large protein molecule called adenyl cyclase, and it resides within the surface membrane of certain nerve cells, cells of the heart and cells of the liver. There is a sticking site -- a *hormone receptor* -- on the part of adenyl cyclase oriented *outside* of those cells. It happens that there are other kinds of sticking sites on adenyl cyclase, including one oriented *inside* the cell. But focus on that first site, the hormone receptor. The hormone molecule that sticks there is adrenaline, a fairly small biological molecule. It's a natural component of your biochemistry. Everyone is familiar with adrenaline. When we get a good scare, adrenaline is released into the bloodstream. The hormone reaches the receptor of adenyl cyclase and it sticks there, in the sense of case 2 above. And while it is attached to the receptor, that special site of adenyl cyclase *inside the cell* becomes active, as in case 3 above. A specific chemical reaction thus happens *inside* the cell, which in turn sets off another chain of events, all involving further examples of 2 or 3 above (we will not go into those, but they lead to the ultimate effects). The end result is an increased heart rate and in the liver, mobilization of sugars as a source of energy. These events prepare us for a desperate run, such as fleeing from an enraged bull or a brush fire.

Here is where some abuse drug substances come into the picture. The molecules of adrenaline, amphetamine and methamphetamine are very similar, and because of that similarity, all three are able to bind with the adrenaline receptor. We say the amphetamines "mimic" adrenaline, and they trigger the receptor the same way the natural hormone does. Thus, they increase heart rate, etc. In this example the drug *activates* a biological function. But there is one difference: molecules present in the medium, belonging to case 3, rapidly convert adrenalin to an inactive form. The amphetamines hang around a lot longer. Also, the amphetamines interact with other binding sites throughout the body, notably in the brain, which leads to the effects that encourage continued use and dependency. The high is euphoric; the low is unbearable.

Other drugs shut down functions. In a second case completely unrelated to the first, an example is found in gram positive bacteria, some of which are human pathogens. In these bacteria a special cell wall material known as a *peptidoglycan* is manufactured by the bacterium and deposited as a protective outer cell wall. The bacterium makes the peptidoglycan in a *multistep process*. The purposeful molecules of the bacterium are special proteins known as enzymes, which cause specific chemical reactions to occur in accordance with case 3 above, and they work *in sequence*. The first enzyme in the sequence sticks to a simple molecule and converts it to a second substance, which is picked up by the second enzyme and converted to a third substance, and so on (It's a metabolic process of *biosynthesis* -- building up rather than breaking down.). The final product of the chain is the peptidoglycan, which is necessary for the bacterium's integrity.

A well-known drug retards peptidoglycan synthesis. Penicillin is an antibiotic, and it binds to *one* of those peptidoglycan-synthesizing enzymes. Penicillin *reduces* (slows) the enzyme's activity. Thus something useful is evident: when penicillin is present the bacterium does not assemble enough peptidoglycan in its outer cell wall -- the cell wall is weakened. The accumulation of materials that should have been converted to peptidoglycan also causes a problem for the bacterium. Humans do not have peptidoglycan cell walls, and we are not affected much by penicillin (although a few individuals are very sensitive to penicillin and go into anaphylactic shock when they are injected with the drug). From the point of view of the bacterium, penicillin is an outright *poison*. In this case a medicinal drug achieves a desirable effect by shutting down an essential reaction *in the bacterium*. The bacterium does not lay down enough cell wall material and may burst open because its cell wall is thus weakened. It dies, or failing that, at least the process of cell division is slowed down enough that our immune system eventually copes with the invading bacterium.

A third example is the blood cell protein known as hemoglobin. It's the red stuff. Hemoglobin falls into case 2 above. The iron atoms in the hemoglobin protein, four of them, are binding sites (i.e., sticking points) for molecular oxygen. The purpose of hemoglobin is to carry oxygen from the lungs to all the cells of the body. The binding is reversible; hemoglobin loads up with oxygen in the lungs and dumps it in the various organs of our body. Everything is fine as long as that is working right, but hemoglobin is affected by carbon monoxide, a molecule almost as simple as one can be, just one atom of carbon and one of oxygen. Carbon monoxide binds tightly with the iron atoms of hemoglobin -- it sticks to the oxygen carrying sites so that oxygen can't get in. Thus it is a poison and leads to asphyxiation. Carbon monoxide is to *humans* as penicillin is to *gram positive bacterial species*. Drugs and poisons work the same way. The only distinction is the *effect caused*. Other examples might be cited, but the basic concept should be evident.

There are many drugs and poisons to consider. Alcohol is just another drug from the point of view of a chemist, because it interacts at a special binding site (i.e., a sticking point) that stimulates the release of a neurotransmitter substance known as GABA. GABA causes you to relax and feel sleepy (and of course, GABA targets *other* binding sites, etc.). Alcohol tends to be treated as if it were not a drug, and that is a misconception. As with all other drugs, overdosing with alcohol will kill you. The abuse drugs, which are psychotropic, bind to receptors in the brain, thus altering *consciousness*. All drugs (psychotropic agents, antibiotics, anticancer drugs, anesthetics, anti-inflammatory agents, etc.) have side effects. That is a general rule, and there are no exceptions.

In summary, the molecular machinery of life is a huge complex of binding interactions, all interrelated, to produce a phenomenon known as the living state. Drugs interact with those binding sites, causing altered states.

REFERENCES CITED -- Chapter 5

1. A study of the situation was published through *Public Library of Science -- Medicine*, an online scientific journal that originated in 2004. The study published in July of 2008, "Toward a Global View of Alcohol, Tobacco, Cannabis, and Cocaine Use: Findings from the WHO World Mental Health Surveys," was sponsored by the World Health Organization, and it involved 54,069 survey participants in 17 countries.

2. Staff writer, "F.B.I. and States Vastly Expand DNA Databases," *New York Times*. A first version of this article appeared in print on April 19, 2009, on page A1 of the New York edition and was corrected on April 26, 2009.

3. Kent Fischer and Jason Trahan, "New drug craze hits DISD," *The Dallas Morning News*, April 28, 2006. Cheese has been described as a starter heroin.

4. The author simply logged into the Indianapolis TV station *WXIN-TV (Fox 59)* web site: *http://www.fox59.com/* -- The keyword "shot" turned up the six shooting incidents (along with vaccinations, etc.). The outcome of such a search changes as time passes.

5. Maurice Possley and Steve Mills, "Crimes go unsolved as DNA tool ignored: genetic profiles in rapes, slayings not sent to FBI," *Chicago Tribune*, October 26, 2003

6. Staff writer, "Police: Okla. Sheriff Ran Sex-Slave Operation From Jail,"

Oklahoma City News, posted April 16, 2008 and updated April 17, 2008.

7. See appeal 1968 OK JUD 1, 448 P.2d 301, October 4, 1968: Sharpe v. State Ex Rel. Oklahoma Bar Association in Oklahoma Court on the Judiciary.

8. Josh Stevenson, "20,000 pot plants seized in Pushmataha Co," *TV Station KXII News*, Jul 22, 2009. There were other busts in nearby counties, but the one in Pushmataha County intercepted about $20,000,000 worth of high potency marijuana. In Bryan County the drug task force had found "...*236 marijuana plants, potted and scattered along Wilson Street just outside of Durant*." These plants had been grown indoors in containers, perhaps in a barn or something like a chicken brooder house, and they had been well cared for. It was not known if the dumped plants were the result of criminal competition or fear of being caught. Another bust took place in Marshall County. See: Rita Kotey, "More marijuana found, destroyed in Co.," *ibid.*, Sep 1, 2009; and Tom Johnson, "Over 1,100 marijuana plants found, destroyed in Marshall Co.," *ibid.*, Jul 23, 2009.

9. JONES v. STATE, 1982 OK CR 178, 654 P.2d 635, Case Number: F-81-159 Decided: 11/11/1982, Oklahoma Court of Criminal Appeals. This document was found online through the Oklahoma State Courts Network (OSCN). According to some of the testimony, accomplice Charles Maines delivered the *death blow*, that is, he shot Metcalf and Fielder *again* before leaving the crime scene. One of the prospective jurors who was not selected said that during the screening process, when Maines came into the Durant courtroom wearing a collegiate sweater, a middle aged woman who was sitting to the left of him said aloud, "*Oooh, he looks so young!*" And another lady behind her went: "*Shhhh! Hush; we aren't supposed to talk!!*" On hearing what the first one said, he thought "*Yes, lady, that's just the response his lawyers want from you.*" Maines was used as a witness, but a search of OSCN did not turn up a conviction for him. Kay was set free.

10. See 786 F2d 977, United States v. Hampton, No. 84-2704, United States Court of Appeals, Tenth Circuit. March 11, 1986.

11. Staff writer, "Federal officials investigate big bank deposits made by reputed drug-cartel member," *Deseret News*, Salt Lake City, Utah, April 18, 1988; Staff writer, "Mexican rancher is murder suspect: DEA says 10 deaths drug related," *The Oklahoman*, May 5, 1988; Anthony Thornton, "Drug kingpin, 4 others indicted in money laundering scheme," *ibid*, Jan 20, 1989. Jose' bribed his way out of a Mexican jail, where he was awaiting trial for

murder, then fled directly into the United States.

12.   A court record of *one* of the Contreras-Subias appeals is worth examining, and it provides the necessary keywords for a complete internet search of the large scale drug trafficking and money laundering scheme: United States of America, Plaintiff-appellee, v. Elbert Johnson, Defendant-appellant.   United States of America, Plaintiff-appellee, v. Jose Leonardo Contreras-Subias, Defendant-appellant.   United States Court of Appeals, Ninth Circuit. - 967 F.2d 594 Argued and Submission Deferred Feb. 5, 1992.Resubmitted April 2, 1992.Decided June 3, 1992 Before WALLACE, Chief Judge, and JAMES R. BROWNING and SKOPIL, Circuit Judges. In the Oklahoma part of the trials evidence showing that Johnson and Contreras-Subias laundered the proceeds from drug crimes by purchasing real estate in the United States. The co-defendants (Johnson and Contreras-Subias) "were not prosecuted for substantive drug offenses in Oklahoma," that is, the case was about money laundering. Also involved in the laundering process was a man named Filiberto Montoya and a woman, Rosario Montoya. See: 45 F.3d 1286 U.S. v. MONTOYA, Rosario MONTOYA, DefendantAppellant. UNITED STATES of America, Plaintiff-Appellee, v. Filiberto E. MONTOYA, DefendantAppellant. Nos. 93-50411, 93-50440. United States Court of Appeals, Ninth Circuit. Argued and Submitted March 9, 1994. Decided Jan. 12, 1995.

13. Nicolas Rasmussen, "On Speed: The Many Lives of Amphetamine," New York University Press, New York and London, 2008.

14.   "Drug-Related Crime," Executive Office of the President, Office of National Drug Control Policy (ONDCP): Drug Policy Information Clearinghouse Fact Sheet, March 2000.   Other such fact sheets are forthcoming.

Chapter 6 - Living with guns in America: why civilians have guns

"A well regulated militia, being necessary to the security of a free state, the right of the people to keep and bear arms shall not be infringed."
- Second Amendment to the U.S. Constitution

The right to bear arms

This short chapter is about our right to have guns and why that freedom should continue. Guns have *many* uses besides the one that usually comes to mind: *i.e.*, humans killing or injuring other humans. Firearms should be thought of as *tools for survival*, but there are even recreational uses. Innocent citizens ought to have the right to defend their lives against violent criminals, and that situation is the focus of this book. But the right to own firearms and the self-defense laws are not quite the same thing. Those self-defense laws concern only one application of firearms, and they even consider the use of weapons other than firearms. If those laws have failed to accomplish their intended purpose because of inappropriate wording or through misapplication, that is a *separate issue*. A failure of any of those self-defense laws does not imply a failure of the Second Amendment.

The Second Amendment was well-conceived, and its loss will signal the end of American freedoms. When we lose the Second Amendment, the other freedoms and rights will suffer the same fate. We should be thankful that the Bill of Rights allows a *responsible* citizenry to own guns. The Second Amendment is the kind of thing that only happens in a free society. Totalitarian regimes rule by force, and in a totalitarian state guns are among the first things to disappear from the hands of law-abiding citizens, followed by people deemed to be inconvenient to the regime. Having access to guns means that we can defend ourselves and our families and participate in recreational events such as skeet shoots and marksmanship competitions. The states still issue hunting licenses.

An armed public competent with guns also means that the nation -- America -- has a special manpower resource for defending itself against aggressors. *That was the primary idea behind the Second Amendment*, and its authors meant the general public, not the National Guard. Those who backed the amendment had not forgotten the experience of being subjected to English domination, made possible for one thing by those Americans who remained loyal to the crown -- and others who were just plain indifferent. The term "enemy" thus had a broader definition: "...both foreign and *domestic*...". This thinking can be traced back to the American Revolutionary War, and it continues in many minds, with good cause. The author remembers the oath he took in 1961:

"I, _____, do solemnly swear (or affirm) that I will support and defend the Constitution of the United States against all enemies, <u>foreign</u> and <u>domestic</u>; that I will bear true faith and allegiance to the same; and that I will obey the orders of the President of the United States and the orders of the officers appointed over me, according to regulations and the Uniform Code of Military Justice. So help me God."

That is a nationalistic viewpoint, and those who want to dissolve the borders between the nations view such thinking as archaic; but they should pay attention to what is in the history books. The concept of a unified world has been around a long time, and attempts to make it happen have always failed, causing the worst kind of wars in the process.[1] In fact, those leaders who have tried to pull things together found it necessary to resort to force against those seen as decadent, meaning entire nations *and* individuals. There is abundant turmoil in today's world, and it will work against any hope of a workable global unification in the near future. We still need the Second Amendment.

Even if all the guns were rounded up and destroyed, violence would not go away. It would be accomplished with knives, sticks and rocks. Take away the knives and that would leave a world literally full of loose rocks and sticks from fallen tree branches! Lock them in a courtyard with bare walls and a smooth concrete floor and the bad ones will use their hands and feet. The problems are caused by attitudes and motives. But the gun is more deadly than a knife. Even so, it is suspected that the American public will own guns for a long time.

America is not the only nation that allows its citizens to have firearms, but even in America there are places where gun ownership is substantially restricted. In Switzerland all healthy men between ages 20 and 42 are candidates for conscription. The ones conscripted enter a short period of military service and training, then become part of the militia. They keep government issued firearms in their own homes. Switzerland has a very low crime rate.

The Czech Republic has surprisingly liberal gun laws considering its location within what had been the old Soviet Bloc. Citizens without criminal records may acquire firearms, and handguns may be carried concealed. The murder rate in that country is low.

The United States is often portrayed as a worse case nation regarding violence, and the easy availability of guns is usually blamed for that. Yes, there is too much violence in America, but we are nowhere near the top of the list based on homicides per 100,000 people. The table on the next page shows that the situation is much worse in nations like Mexico and Russia, where gun ownership is more restricted than it is here. One cannot claim that private gun ownership causes violent crime, because the numbers simply do not support that viewpoint. In fact, just the opposite seems to be true. A bumper sticker often seen in the United States summarizes the reason behind the phenomenon: "*If guns are outlawed only outlaws will have guns.*" Restrictive gun laws correlate with high crime rates. The reasoning is a kind of vicious circle: restrictive gun laws impact the innocent citizen, not the felon; such laws encourage the felon. Crime thus increases and the clamor for gun confiscation begins to be heard (*which further abuses the victim even though the real problem is the criminal's attitude!*). The most significant underlying factor of crime in the United States is *illegal drugs*, which was the conclusion of the previous chapter. New Orleans Police Chief Riley once said this during a CNN interview: "90% of all murders are drug related," and he should have known; New Orleans leads the entire nation in the matter of violent crimes! Drug and alcohol abuse is rampant in that city.

Things have changed since the year 2000, and the table

265

presented here is somewhat dated. Based on sources other than

Murder rates per 100,000 per year.

Country	Murder Rate
Colombia	62
Jamaica	32
Russia	20
Mexico	13
Lithuania	10
Costa Rica	6.1
United States	4.3
Finland	2.8
France	1.7
Czech Republic	1.7
Canada	1.5
United Kingdom	1.4
Switzerland	0.92
Japan	0.50
Saudi Arabia	0.40
Qatar	0.12

Source of the tabulation: *The Seventh United Nations Survey of Crime Trends and Operations of Criminal Justice Systems, covering the period 1998-2000 (United Nations Office on Drugs and Crime, Centre for International Crime Prevention).* The UN isn't the only entity that compiles such data, but *that* source was selected because the UN can't be accused of going easy on the United States. In fact, if it were up to the UN there would be no Second Amendment to our Constitution. Other compilations agree reasonably well with the UN data.

the UN, the United States has witnessed a slight downward trend in homicides, and it would probably be a lot lower in the tabulation if its drug abuse problem didn't exist. The United Kingdom has witnessed an increasing homicide rate and might eventually compare with America's murder rate. Russia and Mexico have also moved upward in the table, and South Africa apparently has replaced Colombia for top position. The weighted average of the entire UN tabulation is 10 homicides per 100,000. Places like Qatar have very low homicide rates, but if you get out of line in Qatar or Saudi Arabia, the penalty might be a hand cut off or even crucifixion! Guns do not seem to be in short supply in the Islamic countries.

When guns are essential tools:

The Europeans who settled the land now known as America learned quickly that the gun and the axe were the two most important tools for surviving. If our assets of high technology are ever removed, things could go back to those realities. And if that ever happens, just finding food could be the major preoccupation of our efforts. The human species is omnivorous, which means that its diet must contain both vegetables and meat.

A healthy diet tilts toward plant products, but a purely vegetarian diet leads to nutritional disaster. Some vegetarians and animal protectionists dispute the idea and even think their views should be imposed on everyone else; however, biologists and biochemists -- most of them -- know better.

If we went back a century and a half to a time when many Americans still lived rural, we would notice that the food on the dinner tables often included harvested wild game -- deer, game birds, squirrels, rabbits, etc. The long gun was the tool for putting that kind of meat on the plate. They fished for food, too. There were no radios, no electric lamps, no phones. Wood stoves were common. In the Ozarks they built small but sturdy pen cabins, for warmth in winter and protection from the "booger bears" in those woods (the term means anything from a black bear to a bobcat -- a beast to avoid). The early Arkansans encountered a special problem: malaria.

The Native Americans and the early settlers absolutely had to hunt and gather to survive. For the settlers it filled the gap until land could be cleared for agriculture. They knew a lot of practical methods that are all but forgotten today. For example, the common hickory nut of the Ozark Plateau is good food, but you could starve to death going at them with a nutcracker (for example, using a hammer on its thick shell, then digging out the nut meat, piece by piece). The Native Americans gathered the nuts, washed them in the creek, then crushed them in a large wooden mortar. The coarsely ground mixture was then boiled with water and the shell parts floated off, or better, filtered through a mat of dried grass stems. When the rest is cooled you have a very rich milk-like product to consume in various ways. You can drink it or combine it with other foods or boil it down to a nut butter. Future generations may never experience the very delicious flavor of the diminutive chestnut of the Ozarks, the chinquapin (Castanea ozarkensis), because it succumbed to the chestnut blight. Grafting may be the only way to save it from extinction.

The early settlers of North America knew to look for game and edible plants along the small streams. They knew how to find food there. They were aware of the *when and where* of nature's daily and annual cycles. Do you know when morel mushrooms are in season? Could you identify one and not confuse it with any of the poisonous species? Do you know when persimmons are ripe enough to eat, or how to get close enough to a rabbit to take it with one shot from a .22 rifle, or even a pellet gun or a thrown rock? You say, "*Ah, but I'll never be found in that situation.*" Perhaps not, but we can't know the future. There is wisdom in staying closer to the land, the way the

Amish and Mennonites and Native Americans lived.

One thing is necessary in that setting: all wild game and most plant products (both the roots and upper parts) need to be cooked. The wild meat -- from frogs, fish, squirrels, whatever -- should be cooked *well done*, otherwise you will likely encounter a pathogen or a parasite. Some wild fruit such as the pawpaw can be eaten out of hand when it is yellow-green and fragrant in mid-September (The pawpaw is *the* exotic fruit of North America, with a taste almost identical to its elegant cousin in Peru, the cherimoya -- the author has tried both.). But even there, at least wash wild fruit such as pawpaws and persimmons in cool water that has been boiled beforehand, the way you would wash an apple or a pear bought at a food store. And you will indeed need a supply of drinking water sterilized by boiling. Only a fool sips directly from a stream or a spring because he thinks it looks crystal clear and inviting.

Surviving the worst times

A degree of subsistence living was still happening to a lesser extent mid-way through the 20th century, and the practice has not entirely disappeared in 2009. Today we depend on a technology that is fragile at best. We buy food at a supermarket and never give much thought to the mechanized processes behind it. The process of plowing and planting, cultivating and harvesting requires fuel for the tractors and trucks. Farm animal care consumes energy, too. You also have to factor in the refrigeration and heating at the warehouses and slaughterhouses and canneries, then consider the process of moving those products overland to distribution warehouses and finally, to food stores. That consumes fuel, too. Don't overlook the computers and communication systems, various electronic devices and even the Earth satellite-based global positioning system. Those things keep the system working. You don't have to wring the chicken's neck, pluck the feathers or do most of the other steps between a live chicken and food on the platter, and it is easy to believe that day-to-day life will always be that way. But what happens when something pulls the power plug?

Early in 2009 a severe ice storm descended on Southern Missouri, Northern Arkansas and Kentucky. Electric power and phone service was lost for days, and that wasn't the result of a few lines down here and there. Literally miles of utility poles had been snapped like so many match sticks; the infrastructure had been hard hit, and it took *months* to complete all of the needed repairs.

Citizens with normally comfortable natural gas central heating units found themselves shivering as the cold crept indoors, because central heating does not work without electric power to the blower! The gas supply was still there, but for many (those without simple space heaters) it was useless without electricity. Some resorted to potentially dangerous kerosene heaters while others rolled out noisy electric generators and worried about how long their supply of fuel would last. The rest took refuge in schools and other public buildings. There was some concern for food availability, so refugees were asked to bring their own food to the public shelters.

For most, the crisis was over before the situation became grim; people helped each other, and that was group cooperation and survival at its best. The same was mostly true in Florida during the 2004 sequence of three destructive hurricanes (Charley, Frances and Jean), but in New Orleans, after Katrina, *there was plunder and worse.* FEMA did not do a very good job in Arkansas and Florida, and their record in New Orleans was fully *dismal*, not surprising in view of their own lack of preparation, the intensity of the storm and flooding and the serious drug and crime problems that existed in New Orleans before the Hurricane arrived. Cooperation of the civilized kind was in short supply in New Orleans; too many people had an attitude problem. The lesson is clear: rely more on local resources; work together with your neighbors, and be well prepared. The thing that happened in New Orleans will happen again. It always does in spite of politicians telling us not to worry, that we'll be cared for. They never have been able to deliver on such promises. And you will need a means to defend yourself if things get as bad as they did in New Orleans. If you end up in some Katrina-like disaster someday and don't have a gun, you'll wish you had one.

If a rogue nation manages to detonate a large nuclear weapon about 250 miles above Kansas, the whole nation will take a severe hit. The very brief but intense electromagnetic pulse (EMP) from such an event is expected to have far reaching and long lasting effects, as we learned from experiments like "Starfish Prime," conducted during the early 1960s. The Starfish test involved detonating a 1.4 megaton thermonuclear bomb 399 kilometers (248 miles) above the Earth's surface, and there is an optimum altitude for energy coupling (probably classified!). In a deliberate EMP attack we may expect that electric generating plants will be damaged and unprotected electronic circuits, computers and communications devices will be fried. A lot of infrastructure will be lost. As a result, many ordinary citizens will find themselves in the middle of an extended loss of services. Access to food in urban areas might become critical, with people literally starving to death, and robberies, thefts, intrusions and other kinds of crime would probably increase. The more rural dwellers might find themselves reverting to a subsistence mentality. They would be thankful to have a gun and enough line and fish hooks for such purposes.

Wide-ranging disasters have occurred all through human history. After the collapse of the Soviet Union the Asian people of the Chukotsk Peninsula, the part of Siberia nearest to Alaska, had to revert largely to subsistence living, because even ordinary bread was in short supply. Guns that were hidden for decades were used to hunt game. A bacterial pandemic caused by the species *Yersinia pestis*, the black plague, wiped out a third of the European population during an earlier time. The big war ending in the 1940s also trashed Europe. In the wake of World War II, American GIs tried to share their food with starving Europeans, because substantial help did not materialize overnight. Our soldiers witnessed those privations. It was worse in some places than others.

Driving down the streets of any small town in a rural setting, one does not see many meaningfully large gardens. In the 1940s and 1950s there were vegetable gardens of varying sizes in *most* of the small town yards. These days even the people that live out of town do not necessarily tend gardens. The rural dweller might hold a job at a Home Depot or an insurance agency in a town 25 miles away. *"Why bother with an old fashioned garden? All that driving and a full work day at the other end wears us out. We buy our stuff at Wal-Mart or Town and Country stores. This is 2009."*

The following thoughts had been entered into a diary, which amounts to notes of interest -- not hardbound -- that the author occasionally creates with Wordpad and saves to a laptop disk file named "GENERAL:"

"Twenty-four hours after writing that remark about buying everything needed at food stores, I had to drive from Cotter, Arkansas through Melbourne and Cave City to Strawberry, Arkansas. Rural homes along that route are mostly well kept and have neatly groomed yards. This time I paid more attention to the rural homesteads than I usually do. Less than five percent of the dwellings along the highway had visible gardens. Oh sure, a lot of the rural dwellers keep a few cows. They'll have beef, beef and more beef when the chips are down. Arkansas raises zillions of chickens. Those chickens live in brooder houses, and they have to be fed, too! But a better human diet also needs vegetables and grains. Where would the plant products come from if the infrastructure collapsed? There are soybeans in the delta country east of the Ozark escarpment -- rice, too; how do you get those things to starving people elsewhere in the state and in nearby states if gasoline is in short supply? During the Great Depression, produce rotted at the source while people suffered malnutrition."

Gardening novices are often surprised at what their yard-sized plot can yield even with minimal care: okra, tomatoes, sweet "taters," Kentucky wonder beans, squash, purple hull peas, etc. Indeed, this is 2009, and self sufficiency, food canning, storing grain, etc. is no longer an ethic. The need for a long gun and a supply of line and fish hooks is minimized by a lot of people. But we'll be hanging our rear ends over the cliff if something more widespread than Katrina ever happens.

How will you handle it if an armed group decides to let you tend the garden and then plunder its products (canned goods, dried food, grain, etc.) when it's harvest time? That was a way of life in feudal Japan. It was like that in Mexico, too -- maybe still is. Arkansas was a confederate state, but during the Civil War confederate soldiers raided the creek and river bottom farms of the Arkansas Ozarks; other plunderers known as "jayhawkers" did the same thing, only they added murder to their crimes (The jayhawkers were not soldiers.). After that the traumatized natives considered all soldiers and strangers as possible enemies,[2] who threatened death by starvation. Don't forget the squirrels and rabbits and birds; they will raid your garden, too, but they might be a good thing if you have the time...just pick a strategic spot and wait with a Crossman air rifle. The garden is bait, and their meat is thus added to the diet! In those bygone days the women and the children kept an eye on the garden. But you might not have much time for that sort of thing. It's sobering.

Even if the United States never experiences a deliberate EMP attack, natural phenomena are capable of causing severe damage to electrical and electronic equipment. On September 2, 1859 -- *before* the Civil War -- astronomers observed a strong solar flare on the sun's surface. As it happened, the Earth received the full blast of charged particles spewing out from that eruption. Particle radiation arriving from the Sun produced red auroras in Cuba and at points even further south. It is unusual to see auroras much further south than central Missouri (roughly latitude 38 degrees). The resulting geomagnetic storm, which was detected by the crude magnetometers of the time, was unlike anything witnessed afterwards, and other than the auroras, nothing of the kind could have been noticed before the technology of wires. This event took place in a time frame well before fragile electronic circuits, when communication was by overland mail and telegraphs.[3] It could repeat without warning, and compared with other possible widespread disasters, it is a more probable hazard.

The telegraph wires were electrified, alive with strong

induced currents, and the effects lasted for *many hours.* Telegraph code operators received shocks, and sparks set their paper message forms on fire! Such high voltage jolts would destroy unprotected electronic circuits, computers, etc. It is estimated that if an event like the one in 1859 happened today, the electric power, communications and data processing infrastructures would be severely damaged. Replacement and repair estimates range between one and two *trillion* dollars. For comparison, the US budget deficit in September of 2009 had reached 1.4 trillion dollars in the wake of the worst economic downturn since the great depression. If that was enough to cause worry for our children's future, what happens after a second disaster of that magnitude, *one that actually destroys physical devices?* It was bad enough when real estate and investment portfolios suddenly lost value *on paper.* We don't know how long it would take to repair *actual physical damage* caused by an intense solar flare, and the effects would be virtually global.

And there are other possible mega-disasters: viral pandemics, climate changes (warm or cold, wet or desiccating), large meteor strikes (like the 15 megaton Tunguska event in Siberia on June 30, 1908, or even worse impacts), super-volcanic eruptions (like Tambora in 1815, which ejected 36 cubic miles of material), nuclear warfare (which will not kill everyone), super-terrorism (which must not be underestimated -- see end note (a) of chapter 2), mega-tsunamis (with 500 ft waves, or worse, that can come *far inland*), and regional earthquakes. The New Madrid fault zone of the boot heel region of Missouri comes to mind as an example of a regional earthquake. The flurry of severe earthquakes starting in 1811 and continuing into 1812 was not localized like the ones in California, and they were more destructive. The effects were felt as far away as Maryland. Geologically, the New Madrid quakes were caused by a new and very active fault zone, which is known to cause massive, recurring earthquakes, and if a new outbreak of quakes began today the affected region would include cities like St. Louis and Memphis. The quakes were terrible enough in 1812, when the region had few inhabitants and no large cities. People died even in that one. The New Madrid fault zone has produced the strongest quakes thus far witnessed in the United States. But while it is known that the Earth has undergone many cataclysmic events in its history, most of the events that involve a whole continent or the entire globe are so infrequent that they are not plausible concerns.[4] It's the man-made disasters and the infectious diseases that are worth worrying about.

Anyone who thinks the 21st century can't bring tribulations

equal to or worse than those of previous centuries is living in a dream world. This book will not pay further attention to such disasters because that is not its purpose, but the prospect of such events *is relevant* to the issue of guns and other weapons and self-defense. The issue is not politics of one kind or another but how ordinary people survive when the odds are against them. We learn that guns are *not* obsolete tools even in the 21st century. In an extended crisis, where outside help *never* arrives, groups tend to form, probably most with civilized purposes, but others will do so for the wrong reasons. *Guns will be involved one way or another.* This will be true in both urban and rural settings. Thus, the Second Amendment is a provision for citizens that are left to fend for themselves, until order is restored. Be thankful that we still have it.

Other uses of guns:

For some individuals, shooting is a sport like golf, tennis or archery. Those who participate are not necessarily hunters, and they develop skills, compete in matches, etc. They do not plot murder. They are not burglars or robbers. What they do is a form of recreation. Marksmanship is a volatile skill for most of us; if it isn't practiced frequently the skill fades. Some just "plink" at tin cans with a .22 rifle; it's even fun. Accurate shooting seems to take more self-control than riding a bicycle, driving a car or even flying a small aircraft.

A strong case can be made for teaching young people to handle a gun safely under controlled conditions, involving them in target shooting events on a proper firing range. The National Rifle Association sponsors good programs of this type. Curiosity about guns is channeled in a positive direction, and that's better than ignoring a fascination with guns that gets your child involved with a gang behind your back. It's like teaching him or her to swim before falling into deep water with no one around to help. There is no guarantee that it will work in every case, but firearms training usually has the desired effect.

There is no doubt in the author's mind that his early involvement with hunting engendered a responsible attitude. There were rules of conduct such as: "Unless it is vermin, never kill what you don't intend to eat." and, "Even if you see the target, be aware of what else is in that path." "Never shoot toward sounds or at movement behind brush." "Know where all the others are," etc. All of these are common sense rules. Breaking the rules could and likely would exclude you from any future hunts; the hunt is a social thing, and the participants expect reliable behavior from each other.

Finally, there are some who just collect guns, often vintage guns. It's an expensive hobby, but such individuals preserve artifacts of our history.

When guns work against our best interests:

Unscrupulous people resort to the use of terror, and there are two kinds: one happens when a relatively weak faction resorts to violence, often against innocent people, to bring attention to their cause, hoping that it will bring about a desired kind of political action. We call that "terrorism." The other happens when a state rules its subjects by terror. We tend to ignore the latter kind and focus on the former, but the latter kind makes far more people miserable. Nations that use terror to control subjects use it frequently and visibly, lest anyone misunderstand.

Confiscation of firearms has been a characteristic of dictatorships, such as in Hitler's National Socialist Germany and the communist states of Eastern Europe. *"We are taking your guns for your own good. The state will protect you."* That's the logic dictators use, and the anti-gun advocates in America are saying the same thing today. Even the United Kingdom's government takes that position. If the anti-gun people succeed here in America, will we end up like Jamaica, with a terrified populace? In Jamaica only the police have guns, and they are *very corrupt.* Jamaica has a high murder rate, and the police are doing a lot of the killing.

In Nazi Germany, once the state had absolute power, Jews and others deemed unfit to live could be rounded up and shipped to death camps. The result was the Holocaust. A university colleague told of her family's experience in Czechoslovakia under Nazi occupation. Her father had a shortwave radio, and one of her sisters mentioned it to a neighbor, who reported it to the Germans. German troops then came to their home, where they confiscated the radio, took the family outside, warned them all, and at gunpoint threatened to kill the father if such an incident ever repeated. They were not Jewish; no one was safe during that time of terror. You have much to fear from tattle-tales in a totalitarian regime! If America ever makes the mistake of forfeiting its Bill of Rights, oppression is the only possible outcome.

Before Glasnost a similar testimony came from a Russian speaker, one of the "*Siberian Seven*" that Ronald Reagan pleaded for and succeeded in freeing. Someone in the audience taunted the Russian with a question: "*Surely you don't expect us to believe that all those bad prisons in Russia actually existed?!*" The Russian's lips curled into a sneer. He looked straight at the one who asked that question and replied: "*You obviously haven't lived in Russia. I have. I tell to you, all of Russia is a prison!*"

The man had even been in a gulag, so he must have known what he was talking about. He also added, "*In Russia the workers pretend to do their work, and the state pretends to take care of them.*" The author was sitting in *that* audience and heard the dialog quoted here (and that was before his hearing began to decline; he heard what the Russian said very clearly). It may take another century of error to realize that socialism is a failed concept. The Russian experience apparently hasn't been enough for some individuals.

It was shown in the previous chapter that drug abuse is the big problem in America. Drugs are behind *many* crimes, including home intrusions. Some writers attribute the crime problem in our cities to poverty, and yes, criminal behavior does correlate with poverty. *But the use of illicit drugs is a choice by individuals, not something imparted to everyone in a group.* The author and *many others* who came from poor families, did not become entangled with drugs or alcohol abuse. We chose a different way of life. Focus attention on the people who become wealthy by producing and distributing those illegal drugs to impoverished people. They make hard lives even harder.

What works in a rural region or small town setting may not apply in a city. Would you prefer to be in a city when the shoe drops...or in a small town instead?

Concluding

In conclusion we see that civilians own guns for a variety of reasons. Most gun owners keep firearms as a means for self-defense. Additionally, some use them for recreation and sports, including hunting. Others view them as a tool for subsistence, a contingency for severe times, such as wars and natural disasters. Still others collect them in the manner that some people collect old coins or stamps. An armed citizenry is a significant component of national defense, even in the year 2010. And of course, criminals have firearms for the wrong reasons.

REFERENCES CITED -- Chapter 6

1. Kenichi Ohmae wrote two books concerning globalization: "The End of the Nation State: The Rise of Regional Economies" (Simon and Schuster, 1995) and "The Borderless World: Power and Strategy in the Interlinked Economy" (Harper-Collins, 1999). Many intellectuals, industrialists, investors, etc. have apparently followed this kind of thinking without much consideration of its long range viability. Another author, Tarak Barkawi, takes a more skeptical viewpoint of these developments. Barkawi calls it the *"false dawn of globalization"* in his book "Globalization and War" (Rowman & Littlefield Publishers, 2005). Quoting Barkawi: *"Evidently, a great deal of state power is necessary to build a globalist world."* Indeed, it does. And nation states still exist and probably will continue to exist for the forseeable future. People prefer to keep their traditions. History is full of attempts to amalgamate whole regions. Alexander The Great and several of the Roman Caesars attempted to control large areas, which required *continual warfare.* Did any of those efforts produce a lasting result? Charlemagne incorporated Western and Central Europe into a Frankish Empire, and he, too, was at war

continually. His campaigns were far reaching (and sometimes disastrous, such as his contests with the Saracens). Napoleon tried the same thing and set Europe on fire. His efforts came to nothing. So did those of Adolph Hitler, who perished in his own scheme, and there are a few still living who witnessed *that* disaster firsthand. What became of Stalin's expansionism? Where is the Soviet Bloc today? The conclusion: attempts at globalization generally cause the worst kinds of wars, and alliances are only temporary things. The only factor that has changed dramatically in recent years is our ability to wage destructive warfare.

2. John Quincy Wolf , Sr. (edited by his son, Dr. John Q. Wolf, Jr.), "Life in the Leatherwoods," Memphis state University Press, page 4, 1974.

3. Scientific studies of destructive solar flare phenomena are ongoing and international in scope, because this kind of event will have a global impact if it should occur again in our lifetime. Examples of investigations are:

M. I. Tyasto, N. G. Ptitsynal, I. S. Veselovsky, and O. S. Yakovchouk, "Extremely strong geomagnetic storm of September 2 and 3, 1859, according to the archived data of observations at the Russian network," *Geomagnetism and Aeronomy*, Volume 49, Number 2, April, 2009;

and

B. T. Tsurutani, W. D. Gonzales, G. S. Lakhina, and S. Alex, "The extreme magnetic storm of 1-2 September 1859," *Journal of geophysical research*, volume 108, Number A7, pages SSH1.1-SSH1.8 (2003).

In the abstract of the latter reference it was stated that "The 1-2 September 1859 magnetic storm was the most intense in recorded history on the basis of previously reported ground observations and on newly reduced ground-based magnetic field data." and that "...*a storm of this or even greater intensity may occur again.*" However, the intervals between recurrences (in terms of centuries) are not known and are expected to be irregular: "...the probabilities of occurrence cannot be assigned with any reasonable accuracy."

4. R. Naeye, "Real Potential Disasters," *Sky and Telescope*, pp28-32, November 2009. See also J. K. Beatty, "Jupiter Takes a Hit," *ibid*, pp34-39 concerning a comet or asteroid impact on the planet Jupiter in 2009, which happened about 15 years after an even more cataclysmic event, when mountain-sized fragments of the comet Shoemaker-Levy collided with the

planet. Had any of these events taken place on Earth, there would have been serious, worldwide consequences. But Jupiter, owing to its size and strong gravitational field, is much more prone to such impacts than the earth is.

Chapter 7 - Using a gun

"...way out in New Mexico long, long ago, when a man's only chance was his own forty-four." - From the Marty Robbins version of Billy The Kid

This chapter is mostly about gun fighting and the *realities* of using a gun in self-defense. Self-defense is the whole point of the castle doctrine, and while the statistics and real life examples associated with those laws have been worth looking at, this book would not be complete without examining the factual details of a self-defense situation, which can indeed get you into an out-and-out gunfight! The following account explores the nuts and bolts, techniques and consequences of gun fighting.

We could use weapons other than guns to defend ourselves, but the focus will be upon guns. The logic of settling on firearms is simple: a cartridge of pepper spray or a knife isn't going to be of much help if the intruder is a bit out of your reach and is pointing a .45 automatic at your face. If you think you are the type that's willing to meet *that* kind of force with force, then you need to understand the fundamentals of guns. And if you choose the other option -- no resistance -- the intruder will still point that .45 automatic at you. Either way, the possible outcomes are sobering.

For starters, something should be said about outlaws. For sure, the intruder who breaks into your home with bad intentions *is* an outlaw. Also, if you are quick to use a gun without knowing the rules, *you* could end up *being* an outlaw of the 21st century! Outlaws tend to fare poorly in the long run. Let's consider some infamous Oklahoma outlaws.

Territorial Oklahoma was well known for its abundance of bad men, and that beginning is the background for everything that has happened in Oklahoma afterward, including those examples of violence and crime described in chapters 1, 2 and 5. Oklahoma's outlaw problem didn't end suddenly in the final years of the 19th century. An abated level of criminal activity has existed all along, driven by the same motives and attitudes, and the illicit drug activity of the here and now may in fact be hurting *more* people than those early outlaws did. Drug traffickers are the premier outlaws of the 21st century.

Bill Dalton was shot dead on June 8, 1894, not far west of Durant, near Ardmore in Oklahoma, and the outlaw Bill Doolin drew his last breath at a place known today as Quay, near the northeastern border of Payne County (north of Yale), also in Oklahoma. The two men knew each other well.

Bill Doolin came from the Clarksville, Arkansas area east of

Fort Smith, and although he was described as superficially good natured, he was best avoided. He and other ne'er-do-goods such as Bob Dalton, Charlie Pierce and "Bitter Creek" Newcomb left a trail of robberies. The lawmen who came after them at a village called Ingalls thought they had the upper hand, but it turned out to be a disaster. Some claim that a female outlaw, Rose Dunn, participated in the vicious shootout between the Doolin-Dalton gang and US marshals, which happened at Ingalls, Oklahoma on September 1, 1893, when three marshals and two innocent bystanders were killed (one was a child). Others were injured.

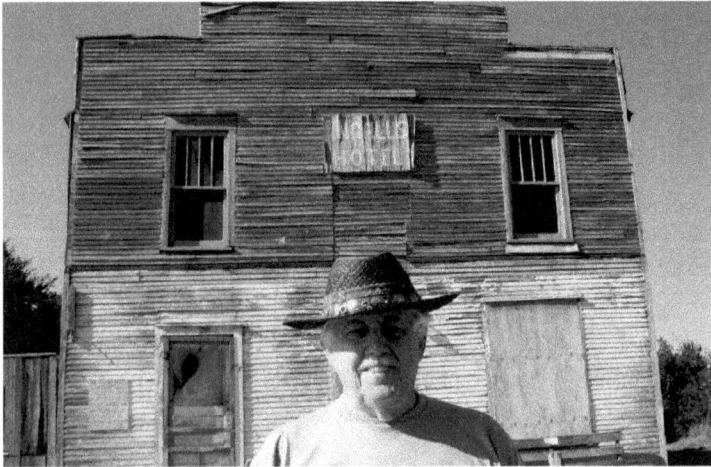

The old Ingalls, Oklahoma Hotel, still standing in 2009.

They went at each other mostly with rifles and shotguns. None of the outlaws were killed, although two got shot up, and Arkansas Tom Jones, who was sniping at the lawmen from the upper floor of the Ingalls Hotel,[a] was captured alive after the others fled on horseback and left him to deal with the posse. He was surrounded. Honor among criminals is like chastity among floozies. They tend to be selfish when the chips are down, as Tom learned that day.

Before the gun battle in 1893 the citizens of Ingalls benefited from the presence of the Doolin-Dalton gang, who after a fashion owned the town. The gunmen were generous spenders, frequented the Ransom Saloon just west of the hotel, and their ill-begotten loot certainly helped the town to prosper. In return, they enjoyed a safe haven, or at least it was safe for a while. During the shootout a resident of the town -- a woman -- refused to help one of the lawmen; it is wrong to think that the locals didn't know what was going on. Almost a century later Jose' Contreras-Subias would be doing the same kind of thing in Southeastern Oklahoma, currying favor with the local people around Stringtown in Atoka County (chapter 5).

The outlaw at Ingalls known as Arkansas Tom Jones apparently killed U. S. Marshals by sniping at them with a rifle from an upstairs window of the hotel, one of those visible in the photograph,[a] yet even after he was convicted, influence was used to get him out of prison early. He had a long sentence but served only fourteen years of it. Tom started a new life as a peace officer but drifted back to his outlaw mode. He was eventually killed by a lawman when he resisted arrest, and that happened at Joplin, Missouri. Most of the outlaws ended up shot to death or at the end of a rope or in jail for life. Only a few like Frank James returned to normal lives.

It's an old story, and it continues today, a bribe here and a whispered suggestion there. Does anyone care where the money came from, or who got hurt in the gettin'? Outlaws are even glamorized in movies and books. In truth they are just greedy cutthroats. Those who condone them come from the same mold.

Bill Dalton and Bill Doolin were members of an especially notorious gang. Some called the gang the "Oklahombres." Bill Dalton, the leader, was not at Ingalls when the shooting started. He missed the battle, and what took place was probably much worse than the OK Corral gunfight in Arizona. But Bill was destined to die violently less than a year later. The Dalton brothers had already suffered their big loss at the Coffeyville, Kansas bank robbery on October 5, 1892, and Bill was the last member of that bunch. On learning of the outcome of the shootout at Ingalls, Oklahoma, Judge Frank Dale was livid, and he told the marshals to "...*bring them in dead. Quit trying to bring them in as prisoners.*" It more or less turned out that way.

The old outlaw stories are interesting, but you might rightfully ask how a gunfight in the streets of a frontier town could have any relevance to the castle law situation, which is (or ought to be) about life-endangering home intrusions. The answer is, "It does indeed." Armed criminals are not constrained by any law. The weapons they carry are not just for show, and many criminals will use deadly force at the drop of a hat if they think letting a victim live will land them in prison. We can say that they operate with a set of prepared decisions. On the other hand the innocent person who is thrust suddenly into a deadly situation goes from the ordinary day-to-day thoughts to the brink of terror in about one second. There is a distinct psychology to it: The mind tends to hesitate and ask, "*Is this really happening?*" But there is no time for that. Those who survive deadly encounters also tend to have prepared decisions. They react. The lawmen who died at Ingalls were no doubt aware that they were going into a dangerous situation, but they lost the element of surprise. The outlaws set up an ambush. They were not ready for that. The criminal is ready to deal with *you*. Are you ready to deal with him?

Everyone has heard of the female outlaw, Belle Starr. She was probably not as dangerous as some historians portray her, being more inclined to lesser crimes such as horse thievery and merely providing refuge for outlaws like Jesse James and Cole Younger -- helping them hide out. But Belle was shotgunned off her horse not far north of what is now called Younger's Bend on the Canadian River (which is near Porum's Landing, not far south of I-40 and Porum in Eastern Oklahoma). It was an ambush; apparently she didn't see it coming. She was buried near the location of her murder on what had been her own property.[1] The site is not available to the public, not even marked as an historic site, although her tombstone is somewhere out there in the brush. Her killer was never identified.

Forget those movies where two cowboys faced each other on a dusty street, revolvers holstered, ready for a fast draw; it was more often a bushwhacking, and shotguns and rifles were the preferred weapons. Lawman Bud Ledbetter was in Henrietta, Oklahoma en route to another Oklahoma destination, hunting down outlaws, and as he walked in front of a saloon on his way to a hotel, carrying his saddle, a band of gunmen in the saloon recognized him and thought he was coming for them. They came out of the saloon, guns drawn and shooting at the lawman. In the resulting gunfight, which certainly took Bud by surprise, he killed all six without being hit himself. He started shooting with a lever action rifle, which he pulled from the saddle he was carrying, and having emptied its magazine, finished with a handgun.

That was an example of a lawman standing his ground. As the story goes, the astonished local constable came up to the lawman and asked (with an accent probably a lot like that of actor Slim Pickins), "*Are ye hit?*" The answer was, "*Ah don't think so.*" Bud was well dressed, and the constable knew he wasn't dealing with a saddle tramp. He asked: "*Who are ye? Yew ain't a lawman -- ah don't see no badge.*" Bud apparently didn't wear the badge when it wasn't official. He pulled it out and pinned it on, saying, "*Ah'm wearin' it now. Ah'm Deputy US Marshall Bud Ledbetter.*" Bud Ledbetter had survived a close call, but he was known to operate with a set of prepared decisions. Even so, the outcome was determined in part by pure luck.

Imagine yourself in the lawman's predicament. Home intrusions often involve more than one perpetrator. Are you comfortable with the thought of *two or more* armed intruders breaking into your home, even if you were waiting with a gun in your hand? The prospect of engaging multiple aggressors ought to be sobering even to those who are well-trained in the use of guns.

Operating out of Ft. Smith, Bud Ledbetter was one of Judge Parker's best lawmen. He attributed his good fortune of the day partly to the fact that the outlaws he'd just killed were full of liquor. Alcohol spoils coordination and reaction time, but drugs like PCP and methamphetamine act differently. What if you had to face *several intruders* who were hopped up on methamphetamine -- fully aggressive -- and you were relaxing in the comfort of your home with a second stiff drink in your hand?

Bud Ledbetter was not opposed to taking a drink himself, but not on duty. Parker recruited him after hearing an account of what had happened in a Coal Hill, Arkansas *tavern* (that's what they were called in Arkansas; *saloons* are an out west thing). Bud had gone in for a shot of liquor, and a mean-spirited coal miner had wiped his dirty hands on Bud's clean blazer, which led to blows. When the fight was over Bud had decked a whole group of belligerent miners using a tool handle that he'd gotten hold of! Others were still cowering under the tables. A local lawman who came into the tavern after the uproar later remarked, "*Ah gawd... Ah ain't ever seen no one handle coal miners that way.*" He told that to Isaac Parker, and after hearing the story, Judge Parker had said, "*I need men like Ledbetter.*" Indeed he did, considering what was happening out in Indian Territory. Parker's lawmen numbered 224, and 64 of them lost their lives in the line of duty. They experienced more deadly encounters than the famed Texas Rangers did.

A relative of Bud Ledbetter, who lived in Durant, once made a presentation at a Kiwanis meeting and told the group, which included the author, that the lawman may have killed about forty men during his career, but in his old age he pined over the fact that one of them had been innocent. That was hindsight working, but his day-to-day manner had been different. There is a point to make from this: gunfight survivors, as well as those who survive other kinds of fights, are not a bit reluctant to injure or kill someone. They shoot or stab and count costs later. They are mentally prepared for trouble and ready to react in an instant. It isn't a universal trait among men and women, so maybe there is some hope for the human race. But the flip side of that hope is this: the person who is able to react quickly and has the means to counter a home intrusion, for example, is more likely to be one of the survivors.

Native Americans contributed their share in the violence. They lashed out at the white men who were taking their land, and they also fought each other. Quanah Parker, a well-known

Comanche leader (who was mixed blood), was greatly feared by all and with good cause. He and his braves had taken many lives, mostly on the Texas side of the Red River. Part of Fort Washita's mission was to protect the Oklahoma Choctaw tribe from the plundering Comanche bands. Eventually Quanah was defeated and forced to subdue his own fighting spirit. He also founded the Native American Church. There is a story of a struggling white homesteader in southwestern Oklahoma near Cache, who was desperate for firewood as the winter's cold approached. He was searching for wood in a land not graced by many trees (those that existed were down in the gulleys). The homesteader encountered an old Indian man holding a gun, who challenged him, *"You are on my land. Why are you here?"* The answer was simply, *"Ah need firewood."* The old one gave him a hard look, then said, *"I will help you find it, but we must take fallen wood."* It was the Indian way. Afterward, the young man asked his other neighbors who his Native American benefactor might be. It was Quanah Parker. The story is not well known, but it surely has a basis in fact, considering who told it -- the settler's grandson.

In the frontier days there was a sort of castle law: if you entered someone's domain, unannounced, and you were a total stranger you would likely find yourself staring down the barrel of a shotgun until you sufficiently explained your reason for being there. Such was the setting of territorial Oklahoma and Arkansas and other places out west. There was deceit and violence everywhere. A life could end in a flash. And yet some did noble things during the frontier days, both the settlers *and* the Indians. The area had been a part of Arkansas Territory,[2] but the Native Americans were there first. Some had lived west of the Ouachita and Ozark Mountains for countless years while other tribes from east of the Mississippi were forced to go into what is now Oklahoma.

For those Native Americans relocated to Indian Territory, it was a land with fewer resources than they were used to, and it was very hard for them. Native Americans certainly fought each other. The trail of tears itself had been a death march. If that situation wasn't enough of a travesty, bands of cutthroats like the gangs of Cole Younger and the Daltons were in Oklahoma after the Civil War, to hide out and cause another kind of trouble. While it lasted the outlaw had a refuge. Then Grover Cleveland opened the Oklahoma unassigned lands to settlers in 1889, which led to land disputes and range wars. The Indians had to put up with all of that until the rule of law finally reached the territory, and even *that development* exacted a price in terms of human lives lost, as lawmen and outlaws fought it out.

Hangin' Judge Isaac Parker sentenced 160 men to die, but only 79 were actually hanged. His marshals and deputies apparently killed a lot more out in Indian Territory. Judging from all the drug labs and marijuana patches in southeastern Oklahoma in the late 20th early 21st centuries, along with the associated violence from time to time, one would say that there is still more than a trace of the old outlaw mentality in Oklahoma. Even a little is too much. When was the last time you heard of a Jesse James style train robbery? Today it's things like making or trafficking cocaine or meth, because that's where the money is. That's where the outlaws are today.

Oklahoma is not a special case. In Territorial Arkansas, the Mississippi River port town of Helena was notorious for robberies and murders, and along the old military road, the "Southwest Trail" that meandered through the uplands just west of the Ozark escarpment, there lurked frowsy degenerates that would cut your throat for a few coins. Place a United States map on a bed, and blindfolded, play a kind of "pin the tail on the donkey game." No matter where the pin goes into the map, even in a rural location, the natives there will tell you a story about a burglary, arson, drug situation, drive-by shooting, stabbing, murder or a beating -- or perhaps some combination of those crimes. We are not that much better off today than territorial Oklahoma was in the late 1800s, with all of its lawlessness and violence.

There are places in all of our major cities and even in our nation's capitol that a prudent person is well advised to avoid, especially at night. Rural dwellers are not immune to the problem, either. It is not always about a gun. People go after each other with rocks, knives, clubs and poisons -- even bare hands, and some deliberately run over their victims with a car or a truck. It's a worldwide problem, and the toughest imaginable laws have not stopped these things from happening.

The intrusion of such external violence into our homes is what brought about the castle laws.

At least the castle laws allow us to defend our homes. And yet, the castle laws are imperfect, because while they do work as intended in some situations, they permit lawlessness in other cases. Pockets of legal vacuum have thus been created, not big ones like Oklahoma Territory used to be, but a lot of small ones the size of a man's property. This viewpoint will be justified further in chapter 10.

The problem is not guns or knives as such, but the *motives and actions* of individuals. Unless someone falls on a knife accidentally, it is not inclined to stab all by itself. Neither does a gun pick itself up and shoot you. The situation changes dramatically when a violent individual is holding a gun or a knife. Felons and unstable people thus lose their right to have a gun. We shouldn't allow a toddler to have access to a gun, either. Responsibility is a rigid requirement where guns are concerned.

Maybe by the time this book is published we will still have the right to own a gun (or choose not to). If the choice is "*yes, I want one*" then gun safety and the way a gun is used defensively is where you need to be doing your homework. If you are not interested in having a gun it is still worth knowing what's involved when others choose to have one, for whatever reason. Even for those who consider themselves *expert* with a gun, a review of the fundamentals from time to time is a good idea.

Even if you abhor guns there are some things you need to know

If you don't like guns, that is your right. Who can fault the person who tries to avoid trouble? Some of us believe the right to keep and bear arms should stand *as is*. We think there are several good reasons for taking that position. Others think that private firearms ownership is archaic and favor strict regulation of firearms. They support that position with a *different* set of reasons. There seems to be no middle ground in the debate. A view taken by this book is that the castle laws and the right to keep and bear arms are not quite the same thing. The Second Amendment gives law abiding citizens the right to own firearms. It was well-conceived, and it has been one of the unique features of American democracy. The castle laws, as written, basically allow citizens to injure or even kill someone on their own property and not have to worry about being prosecuted for offenses ranging from aggravated assault to first degree murder.

Even if you dislike guns, there are things you ought to know about them, because the violence happening in the world today is not going to disappear overnight. The United Kingdom supposedly has strict gun laws, but the drive-by shootings of street gangs continue to happen there. In September of 2006 a 15-year old boy with the unlikely name of Jessie James was killed in a hail of bullets as he biked his way home from a party. He had no gang connections. His mother likened their part of the City of Manchester to a war zone. Burglaries are frequent in the United Kingdom.

There is a degree of risk in going to a stranger's door, and the castle laws probably increased the risk. But even with that possibility in mind, there is little cause for being paranoid about going to doors; the odds of actually running into trouble are still low, at least in broad daylight. That is probably true even if the person living there has a gun. But again, the person encountered in that situation may not have good judgment *after all* and may even have a mean streak. Certainly you don't want your children to *wander into* a stranger's home. It's the act of going into a home, uninvited, that carries serious risk.

Rick often has this thought: "*If my grandson had not gone into Bud's house in Durant, maybe he'd still be alive. I should have spent more time convincing him just how dangerous it is to venture into someone else's domain.*" If you don't want to find yourself in that situation someday, be sure your children are made conscious early-on of this kind of danger. The outcome usually feared by parents is a sexual molestation, but a shooting death is another possibility that ought to be recognized. The child might encounter a mentally deranged individual who has no sexual motives but is trigger-happy with a gun. There will be examples of this kind shooting in chapter 10.

Another kind of recurring tragedy takes place when a child goes into a trusted neighbor's home and a child that lives there (or perhaps even the child that went in) finds an unsecured gun. The gun is loaded. In 2009 in southern Indiana, not many miles from the Kentucky border, a two-year old girl found a loaded semiautomatic handgun that had been carelessly left within her reach and began playing with it. She died when it went off and the bullet struck her in the head.

There was a situation in Batesville, Arkansas about 53 years ago, one that might have turned into a shooting tragedy. A toddler (let's call him Gary) came out of his home directly across Neeley Street from where an aging couple lived, and he wandered to the street side of his yard, then crossed to the other side. Gary was holding a loaded gun, which no one paid attention to at first. For those that saw the scene, the image of the chrome-plated thing in Gary's hand had probably been taken for a toy cap gun. The older man was working in his vegetable garden, and he barely noticed Gary coming out of his house holding that "toy gun." When Gary stopped he was no more than fifteen feet from the gardener, but there was a fence in the way. It was a summer day with the sun low in the west, and a lot of people were out in their yards, which turned out to be a good thing. Then Gary's older brother came running up the street, pointing and yelling loudly, "*Stop him! It's a real gun!*" A quick-thinking neighbor who was mowing his lawn with one of those old human-powered lawnmowers, who was the second closest, reached Gary first and saved the day. Gary could have shot himself or the man in the garden or the one that took the gun away from him. This kind of thing should not happen, but it does with regularity.

With that type of incident in mind, it should be pointed out that no one paid a bit of attention to a similar situation in Faron's shooting death (chapter 1), which is that a loaded .45 caliber semi-automatic pistol, the same one that killed Faron that December night, might have been within the reach of Faron's daughter. It would seem that the gun had to be loaded and ready, because in the case of Faron's shooting death. Bud was awakened by a knock at the door and retrieved the gun quickly. By one person's account, the pistol was lying on a bedside table, but that's hearsay. If that *were* true, then the gun was within a child's reach. And did any of those rounds fired come close to Rose or her daughter? The author has never been in the house in Durant where Faron was killed, but he has a photograph of it, taken from the street. Carpenters notice where chimneys and plumbing vents come through a roof, and based on the visible evidence in that photograph, the odds are good that there are two bedrooms on the south side of the house (Bedrooms are usually near bathrooms.). The line of fire would have been in that general direction (north to south), and Rose and her daughter were said to be in a bedroom.

Having guns with children present is a special problem.

During the author's child-raising years he kept his guns unloaded and secured, meaning under lock and key, and the cartridges were in a separate location, also locked up. The reality of that situation was that an immediate armed resistance to a sudden intrusion was simply not possible. The emphasis was on locks and other security measures.

Taurus revolvers come with a key that turns a special screw in the hammer. When you insert the key and turn 180 degrees clockwise the screw is extended from the hammer, and it is not possible to pull the hammer far enough back to disengage the hammer safety; if the hammer were allowed to snap loose in that condition the firing pin would not be driven into the cartridge primer, and the gun would not go off. Turning the screw counterclockwise moves the screw flush with the hammer, and the gun is ready to fire. If one wore the key on a chain around the neck and if the gun were kept on a high shelf, younger children would not be able to fire it, yet the proper owner could put it into action in a few seconds. But it might not be enough to defeat curious teenagers or even older pre-teens with precocious mechanical skills! You can't be too careful.

As stressed in chapter 6, expose your children to firearms under controlled conditions; it takes away the novelty of a gun. Faron (chapter 1) was given such training. He passed a state-sponsored gun safety course, and Rick observed that Faron was not only a good marksman but also a careful hunter. He didn't go into Bud's house in Durant carrying a gun. Faron simply wasn't obsessed with guns.

Some individuals with guns go over the edge with very little provocation. In suburban Columbus, Ohio in 2006 a group of high school girls went to a house across the street from a cemetery. The house was imagined to be haunted even though a man named Allen Davis actually lived there. On a dare, some of the girls ventured a few footsteps into the property, then fled. They heard pops, which they thought were firecrackers going off, but it was the owner shooting a rifle at them from a bedroom window. They returned to their car and circled the block. During the second pass, *which was in the street, completely off the man's property*, the pops were heard again, and one of the girls, seventeen-year old Rachel Barezinsky, took a bullet in the head.[3]

There are people out there that will shoot you first and face the consequences afterwards; they have no concept of what constitutes a genuine threat and what their limits are. Now that many states have castle laws, are the citizens being educated as to what they can or cannot do? Does everyone know a set of *rules of engagement*? Or do we just go at it as we please and find out the hard way? Davis claimed that he shot in self-defense! But you don't discharge a gun at a person or a car passing your home *in the street or even on the sidewalk*. Common sense should tell you that. Neither should we shoot at someone just because they walked onto our property, although we ought to call 911 -- gun or no gun -- if they are breaking into an outbuilding or the home itself.

A rule of *equitable force* should apply, but the castle laws described in chapter 3 leave the choice of shooting or not shooting entirely to the homeowner. The castle laws basically did away with the equitable force concept. You can gun someone down for merely coming into your domain, and chapter 10 will present some disturbing examples of shootings of that type that were *not* examples of self-preservation. Where is the rule of law and accountability in those situations? Nuclear World War III would already be in the history books if our national leaders had not been applying a concept of equitable force over the years. The use of deadly force should require the presence of a genuine deadly threat, and it should be limited to the insides of our homes. The real issue, as in all things, is responsibility.

There are other situations where certain individuals have

concealed carry permits and can take a handgun beyond their own property. Those individuals have been subjected to a training program and have been made aware of a set of *rules of engagement.* They pass an FBI background check. There are restrictions on *where* those concealed guns can go. Responsibility is *required* of the one carrying a concealed weapon. There should be a similar set of rules for home defense. Otherwise, we really are going to find ourselves re-living the wild west mentality on a grand scale. This is why the castle laws of some states have built-in problems.

If *one man* will shoot into a street from his house, *how many others* are there that would take a shot at you if you came to their door? That happens, too. The Ohio example shows us how it is possible to encounter a homeowner with a gun, who has a willingness (even an apparent eagerness) to use it. *Ohio was not a castle law state when that shooting incident happened,* although a castle law went into effect in Ohio in September of 2008, so problems of this type are not unique to castle law states like Oklahoma. And the Allen Davis case[3] was only one of other similar shootings. Allen Davis was charged with murder, and he should have been; he might have been charged even in a castle law state, but that would depend on the thinking of the local district attorney. Some district attorneys also lack common sense or shun a troublesome case and play to the letter of the law even though better judgment is called for. But the laws do not say that a prosecutor can't charge a shooter if something looks wrong; it's simply that the burden of proof is now upon the prosecutor rather than the one who killed someone in the name of self-defense.

Avoidance of trouble has to be your priority if you don't want a gun. The truth is, avoidance of trouble should even be the priority of the person who keeps a gun in the house! You will not be armed, but the burglar who wants into your place may be. If you don't depend on heavy doors and good locks to make it harder for an intruder to reach you, you may someday find your own life and the lives of those you love in the balance. It was alleged that the trucker serial murderer of New Jersey[4] went door to door, trying doorknobs at random until he found one open. "*New Jersey authorities said Lane parked his rig at a truck stop in Bloomsbury and checked the doors of nearby homes until he found the unlocked entrance of Massaro's home.*" Burglars do the same thing.

We are not in a high crime area, but there are locks and chains even on our storm doors. That way, when the glass panels are moved a foot or two to expose the screens and let fresh air pass through the house during the spring and fall months, someone can't casually walk into the house. Those measures would not stop a career criminal from getting in, but the sounds of breaking glass and ripping screens will buy a little more time than an unlocked door. Individuals who live in high crime areas need to be much more serious about security. In that case a specialist ought to be consulted to evaluate the particular security situation because the needs vary from home to home.

Does this mean that every door will eventually have a steel portcullis so that our private homes *actually look like the old castles*? One really hopes not, but if we don't do something about the drug problem and its associated violent crimes, that's where we're heading. The author was an invited speaker at a chemistry conference in Lima, Peru in 2007 (Sociedad Qui'mica Del Peru', 23rd Congress), where he took note of the fact that even the universities were walled-in or fenced (like a fort), with armed guards patrolling. It seemed that our gracious host was always driving us from one secured compound to another one! Lima is an interesting place, full of wonders for anyone who has never been there, but there is a lot of crime in Lima. We stayed in Miraflores, not far from the bluff that overlooks the Pacific Ocean. The guards in front of a certain Miraflores hotel carried submachine guns, and Miraflores is an *affluent* place.

The downside of depending on locks and security measures and calls to 911 is that the police might arrive too late, and locks can be breached or doors battered in. Be aware of that. You'll be on your own if the intruder gets in, but there is a recommendation for that situation. The author and his wife were at a Christmas party in Arkansas in 2006, and one of the fellows invited to that party showed up late. When he finally arrived everyone realized that he was shaken. As it happened, he lived near Mountain Home, and unknown to him, a certain man had gone on a rampage in his neighborhood and terrorized several people.[5] The police were out looking for the troublemaker when he barged into the man's home holding a gun. On seeing an armed man coming into his home through *one door*, he fled through a *different door*, i.e., he went outside and put distance between himself and trouble. The police finally subdued the belligerent one, and no one was killed or seriously injured. That homeowner made a good tactical decision by *leaving his own home* (disregarding the "*stand your ground*" concept, for what it's worth), but it can't be promised that a hostile intruder will not shoot you in the back if you try to run in that kind of situation. Also, the option to run isn't going to work as well in a fifth floor apartment.

How to treat a gun if you intend to have one: gun use and gun safety

The author was introduced to guns when he was not even ten years old. His grandfather put a single shot .22 rifle in his hands and taught him how to aim it and be safe with it (meaning not only for his own safety but also the safety of anyone nearby). In some states today teaching a seven-year old to shoot a gun might be counted as child abuse, but grandfather was born in 1886, *before* the famous Ingalls, Oklahoma shootout, when the public mentality about guns was very different. And he did not just hand a child a rifle and let him run free with it; access to a gun was supervised until the boy was old enough to be trusted. There was merit in that kind of training. The youth was made aware of the actualities of guns, and for one thing the *novelty* of a firearm was worn off. Grandpa never said it, but he, too, was probably taught to use guns at an early age.

The author thus grew up with guns and a set of rules: We should assume that all guns are loaded, and if someone passes a gun to us, we should immediately check to see if it is loaded. Never point the muzzle at yourself or anyone else, and if a gun's muzzle is accidentally allowed to contact the ground, also assume that dirt or mud has gotten into the barrel. If you try to fire a gun with a plugged barrel, it will very likely blow up, possibly killing you or someone standing nearby. During a group hunt such an incident was witnessed when the barrel of a shotgun split open on firing; the muzzle end of the barrel looked like a peeled banana afterwards! Fortunately, no one was hit by the flying metal splinters. Apparently the bore of the barrel had been plugged with clay, because a smudge of clay was visible on what was left of the muzzle end of the shotgun.

Also, if you pull the trigger and the gun makes a weak "*pop,*" set the gun aside so that it is not pointing at anyone. Later, open the action, eject the round in the chamber and check the barrel for an obstruction. Faulty cartridges lead to what is called a *squib round*, one that does not have enough power to shove the bullet or a shotgun's wadding through the barrel. In that case, if you try to fire the gun again, it will blow up. So if you intend to have a gun you need to be sure that the gun barrel is not obstructed before taking it out on a hunt or to a shooting range -- a beetle might have crawled into the barrel since the last time it was used! Always open the action and check for obstructions before loading a gun. A fresh plastic sandwich bag covering the muzzle of the gun you keep ready for defense is a good idea. The bag should come off before you shoot the gun (because it obscures the sights), but even if it's still on, the thin plastic will rupture without any risk of blowing the gun up.

Guns are always cleaned and inspected after every hunt or trip to the shooting range. You unload a gun before you clean it. And you *never* horse around with guns or allow them to be accessible to unsupervised children. When the author's grandchildren visit, the gun that is kept at the ready goes into lockdown. Kids today are saturated with TV violence, and school campuses can be scary places at times. Anything can happen if juveniles are allowed unsupervised access to a gun. Today's young people didn't come up the way an earlier generation did.

It would be better to put all youths through a state-sponsored firearms safety course or the kind of thing the National Rifle Association offers.[6] Rick had been a member of the NRA, but he chose the Oklahoma firearms safety course for Faron. The course didn't keep Faron from being killed by a gun, but the thing that actually killed him was the motive of the one who unlocked a door and pulled a trigger.

The author's people were *poor*, and family members literally hunted to put meat on the dinner table. Grandmother kept a small flock of chickens for eggs and meat, to supplement the pork and beef cuts bought at a food store. They fished and had a garden plot, too. Through hunting the author became skilled with a rifle, but he never had much interest in handguns of any kind, because they are inherently inaccurate compared with a rifle or even a shotgun. The length between the front and rear sights is known as the *sight radius*; *longer* translates to *accuracy*. Revolvers and pistols are very short. With any kind of gun, skill fades as the aging process takes hold, and even young people lose shooting skills without continual practice.

There is an old hunting ethic: *you don't take what you don't intend to eat.* Men who "*hunted for the sport*" and gave the game they took to others really irked some hunters. Individuals who did careless things were generally not invited to participate in further group hunts. The author remembers a particular deer hunt in Oklahoma. His stand was behind some branches, and while awaiting hopefully for a deer to show up a coyote came out of the eye of the wind and wandered in his direction. It didn't notice the outline of a human behind those branches until it had approached to within ten feet. Then it took off running. The friend nearest to the stand yelled, "*Why didn't you kill that damned coyote?*" The answer was, "*I don't eat dogs and coyotes!*" A Native American in the group was laughing, because he frowned on unnecessary killing. It had been the ethic of the Ozark Hills; maybe our people learned that from *his* people, or at least some of them, because by other accounts the Navajos ate dogs!

Similarly, there was once a chance to take an armadillo, and some Texans and Oklahomans had reported that the meat is good tasting. It had emerged from the brush, rooting in the ground like a pig hardly 30 feet away, and it was not paying much attention to the man with a rifle. But on recalling that the armadillo can carry *Mycobacterium leprae* (the leprosy bacterium), and taking a closer look at the beast's armor plating, the thought of taking on an armadillo and dressing it out for cooking simply evaporated. It was the beast's lucky day.

Hunting may seem a little off-track, but there is a point to make: The author knows a few things about finding and taking game, even dressing out the meat and cooking it, but other than spending some time on a military shooting range practicing rapid-point firing methods with a handgun, he's no expert in the matter of mortal combat with a handgun. *Neither is the average person out there, and that has considerable relevance to home defense, the castle laws and the issues of this book.*

Choosing a self-defense gun

The Air Force's specialization is not like that of the Army or the Marines because small arms are secondary considerations, but when the author went through Air Force military firearms training at Officer Training School (Medina Base and the old range at Kelley AFB) his instructor preached *marksmanship*. The instructor was one that had been caught in the deadly fighting of the Pusan Perimeter at the start of the Korean War. He knew his specialty, and there was no trouble understanding what he intended for us to learn. He even put an M-3 submachine gun in front of us, just to demonstrate how inaccurate fast firing weapons can be, and the experience did a good job of convincing everyone that aim is important. Machine guns and submachine guns are military weapons, and that's where they belong. The skilled shooter with a rifle or a shotgun, who aims every shot, is much more to be feared than the one who sprays bullets around. A well-trained soldier with good fire discipline, who carries a semiautomatic rifle, is formidable. You will hear a distinct pause between every round he fires, as he comes back on target. It's not the "WHOOM-BANG-BOOM-BANG-BOOM" stuff of a Rambo movie. An experienced rifleman isn't seeing how fast he can empty the magazine; he's actually trying to hit his enemy.

But a close-up gunfight involving handguns is different in nature. Handguns are appropriate in close quarters, which is the home defense situation. Speed and special techniques for controlling the aim of handguns apply (more about this below).

A case can be made for medium powered carbines as defensive weapons in the home setting. A carbine is a short barrel rifle, and many medium powered carbines will match or outdo the most potent handguns in shocking power. They are easier to aim accurately and yet their shorter (but legal) barrel is easier to maneuver than a long barrel rifle. Rifles, especially high powered rifles, are not recommended for home defense. A rifle bullet has too much penetrating power and can go through very thick walls, even some kinds of masonry. Bullets from handguns will also easily penetrate drywall sheets.

Shotguns are considered by some to be good defensive weapons, but like long barrel rifles, they are clumsy in close quarters. You don't need to load 00 buckshot for home defense. Even waterfowl loads are brutal a few feet from the muzzle. Shotguns certainly are destructive at short distances, but they, too, have to be aimed like a rifle -- the shot pattern doesn't spread much in twenty feet. There is a common misconception that one only has to point a shotgun in the general direction of the opponent and pull the trigger. It isn't true, and if you try it in a gun battle your opponent will likely put you down before you manage to hit him.

Most experienced shooters think a handgun is better for home defense,[7] because of the inherent proximity to a target. The choice of a handgun is up to you. *The author does not prefer any handgun (that's the hunter thinking)*, but if he had to choose among handguns, a revolver with both single and double action modes would be the pick (this rules out hammerless revolvers). Revolvers are simple guns, and they do not tend to jam the way some semiautomatic pistols do (although a quality semiautomatic in good repair shouldn't jam if premium ammunition is used). But revolvers have a limited capacity, usually five or six rounds in the cylinder. Most gunfights are over after about two or three rounds fired. Some .22 revolvers have seven or nine round capacity, but a .22 bullet is not a man-stopper unless it hits the brain or the heart. The Smith and Wesson TRR8 in .357 magnum caliber is a *potent* revolver, probably too much so for the average home defender, and its cylinder holds eight rounds. At about $1,400 it's a bit pricey. The table on the following page compares several kinds of handguns. All of the guns in the table are lethal if the bullet hits a vital organ, but the three handguns in the top group are considered to be too weak for self-defense. A .22 caliber revolver or automatic would fall into that group, too. Those guns do not have enough stunning/shocking power (see endnote d of chapter 1).

Guns in the bottom group certainly have shocking power, but they also "kick" harder and produce an awesome muzzle blast -- very intimidating to inexperienced shooters and some veterans, too. Because of the harder recoil the muzzle flips up when the gun goes off, and it takes longer to get the sighting back on target. Thus, the guns in the bottom group are not recommended by many firearms instructors. If you want to be macho like Clint Eastwood, fine -- go for it, but try out a .44 magnum revolver with premium magnum loads on a shooting range before you actually buy one. The experience may change your mind.

Handgun Type	**Muzzle Energy (ft-lb)**
25 automatic	65
32 short revolver	90
32 long revolver	115
38 special revolver	372
9 mm automatic (parabellum)	382
45 automatic	411 (185 grain bullet)
327 magnum revolver	486 (115 grain bullet)
357 magnum revolver	583
44 magnum revolver	729 (Dirty Harry gun!)

The middle group contains a better selection of self-defense guns. The 327 magnum revolver is a fairly new design intended for self-defense, and the *low recoil* Federal Premium personal defense cartridge with an 85 grain Hydra Shok bullet may be a better choice of ammunition than the Speer Gold Dot cartridge noted in the table (see the photo of a 327 magnum revolver and its ammunition). The 85 grain bullet attains a muzzle energy of only 370 ft-lb, but that small but very fast bullet (1,400 ft per second) has a lot of shocking power. The 327 cartridges contain a fast burning powder (though not so fast as to imply *detonation*, because that would blow the gun up). It's the powder's burning rate and the choice of bullet mass that allows high velocities from a gun with such a short barrel. For purposes of target practice, the gun also accepts the less expensive .32 short and .32 Smith and Wesson long cartridges. A Taurus 327 magnum can be bought new for about $380 before taxes. Variants of some of the guns in this table are designated +P (but none of those are shown here); +P and +P+ means higher chamber pressures and thus more energetic bullets. The more energetic cartridges can only be used in a gun intended for them.

Photo of a .327 magnum revolver beside a box of its cartridges. The lightweight .327 bullet is supersonic. Many handgun bullets are subsonic but much heavier.

Never buy a vintage revolver that doesn't have a hammer safety; it is a feature that keeps the firing pin from being driven into the cartridge primer if the gun is dropped on its hammer.

In the single action mode the gun's hammer is pulled back to cock it, then a pull on the trigger fires the round. Assuming you are a right-handed shooter, re-cock the gun with your left thumb. The cocking and firing procedure can be repeated, and the relatively light force required to pull the trigger does not spoil the aim. In the double action mode you just aim and pull the trigger. It takes more force to pull the trigger in double action mode, because the hammer is being forced against its spring, and this tends to spoil the aim for most shooters. Some shooters do well with the double action mode, but the author is not one of them.

It is important to know a lot about your gun, which requires that you spend plenty of time on a firing range. Go out with someone who really knows guns. If you are unwilling to do that, if your plan is to simply buy a gun, load it and put it in a sturdy locked cabinet (or worse, an unlocked drawer with kids around!), *then you probably have no business even owning a gun.* That is the opinion of a lot of people who use guns regularly. People who buy a gun and set it aside probably tilt the gun over sideways when they shoot it, like a pimp in a *Walker Texas Ranger* TV series, and they are likely to say things like, "I loaded the gun with bullets." (They are called cartridges!) Such individuals are possible accidents in the making, and they are likely to injure or kill themselves or some innocent person when they think it's time to bring their gun into action.

So you need to know about *primers*, *cartridges*, *bullet types, brass* and *gilding metal* along with the features and functioning of the gun itself. Learn how *everything* works. A gun owner should know how to properly *open and close* the *action* of a gun and load it with the *correct ammunition*; how to inspect the gun for possible problems; and how to *field-strip* the gun, clean it and reassemble it properly. The terms may seem bewildering at first, and maybe you didn't know that a "round" fired means just one bullet into the target and not a box of twenty (like a round of beers with the boys!). Do some serious background reading. [8] *Please do it!* You must become proficient with a gun if you intend to have one.

Using the gun

Innocent citizens sometimes do find themselves in life threatening situations through no fault of their own. They hear about repeated muggings and intrusions in their neighborhood and wonder if they are next. Thus, many law-abiding individuals have had enough, and they buy a gun. Perhaps you are considering the option or have already acted on it. In that case, if an uninvited intruder with hostile intent shows up, at least your encounter *might be* on more level ground. But be prepared for the reality of the situation: you will suddenly be in a latter day version of one of those wild west scenarios, the kind described at the beginning of this chapter. *You need to know yourself, especially your limitations.* Be completely honest with yourself: can you be cool when someone is pointing a gun at you? Or will you fall apart? You need to keep a set of rules -- in your head -- of what should and shouldn't be done in an encounter with a dangerous intruder; in other words, have some kind of contingency plan, including *avoidance* considerations. All gun owners need to be *proficient* and *safe* with their gun.

Shooting at tin cans, known as "plinking," is not the same as countering an assailant while he is trying to kill you. The first kind of activity is a way to improve marksmanship, and it needs to be done because shooting skills fade without practice. What is known about the second kind of activity is fully sobering. First of all, gunfights tend to happen in close quarters and under conditions of poor lighting, and they develop *very rapidly*. Fractions of a second can mean the difference between living and dying. The one who is ready to shoot rather than scramble to retrieve a gun is much more likely to survive. If cover that will stop a bullet is available, get it between you and the assailant. The concept of positive control -- making sure that the person you are engaging in mortal combat is indeed a real threat and not a family member or any other innocent person -- is something to take very seriously. It is an *intense psychological situation*, as any combat veteran or gunfight survivor will tell you.

It is healthy to admit limitations. In any case, *avoidance* of trouble should be the priority. With that in mind, even if you live in a castle law state, *just forget what your castle law claims to allow you to do. Use your <u>common sense</u>, because after the odor of burned smokeless powder dissipates, you may find* *yourself facing a manslaughter or murder charge even though you thought it really was a desperate self-defense situation.* It has happened. The prosecuting attorney of *your* county might be hard-nosed -- a doubting Thomas -- while the one in the next county might have accepted your story and let you go. Those wild variations in justice were pointed out in the introduction to this book. More detailed examples will be examined in the final chapters of this book.

If you live in a high crime area and your doors and locks are easily defeated, *shame on you!* If you have a family you are risking their lives, too. Even if you manage to produce a loaded gun when an armed intruder suddenly appears one day, there is no assurance that you or someone you love will not be in the next day's obituary column. *Before confronting and engaging an intruder, depend on locks and a call to 911 if there is time for a call.* A gun should be used *only when there is no other choice.* Regardless of what your state's self-defense law says, *never open fire unless you are actually under attack.*

You have to be willing to inflict serious injury or even death if someone is shooting at you. You have to hit a vital organ to bring down a dedicated assailant. Are you really willing to do that? Intentional wounding shots are out of the question, because they may not incapacitate the one shooting at you and are demanding of aim. Speed is more important than pinpoint marksmanship. If you expect to survive a gunfight, you'll have to focus on *directing your fire* as well as you can while your opponent's bullets whiz by you or even hit you. That was a characteristic of the lawmen of the old west; combat proven police officers and armed forces veterans still living in 2010 will tell you the same thing. For those of us who have never been put to the test, saying I'll do this or that is only vain speculation. There is a tendency to shoot wildly rather than aim, and it will be essential to suppress the tendency in a shootout. These are the realities of an armed confrontation.

Detailed recommendations concerning the use of a gun in a shootout is not the intent of this chapter. One should read the accounts of those who were experienced in gunfighting techniques.[9] However, two tactical considerations are *paramount* and should be stressed: one is that *you need to know where your family members are located*, and the other is that if you are aware of an intruder moving around but have not made direct contact with him it *is better to stay put* and try to have someone make that emergency call rather than go looking. The one moving around is at a disadvantage, so let the intruder do the moving. If there is any doubt at all about the positions of the ones you are defending, you'll have to be especially careful of what you shoot at. Shadows and poorly illuminated shapes do not qualify as targets. Positive control requires that *you see well enough to be sure of who is out there.* Nothing less is acceptable. There is merit in having remote controlled lamps in our homes, or at least in leaving night lights on -- something more reliable than the simple types that plug into a wall socket and are easily defeated by a prowler.

The way the gun is handled is another consideration. Your index finger should not be on the trigger until you are ready to shoot. It should be outside of the trigger guard, perhaps lightly touching the front edge of the guard and thus approximately parallel with the gun barrel. Use a two-hand grip on the gun.[9] Before you are ready to shoot, hold the gun closer to your torso with the barrel tilted downward toward the floor a little ahead of you (but not straight down for obvious reasons!), and maintain that two-hand grip. When you are ready to shoot, pull the gun up to chin level and thrust forward, extending your arms fully outward toward the target and pulling the trigger as you extend. This creates a sturdy triangle between your chest and your two arms, and your aim is thus more steady than if you held the gun with just one hand. You control your point of aim with your *whole body.* After the shooting is over, always move your finger back to that safe position.

Try it: unload the gun (make very sure!), stand erect, and with just one hand holding the gun, pick a target. Do not point even an unloaded gun at anyone, or at a wall if someone might be on the other side! Pick an inanimate target. Line the sights up on that position (see the sighting diagram) and try to maintain aim for several seconds. Notice that the gun tends to wobble a bit, especially if the gun is a heavy one. Then do the same thing with a two-hand hold, with the arms well extended from the torso. Your aim ought to be more steady than it was with a one-hand hold, and it usually is. It is not necessary to pull the trigger in this experiment, and "dry firing" (as it's called -- pulling the trigger without a cartridge in the chamber) is not good for most guns. A two-hand hold is assumed in the remaining discussion. The gun should be in the downward position when you are cocking, moving the slide of an automatic, loading or unloading. Uncocking a gun -- easing the hammer down when there is a live round in the chamber or cylinder -- should also be done with the gun in a muzzle downward position; it's best to learn proper technique from a qualified instructor.

In the case of a revolver the double action mode using *point firing* techniques[9] is called for when the distance to the target is between that of a handshake and 15 feet (It's a disturbingly frequent situation in real life gunfights, and about 75 percent of all police gunfights happen at ranges less than 20 feet. That's exactly what applies in a home defense situation.). The gunsights are not used, and the barrel of the gun is pointed *instinctively* toward the middle of the opponent's chest, more or less as if you were pointing your index finger at that spot. Keep your eye on the target, extend your arms from the chin outward to form the triangle with the gun a little below the line of sight. As the gun goes out to form that triangle, the trigger is squeezed smoothly. Ideally the gun goes off just as the triangle is completed. Speed is much more important than fine accuracy. So is having the gun at the ready *before* things start getting out of hand. Point firing needs to be a reflex, and if we don't practice point firing with silhouette targets about fifteen feet away we will have to depend on pure luck in a real shootout. It is not something to gamble with. For longer distances, bring the gun up to a true aim and use single action, re-cocking with the left thumb after each shot is fired (Assuming the right index finger is on the trigger; left-handed shooters reverse the hold and cock with the right thumb.). Longer distances means beyond 20 ft.

It's a trade-off: speed up close; accuracy further out. If cover is available, get as much of your body behind it as possible (*Cover* means an object that stops bullets, as opposed to *concealment*, which is about hiding.). Give yourself every possible advantage if someone is shooting at you.

Semiautomatics have a larger magazine capacity, and some who use them put a cartridge in the chamber, pull the hammer back to the half-cock click and put the safety on. Most shooters don't find the idea of carrying a gun with a cartridge already in the chamber very reassuring, and they prefer to leave the chamber empty but with the safety off (whether or not the safety prevents moving the slide) and with the hammer not cocked. *If the gun is not a double action semiautomatic,* pulling the trigger with the magazine inserted but without a cartridge in the chamber will not fire the gun, so the empty chamber is of itself a very good safety. When the gun is needed, angle the muzzle downward, as described above, pull the slide fully back and let it snap forward. That simple maneuver chambers a cartridge and thus arms the weapon.

Double action semiautomatics are fairly common these days, and the first pull of the trigger requires more force, because it's working against the recoil spring. After the first round is fired the slide flies back, then forward -- very quickly. The empty cartridge casing is ejected, a new cartridge is stripped from the magazine and the hammer is cocked simultaneously; the remaining rounds will fire with a light trigger pull. Thumbs, fingers and other body parts have to be well clear of the slide when shooting a semiautomatic pistol, because the slide moves back with considerable force when the empty cartridge casing is being ejected. Shooting techniques are similar to those described for revolvers, except that you don't have to re-cock a semiautomatic pistol. After you are finished with firing one of these weapons get your finger off the trigger! Point the gun in a safe direction, put the safety on, pull the magazine (first), then carefully eject any round left in the chamber. *Make sure* that the chamber is empty. *Double check* for an empty chamber, and do that without a magazine in place *before* you store the gun. Or if you are returning the gun to the holster (as in a concealed carry), do that empty chamber check, be sure the slide is forward and *then* insert the loaded magazine.

The triggers of double action revolvers and automatics can be snagged, causing an unintentional discharge in spite of their harder trigger pull, so running and banging into things with a gun like that stuffed between your shirt and your belt is not a good idea. It's a good way to blow off part of your butt (or worse). It's better to have the gun in a proper nylon or leather holster that fully encloses the trigger.

When firing any gun for accuracy (with sights), the trigger should be squeezed progressively, rather than given a sudden, hard tug. Suppress flinching. You should concentrate on keeping the sights lined up, starting with the front sight visible. Proper sight alignment is as shown in the following diagram:

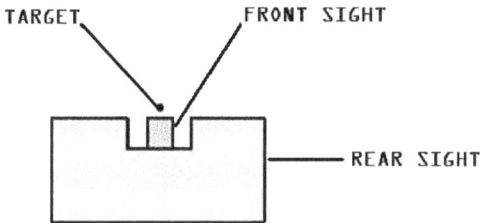

Sighting alignment illustration. The front sight should be centered in the rear sight slot, with the tops of both sights on the same horizontal line.

Practice on a proper range -- one with a bermed earth backdrop that is free of stones or other objects that might cause a bullet to rebound back to the firing line. Use less powerful loads. They are cheaper. But fire magnum loads occasionally for familiarity. If you don't practice with live ammunition you will not have a clue if trouble ever comes to your door. For defensive purposes, load your gun with the most magnum ammunition that it will safely accommodate, but be aware that a bullet's placement is more important than its potency. Make sure your defensive ammunition is fresh. Hollow point bullets and wad cutters are more destructive than round nosed bullets. Wad cutters (flat nosed bullets) are intended for revolvers, and they are used mostly for target practice, because they cut neat holes in a target. They tend to foul the barrel with soft bullet metal if you shoot many of them (The fouling can be removed.). Hollow points -- bullets that expand on impact and thus have more shocking power -- work best in revolvers. Semiautomatics generally work better with fully jacketed round nosed bullets but there are specialized hollow points intended for automatics. Again, take your pick from the table, but be aware that too little or too much firearm power may work against your survival.

Those stand-your-ground-anywhere situations

Something should be said about the *other situations* allowed in most of the castle law states. In those cases the law applies even in your car or at your workplace (assuming that a gun may be carried in your car legally, and that you own the property of the workplace, or that your employer who owns the business allows you to have a gun there). You are not required to retreat in those states.

Keep this in mind for situations at the place of business: if you decide to engage armed robbers and during the shooting contest one of your stray bullets hits an innocent customer, odds are good that you will not have immunity to criminal or civil prosecution for *that* person's injuries. The part of your state's law that says, "...*reasonably believes*..." (or something similar) is not going to apply to a sixty-two year old unarmed female customer that has no prior criminal record, especially one who is well known in the community. There is no way to make her fit in as a co-conspirator with the two street punks that came to rob you. What if your bullet goes through the window and injures a child in the playground across the street? Even if the court goes easy on you, your customers might be saying, "*He's trigger happy. I'm going somewhere else.*" Using a gun in places where people congregate is a nightmare. Those who carry a gun *officially* hope it never happens to them. The car situation is equally bad.

It is *not* a good idea to be inside a car when someone is outside pointing a gun at you. Try this simple experiment: go strap yourself into the driver's seat of your car. Have a friend stand directly in front of your car. It's not hard to point your finger at him, so you might be tempted to take a shot at him through the windshield (but guess what flies everywhere if you do that!). Shooting through glass can deflect the bullet's path. Have him also run behind the car and try to keep up with him;

that's when you'll notice the blind spots as you struggle to turn around in your seat. Now imagine all of that with bullets whizzing through your car and glass shattering and your own gun going off deafeningly in a small space, making your ears ring for a long time, perhaps forever. (The author suffers from tinnitus and a serious hearing loss. A doctor told him that it was caused by working around noisy construction tools when he was young - - probably by guns, too.) The stand-your-ground concept of most castle law states may give you the right to self-defense even in your own car, away from home, but the reality is that you are definitely not in a good situation if you are sitting in a car when the shooting starts! The one outside with a gun has more freedom to maneuver than you do, so your best bet is to drive away if you can, or better yet, let avoidance be your primary mode of defense.

The kinds of trouble warranting self-defense out on the road are mainly those of carjacking and road rage. Carjackers are notably inclined to violence, because their crime is a more serious felony than mere car theft. A carjacker might kill you to avoid a long prison sentence. You would likely be dealing with more than one carjacker, and your odds of being shot are substantial if you attempt to mount a self-defense. A carjacking can turn into a kidnapping. In the case of road rage you will be dealing with an irrational person; anything can happen. Watch out for parking lots. Some appropriate parking lot recommendations are summarized here:

1. Pay attention to the situation that you are driving into. Avoid parking in a secluded location (with obscuring hedges, etc).

2. Be wary of people standing idle in a parking lot or who are sitting in a nearby car, who might be waiting to jump you.

3. Be even more wary of people who approach your car.

4. Spend as little time as possible entering or leaving your car; waste no time starting the engine and leaving.

5. Avoid unlit areas.

6. Some parking lots provide valets and escorts; consider using them.

7. Look inside, around and under your car as you approach it.

8. If an armed carjacker approaches with a gun, give him the keys and walk away from the car if he'll let you.

9. If you are kidnapped -- which is a real possibility in carjackings -- be compliant but cool. If you can get away from your abductor near a busy location, head *toward* the crowd.

As for intruders in the workplace, there are some general recommendations, and the following is a condensed summary some points offered to the public by Sgt. Tim Phillips, a Baxter County (Arkansas) Court security officer:[10]

1. Don't escalate a situation; lives are more valuable than property.
2. Install a video surveillance system. (These are not terribly expensive, and the author has such a system at his own home.)
3. Watch out for suspicious behavior -- a customer who lingers too long and is looking for cameras, etc.
4. Have a way to signal an employee to get tag numbers if 3 (above) is noticed. With a good video system that includes customer parking areas in the surveillance, it could be automatic.
5. Lower shelf heights and convex mirrors let you see more of what's going on in your store.
6. A wireless alarm to local law enforcement is a good idea.
7. Convey your security plan to employees and have emergency numbers other than 911.
8. If you are in a strip mall, organize a business watch group and post signs to that effect.
9. Have good parking lot lighting and put motion-activated lamps in alleys, etc.
10. Secure your phone communications. A cell phone is a must.

Landline phone wiring and electric power can be disrupted.

Using a gun in a public place carries a lot of responsibility because of potential harm to innocent bystanders. Take that into consideration before you choose to confront intruders at the workplace.

Common sense

Don't be trigger happy. Use a gun *only* if armed and aggressive intruders bash their way into your home. You'll have the moral right to defend yourself in that case. The truth is, that right existed in most places even before the so-called castle laws came into existence. It might be your own funeral if you think you ought to confront prowlers *outside* your home. Even if you don't get killed for pushing your luck, you could go to prison for misjudging what you could or could not do under your state's castle law. Leave that kind of situation to the police. If your home is easily broken into, odds are good that an intrusion will catch you with your pants down, with no hope of retrieving a gun in time to have the advantage.

More Oklahoma outlaws

There is one more Oklahoma outlaw story to tell, and it is

relevant. Claude Dennis and Michael Landcaster terrorized the public during the late 1970s. Their killing spree across Oklahoma and parts of the mid-south resulted in 20 deaths. They killed people to get a pickup truck or for money or food, and they preyed mostly on *rural dwellers*. Intrusions into homes was the *mode* of their crimes. It got so bad that people would leave food in their trucks along with the ignition key and a note of the type: *"Please take this truck. We don't want to die!"* Russell Washington, who lived near Durant, was one of the few that survived an encounter with the outlaws, and it happened that Russell would be the last citizen victimized. Unfortunately, law enforcement lives were lost in the final shootout, which happened right after Dennis and Landcaster left the Washington home.

Russell Washington and the author attended the same church, and the story was heard from the one who lived it. It happened that the killers got the drop on Russell before he could say, "Jack Robinson." They came into his place near where the Blue River crosses Oklahoma 48, just a few miles north of Durant. This happened on a fateful morning in May of 1978. They might have killed Russell, too, but Dennis remembered that Russell had allowed him to hunt quail on his land at an earlier time. The outlaw simply tied Russell up, took his guns and some money and headed north on Oklahoma 48 in Russell's pickup truck. So much for the self-defense laws existing in Oklahoma at that time; they are of no help if someone gets the drop on you! But Russell got loose and called the police.

Turning east on a gravel section line road that paralleled Oklahoma 22 (it was one mile south of that highway), the killers ran into a highway patrol roadblock. This was not far from a small village known as Kenefic. The outlaws shot their way through the roadblock, killing officers Young and Summers. It was told that the roadblock was almost in front of a home where an elderly woman lived; she had grabbed her shotgun and was heading out to try for a shot, but Dennis and Landcaster took off before she reached a clear line of sight.

The trooper/pilot of an aircraft flying overhead had been advised of Washington's phone call and now had the pickup truck in sight as the outlaws continued east toward the small town of Caddo. The pilot radioed back that he was tracking the truck toward Caddo, and that is where the final battle took place.

On reaching Caddo the fugitives turned into a driveway. The weather was mild, and there were children playing in the neighborhood. The two officers first to reach the site didn't realize that the outlaws had turned off the street, and as they drove by the house they came under fire. Lt. Grimes was killed and Lt. Young was seriously wounded. Grimes was in the front passenger seat, on the side facing the outlaws. It illustrates the principle that the one in an armed confrontation who takes up a fixed position has an advantage over the one in motion, especially if the one in motion does not know where his adversary is located. It also shows the disadvantage of being shot at while sitting in a car.

There probably would have been a hostage situation at that *home*, but fortunately, no one was there; then the other police units converged and caught the outlaws in a cross fire. Bullets flew, but none of the neighborhood children were hit. Both of the outlaws were killed. The dead or injured can often be counted on *both sides* of any armed confrontation. Bear that in mind when you take hold of a gun, and hope that you never have to use it in a conflict. Avoid trouble to the extent that you can -- that's the cardinal rule. Don't pull the trigger until you have no other choice.

During the war protest years Joan Baez portrayed Oklahoma's Pretty Boy Floyd as a sort of folk hero, but if *all* the facts about *him* are put into view, that is like making Claude Dennis a hero for sparing Russell Washington's life! Some extreme right wingers view Adolph Hitler as their hero, and a few hard-line left wingers think Che Guevara was a kind of messiah. Yassir Arafat received a Nobel Prize for *peace*. *If his life exemplified peaceful deeds, what is a warlord like?* Why do we glorify the outlaws and killers?

"*Thou shalt not kill.*" - From the Holy Bible, Exodus 20:13

"*Ye have heard that it was said by them of old time, 'Thou shalt not kill;' and whosoever shall kill shall be in danger of the judgment. But I say unto you, that whosoever is angry with his brother without a cause shall be in danger of the judgment...*"
- From the Holy Bible, Matthew 5:21-22

ENDNOTE -- Chapter 7

a. The photograph of the old Ingalls Hotel was taken on August 30, 2009, just two days before the 116th anniversary of the infamous shootout. The author is standing in front of what is left of the building, around which the fighting took place. The camera is pointing north, and a gravel road runs east-west behind the camera, but the west end was fenced in 1893. The outlaws were bottled up against that fence and had to cut the barbed wire in order to get away. A mortared fieldstone monument, fashioned as an obelisk, honors the three U. S. Marshals killed in the gunfight (Dick Speed, Tom Houston and Lafe Shadley), and it is on the other side of the gravel road, about six hundred feet to the east, near a volunteer fire station. Ingalls is still a living community, although it is off the beaten path. The location isn't marked on the current Oklahoma state highway map, but it can be reached by going approximately ten miles east from Stillwater on state highway fifty-one, then south for a mile.

REFERENCES CITED -- Chapter 7

1. Glenn Shirley, "Belle Starr and Her Times: The Literature, the Facts and The Legends," University of Oklahoma Press, Norman Oklahoma, 1982.

2. S. Charles Bolton, "Arkansas 1800-1860: Remote and Restless," The University of Arkansas Press, Fayetteville, Arkansas, 1998. See the map on page eleven. All of chapter 4 of Bolton's book is relevant to the westward relocation and the problems of Native American tribes such as the Cherokees and the Choctaws. Today's Oklahoma -- excluding the panhandle -- used to be the west end of Arkansas Territory. Because of all the trouble out there, even before the relocation, Arkansas' territorial leaders had been happy to give the western region away when the issue of Native American relocation came up. However, it needs to be pointed out that Arkansans had a part in those troubles. The indigenous and relocated Native Americans slipped across the Arkansas/Oklahoma border to procure illegal liquor from the Arkansans who made whiskey in the Ft. Smith/Van Buren area. The federal government was not a bit happy with that development.

3. Staff writer, "Ghost-Hunting Teen Shot Near Spooky House," *Fox News*, August 23, 2006; this happened at Worthington Ohio.

4. Ralph Ortega, "Judge postpones hearing for trucker accused in Bloomsbury slaying," *The Star-Ledger*, September 04, 2008.

5. John Anderson, "Police: Armed man terrorizes neighborhood," Staff Writer, *The Baxter Bulletin,* December 22, 2006. Jerry Martin was alleged to enter Mountain Home Arkansas homes and point a gun at residents, terrorizing an entire neighborhood.

6. Log onto this website: http://www.nrainstructors.org/searchcourse.aspx. The website finds the NRA firearms education and training sites nearest to your location. First you choose a type of course (e.g., *NRA Basic Pistol Shooting Course*), then use the search engine by *state* or *zip code/radius* to find locations and times.

7. Daniel T. McElrath, "Blocking Home Plate," *Shooting Times*, July 2009, pp40-45.

8. For a good general reference see: John Malloy, "Complete Guide to Guns & Shooting," DBI Books, Northbrook IL, 1995. The 256 page paperback book includes photos and sketches. An on-line glossary of gun and ammunition terms can be found at:

http://www.armsvault.com/gunterms.asp

Other on-line resources can be located simply by typing the keywords gun_glossary or ammunition_glossary when using internet search engines. Consider a subscription to *Guns & Ammo Magazine* and membership in the NRA.

9. The two-hand point shooting methods currently used by police forces evolved from the one-hand instinctive techniques of Fairbairn and Sykes, dating back to the WWII era. See: Capt. William E. Fairbairn and Capt. Eric A, Sykes, "Shooting to Live with the One Hand Gun," Paladin Press, P.O. Box 1307, Boulder Colorado, 1987. Lt. Col. Rex Applegate (OSS) interacted with Fairbairn and Sykes and developed additional methods. See: Fleet Marine Force Reference Publication (FMFRP) 12-80, "Kill or Get Killed." Also: Colonel Rex Applegate and Chuck Melson, "The Close-Combat Files of Colonel Rex Applegate," Paladin Press, P.O. Box 1307, Boulder Colorado. Applegate recommended taking a step *toward* the opponent, so as to face him directly, which supposedly improves the body-referenced aiming. NYPD SOP 9 -- Analysis of Police Combat -- 1969 is a useful summary of these methods, and it even describes gun attachments that supposedly enhance the point firing techniques. There is a DVD instructional program for handgun combat: "Tactical Readiness: Shooting in Realistic Environments," Second Amendment Foundation Personal Firearms Defense DVD Series. The address is: Second Amendment Foundation,12500 NE 10th Place, Bellevue, WA 98005. Shooters argue a lot about which method is best, and most of the methods are similar; so who do you pick for your "expert?" By one definition an expert is someone from the next town, and the author is skeptical about a lot of the claims and gimmicks. Just pick one that seems right to you and try it out on a shooting range. With the range clear and your gun loaded and ready in the two hand hold, pointing downward at about a 45 degree angle, have someone call "GO," and with your eyes focused on the intended bullet impact point, bring the gun up and get off a shot just as fast as you can when you hear the "GO." Speed is the main issue at short distances, but *never* try to do a fast-draw from a holster -- start with the two-hand grip on the gun described above. If you can hit the heart or solar plexus spots on a paper silhouette reasonably well at 15 feet, time after time, then that's your method. Stay with it and practice it often. If you don't practice you will not be ready when trouble finds you. You should be able to obtain free downloads of some of these documents if you keyword by authors or titles through *Google* or *Yahoo*.

10. Staff writer, "Businesses can take precautions," *The Baxter Bulletin*, July 28, 2009

.

Chapter 8 - Views of the public and the legislators

"Never give a child a sword." - An old Roman proverb

There are people who seem to think it's fine to kill someone and claim the law (or what they *think* the law allows), even under very questionable circumstances. Others want evidence of restraint and common sense where the possibility of violence is imminent. This chapter emphasizes public opinions, and is presented as a sort of forum on the subject of self-defense. The quotations are also in italics, to aid their recognition as such. Most of the quotations are from anonymous letters to commentary websites (unless stated otherwise). Errors of grammatical construction and spelling were not corrected; the quotations are presented just as they were found. Bear in mind that we are dealing with *allegations* in most of these cases.

The things people say and what they put in print tells us a lot about them; some closet psychopaths will warn you beforehand.

The embossed metal sign is printed in red and white reflective material so that it is visible at night when headlights illuminate it. It reads: "*NO TRESPASSING. VIOLATORS WILL BE SHOT. SURVIVORS WILL BE SHOT AGAIN.*" You can buy them on the internet. Another sign reads: "*LOVE YOUR ENEMIES BUT KEEP YOUR GUN OILED.*" Obviously there is a market for such signs. Are these signs intended to bluff or do the owners mean business? No doubt many displaying those warnings are bluffing. The sign is meant to intimidate approaching prowlers. But there are closet psychopaths behind some of those signs, be sure of it. And with that possibility in mind, *be careful!* In 2009 there was a totally senseless shotgun killing of a seven-year old boy.[1] It happened at a place beside the Trinity River near Houston, Texas, and a sign bearing the following inscription was seen on the shooters' property: "*TRESPASSERS WILL BE SHOT. SURVIVERS WILL BE RESHOT!! SMILE -- I WILL.*"

They kept their word! The woman fired, handed the gun to her husband and he fired, too; they took turns, one shot each. The boy and those accompanying him were hit by shotgun pellets. The boy died from his wounds less than two days later, and another individual -- an adult family member -- was seriously injured. The two shooters were jailed but allowed bond while an investigation proceeded.

You'd think it wouldn't be hard to conclude that shooting a seven-year old boy for going behind a bush to pee was outside the scope of the Texas castle law, but the initial comments from the district attorney was that an investigation was under way, trying to establish the circumstances leading up to the shooting, e.g., if trespassing was involved, if provocation was present, etc! If it turns out that the two doing the shooting are exonerated to save the Texas law, an immediate battle will be won for the Texas castle law, but the war for public support will be lost forever. Texans and Oklahomans are not stupid, and while they believe in things like gun ownership and self-defense, they can be totally angered by senseless killings. There is no excuse for shooting a child like that.

Anonymous comments were offered concerning the Trinity River shooting: *"Texas. Seven years old. Yep. Even your dumbest of prosecutors should be able to distinguish between a rightful shooting under the Castle Doctrine and murder."*
And another: *"40 yards? Who sees a 7-year old through their shotgun sights and pulls the trigger? That's murder, plain and simple."* And another: *"Texas must be the real 'Island of Dr. Moreau.' Naw, even animals won't kill the helpless offspring of*

their own species for no good reason." And one more: "*It's an objective standard for fear ('reasonably believes'), not a subjective one ('well, it scared me, and so what if no one else was scared') lest Cretans like this would win. I agree that these Neanderthals should be boiled in oil, heads run up on a pike for 60 days, and then imprisoned for life, but this is Texas and Jethro and Granny are likely to be on the jury with Jed as the Judge. Anything can happen, and usually does in this third world theocracy, so you will understand my reticence that justice will...prevail.*"

Most of the debate over this incident centered on whether or not the death penalty should be imposed. The public was sure that it was a murder, and only one contrary comment was found in a search of several media outlets. Ostensibly, it took sides with the shooters, but it might have been a tongue-in-cheek quip.

Another shooting in Texas happened *earlier* in Passadena, a suburb of Houston, thus not far from the setting of the Trinity River shooting incident, and it, too, was outside the scope of the Texas castle law.[2] The shooter, Joe Horn, was nevertheless acquitted by a grand jury (which the DA convened) even though the intruders were on a neighbor's property and did not constitute a threat to him or his home. Here is the transcript of what Joe

Horn had to say. During the 911 call *this* was recorded along with the sounds of the shots being fired:

(START AUDIO CLIP)

(CROSSTALK)

HORN: "OK. He's coming out the window right now. I got to go, buddy. I'm sorry, but he's coming out the window."

(CROSSTALK)

911 OPERATOR: "No, don't. Don't go out the door.

Mr. Horn? Mr. Horn?"

HORN: (EXPLETIVE DELETED) "They just stole somebody. I'm going out the window. I'm sorry."

911 OPERATOR: "Don't go outside."

HORN: "I ain't going to let them get away with this (EXPLETIVE) They stole something. They got a bag of something."

911 OPERATOR: "Don't go outside the house."

HORN: "I'm doing it."

911 OPERATOR: "OK?

Mr. Horn, do not go outside the house."

HORN: "I'm sorry. This ain't right, buddy."

911 OPERATOR: "You're going to get yourself shot if you go outside that house with a gun. I don't care what you think."

HORN: *"You want to make a bet? I'm going to kill them."*

911 OPERATOR: "OK? Stay in the house."

(STOP AUDIO CLIP)

(START NEW AUDIO CLIP)

911 OPERATOR: "I don't want you going outside, Mr. Horn."

HORN: "Well, here it goes, buddy. (You can hear Horn chambering a round)."

911 OPERATOR: "Don't go outside."

HORN: "Move, you're dead."

(GUNSHOTS)

(STOP AUDIO CLIP)

You may draw your own conclusion, but *that* was a murder according to the author's thinking, not self-defense. Maybe it was *murder two* because the time between the decision to shoot and the action was very short; it was driven by anger and bad judgment. But Horn said he intended to kill the men, and that's what he did. It was alleged that he shot the two burglars in the back. It is true that they were committing a crime, but a concept of equitable force was not applied. The crime was not against Horn, and the author of the Texas castle law went on record to say that the law was not intended to cover such situations: *"It was not an issue in this case other than him saying incorrectly that he understood it to mean he could protect his neighbor's property."* (Texas State Sen. Jeff Wentworth[3])

To some Horn is a hero; to others he's a devil. Objectively, he made himself the judge, jury and executioner. The punishment exceeded what the law prescribes for burglars. Can he live with what he did for the rest of his life? A jury has spoken: *he is innocent.* A court dignified their verdict.

And do these shootings actually put an end to burglaries? Of course not. There is a problem here: burglaries keep happening in Texas and Oklahoma and everywhere else, castle laws or not. Perhaps the rate of burglaries has been reduced. But the intent of such a law should be *to protect homeowners who have to defend themselves when they are genuinely under siege,* not to cause an abatement of burglary crimes. No law should protect shootings which involve *criminal purposes.* Two questions posed by journalist Michael E. Young are pertinent, *"Did the castle law ... unleash a flurry of gunfire?"* and *"Are they more likely to shoot first even when safe retreat may be an option?"*[3] The answer to both questions seems to be *yes.* Young's questions and criterion 2 in chapter 4 are essentially one and the same.

The need for a self-defense option in dangerous situations is not disputed. What is seriously in question is the public's understanding of what it can or cannot do. Some citizens seem to think the laws give them the right to shoot someone who only appears to be engaged in criminal activity, even when there is not an actual threat to anyone. This mentality is a sure path to more tragedy.

More closet psychopaths speak out

There is the joke about a Houston judge who dropped charges after a woman explained why she shot a purse-snatcher in the back six times: *"I raised my right hand, pointed my pistol at the man running away from me with my purse, and squeezed the trigger of my pistol six times!"* *When asked by the judge, "Why did you shoot him six times?"* *The woman replied, "Because, when I pulled the trigger the seventh time, it only went CLICK."* And there was this wisecrack from someone who was leaving Texas: *"After five years attending graduate school here in Texas, I'll soon be leaving for a job in the Northeast. It turns out I'll be leaving just in time to not have to worry about getting my head blown off."* Wow! Why is all of this stuff coming out of the Houston area? It can't be good for southeastern Texas tourism.

A pharmacist in Oklahoma City was charged with murder in 2009 after shooting a downed would-be robber five more times.

The robbers were armed, and *they* shot first (although the one that was killed apparently wasn't armed). A shot fired by the pharmacist had hit the unarmed intruder in the head, and that had knocked him out. He should have stopped there. Those additional five rounds came from a *second gun*; i.e., after downing the robber the pharmacist walked back to the counter, picked up another loaded gun, came back to the intruder lying on the floor and pumped five more rounds into his torso. Using force when it *isn't necessary* is *not* self-defense. The incident was recorded by a surveillance camera, and the medical examiner determined that the head shot was not fatal (but it knocked him out) while those additional shots were lethal. Most of the anonymous comments sent to news blogs agreed with the DA's decision to charge the man with murder.

The prospective psychopaths can almost always be spotted in those kinds of blogs; the following two minority opinions were about the Oklahoma City pharmacy shooting: "*i support the pharmacist. period. as for shooting him 5 times- i would have unloaded my entire clip until the person STOPPED moving.if he's still moving-he's still a threat.*" And another: "*Castle Law + Stand Your Ground are two of the best pieces of legislation to come out for quite a while. Obviously it varies from state to state. If your state has these laws on the books, it's open season if someone breaks into your property."*

Open season? Like hunting ducks? Neither of these individuals bothered to view the surveillance tape. The way the pharmacist came back with that second gun gave no indication that he was afraid of being shot by the one on the floor. Hunters generally show far more caution while approaching wounded animals. The man just hurried back to the one lying on the floor and shot him to death. *Anyone* (law officer or private citizen) who chooses to have and possibly use a gun for self-defense risks being held to *standards* concerning *how the gun is used*, although, because of the *variability of justice* phenomenon, it doesn't always happen that way. The pharmacist could be acquitted of what looks like murder to any rational individual even though he has been charged with murder. That possibility is a consequence of the *current* public mood in states like Oklahoma. How jurors think *privately* indeed could affect the outcome of a trial, and it looks as if that *might have* happened in the acquittal of Joe Horn.

When you read through the anonymous comments posted on various discussion websites that debate self-defense issues, you will quickly notice the group that believes it's fine to shoot someone for merely straying onto their property. Yes, the intruder *could be* someone with a malevolent motive. It could also be a neighbor seeking to retrieve his son's model airplane after a gust of wind blew it into the yard. Too many people think the castle laws are about defending property, and that is a very dangerous misconception. Those who would like to keep their right to own guns need to realize that killings of the type just described will be used to justify the goals of the anti-gun movement. With enough of that kind of thing we could see the end of the Second Amendment.

Here is a choice comment from the Trinity River shooting of seven-year old Donald Coffey, but it may have been a tongue-in-cheek remark: "W*e do not know the facts of this case yet. The initial news reports do seem to indicate that these people did not trespass but the facts of the situation can ONLY be ascertained in a courtroom. Depending on whether these people trespassed these people may have been within their rights to shoot as per Texas law.*" Surely *that* was offered as a satirical remark; if not, the person who wrote it suffers from the kind of bad judgment that leads to senseless shootings. Actually, we *do* know the facts of that case. He was shot to death for going to the bushes to urinate! Killing a child for a crime that might have been a misdemeanor in some other place is murder. Saying that the state law might allow the shooting death of a boy simply because he trespassed is mindless. If we've actually come to such a grim situation, then every man's property is a kind of old time Oklahoma Territory in miniature. It is not wrong to make that kind of comparison. Some would twist the law into whatever they wanted it to be, and anything goes -- shootings, hangings, beatings, scalpings, etc. Let's not go in that direction.

Here are a few more comments from a variety of fatal shooting incidents, offered by the "shoot 'em dead" advocates: *"I would have done the same given the circumstances."* The killing referred to in the last comment was a very questionable one. The following commenter didn't know that spouses, children and neighbors indeed have been shot by mistake: *"if i'd had a clear shot at the backsides of my robbers, i would have delighted in taking it. thank God i live in alaska, where you have the right to protect your life and property and that of your neighbors whenever it, not you, is threatened. and i have not heard of a single case of children, friends, or spouses being mistaken for burglars and shot. plenty of actualy, nasty burglers taken down, though :)"* And another: *"If someone is at my house with the intent on harming me or my family, I would shoot until they are stopped. Even if I had to reload the gun."* Finally: *"It is self-defense when you shoot someone for walking into your home uninvited regardless of why they are there."* Even if walking in was by accident? That has happened a few times.

How much of this is vain boasting? Or would these people actually do what they said they'd do? *Some* of them would do it. The facts show us very clearly that they would. Thus, while the public argument is not unbalanced it also includes thinking that tilts toward being just plain trigger happy.

Concerning shooting someone multiple times

Repeatedly shooting a downed intruder is not a good idea. The overwhelming majority of public comments on multiple gunshots is one of revulsion (though comments of the other kind were presented above). The following was offered concerning Faron's shooting death in Durant, Oklahoma. Of five shots fired, four actually hit Faron: "*I just heard this story and I don't believe it was in self-defense either. Shooting 5 bullets into someone tells me that he intended to kill the man. If it was self-defense what weapon did the other man have? There was no mention of him having any weapon, especially not a gun.*" Faron was not armed -- that is a fact. He went to that house bare handed. The members of Faron's family sincerely believe that a premeditated murder was committed. They see it as a failure of the criminal justice system.

Another, from a different incident: "*...sounds to me like he crossed the line. The first shot was self-defense. At that point the* *attacker stopped and anything beyond that is over the line.*"

The following comments were about the fatal shooting of an intruder in a man's back yard in Fort Worth, Texas. The deceased man had no criminal record in Tarrant County: "*I generally like the spirit of the castle law, but 5 times?*"

And a second comment on that same Ft. Worth killing: "*Did anyone stop to wonder why five shots? why not shoot up in the air... or one warning shot something...To aimlessly shoot is not right? I am well aware of the castle law but I think this Homeowner took it too far. I kno Mr. Bullock Personally Growing up in NJ he was always involved always scored above the rest in High School and excelled at everything he did. Something just isn't adding up here... The facts will be revealed...*" And a third comment on the Ft. Worth incident: "*So let me get this straight, I can accidentally walk onto anyone's residential property and be killed for it and it's perfectly legal? Sounds like it grants a murder license to paranoid A-holes with guns.*"

But that's how the Oklahoma and Texas castle laws work. Yes, you can shoot someone for even being in your domain without raising questions. All you have to do is say you believed your life was threatened. The following comment comes close to what the author might have written: "*I'm generally a firm supporter of the castle laws, but seems to me like the perp needs to be actually in the castle or at least in the act of breaking in. Grab your gun, call the cops and if you hear a window break, then start firing. Otherwise, you might hit somebody who was hiding from robbers, or who was fetching a frisbee from your yard, or trying to fetch his cat."* But one who responded was on the fence: *"I'm tempted to agree with you, but once again, no back story whatsoever. If the guy was in the backyard naked wielding a katana, then 5 shots was a dozen shots too few. If he was a lost drunk stumbling home, then it's overkill."*

Concerning opening doors or leaving doors open for intruders -- how the public views that

Although the castle laws generally don't require attention to door security, comments submitted to newspapers and TV station websites the public were found to be overwhelmingly *against* opening the door to trouble, even in castle law states: *"It is strange. Why would you open the door if you think someone is breaking in? But, if the person did chase him around the condo the person living there has every right to defend himself. What would you do in the situation if the person kept coming? You never will know till it happens to you. Him shooting twice I don't think should be an issue if the guy kept coming. But I still don't* understand *WHY he opened the door. If he did come in without permission and was chasing the guy around the condo then he had a right to protect himself. The guy should have left when told to. Otherwise why own a gun if you can't shoot someone who is in your home with the intent to do harm?"*

This one comes from the shooting of Rick's grandson: *"Faron, the victim, DID NOT have a gun. Supposedly, the suspect knew Faron was coming over and loaded the gun, put it in his back and waited for Faron to come over. If they knew Faron was coming over why didn't they just call the police?"* It's a valid question. The castle laws fail if the eligibility for calling an incident "self-defense" is made too broad. Standards of conduct have been effectively removed so that the shooter does not have to face a civil lawsuit. The fly in the ointment comes from assuming that *all* such killings will be motivated by self-preservation. *Other motives are possible,* and the examples presented above show that rather clearly. Psychopaths and hot tempered individuals *find opportunity in the laws.* If justice is something to be honored, then the obvious murders need to be weeded out. Imposing a presumption of innocence in a ridiculous situation destroys public confidence in the long run.

The logic behind the Texas castle law was explained by Texas

Senator Wentworth,*(3)* and it shows how we got into this situation: *"I read in the newspaper a couple of years ago that Jeb Bush, the governor of Florida, was signing the castle doctrine there to allow residents to defend themselves in their own homes, and I thought, 'Isn't that silly? We in Texas have always had that right.' But when I checked, I discovered that through legislative and judicial action in the 1970s, we'd changed the law. Before that, there was no fear of indictment or civil suits if you defended yourself in your home. But we lost that in 1974."*

The 1974 law required Texans to attempt to retreat, and if retreat was impossible, the homeowner had to be sure that the intruder was armed *before* using force. Also, the use of force had to be *equitable*. That a more stringent law went into effect in 1974 is understandable, considering Texas' history of violence; there was a reason. And the senator continued: *"I believe you have the right to defend yourself with any means necessary without fear of being indicted or sued by the intruder or his or her survivors."* The right to self-preservation when it truly is "us or them" isn't disputed. People have been sued for defending their own lives, and that shouldn't happen. Most of us know that civil lawsuits waste money and time and seldom lead to tangible results. The lawsuit doesn't always happen. A better written self-defense law could separate the questionable shootings from those which are clearly cases of self-defense. Something along those lines is needed.

Senator Wentworth should not be demonized; he had the integrity to point out the inapplicability of his law to recent Texas incidents.[3] But the law that he and other legislators created simply isn't working right. Based on Rick's own experience with letter writing, Senator Coates of Oklahoma seems to take a different view, i.e., that if you ignore the unfortunate cases they will simply go away. *Well, we'll see about that.* The senseless and questionable killings are not received well even by Oklahoma's gun owners, the very ones who wanted a castle law. There *will be* a public backlash if a lawless mentality runs out of control.

Comments that question the wisdom of the castle laws

Citizens certainly do see the problem, and the following anonymous comments came from various discussion threads:
"I'm an 'Eye For an Eye' kind of guy, so this law makes no sense as I see it. Basically, if someone in my state murders someone else, they will probably get 15-20 years of jail time (realistically)

and be done in the eyes of the state. However, if they break into my house, steal a pencil, and I shoot them dead (we'll call this capitol punishment), they lose their life and I'm off scott free. Therefore, in the eyes of my state, MURDER = 15 YEARS and MINOR THEFT = DEATH PENALTY. Could someone please explain the logic in this?" It's a good question. It goes right to the heart of what is being called the "variability of justice." If legislators, lawyers and judges want to keep their credibility, they need to pay attention to the views of the ordinary person. *"Castle doctrines are not laws designed to preserve the right of a homeowner to protect his property (except in Texas). Castle doctrines are laws that preserve the rights of homeowners to protect the occupants of their homes from harm or death. In other words, you are not shooting an intruder as punishment for theft of an item, you are shooting an intruder to stop a possible attack against your person or any other person present in your home."* And another closely related comment: *"Castle Docrine is NOT a license to 'murder' an 'innocent' person. Castle Docrine IS protection for a person that has to protect his life, his loved ones lives, and his property..."*. That's almost correct, but only if you ignore those last two words *"...his property."* It is about self-defense and nothing else. It should only lead to the use of deadly force if there is a genuine, immediate threat to innocent lives.

Killing someone over "...*his property...*" is not a valid justification. If the law reduces the number of burglaries or other kinds of crimes, that's incidental -- not a purpose of the law. The courts do not award the death sentence for burglary alone. But if the burglar tries to kill you, that's different.

The following is not anonymous. It comes from a blog site called "TexasFred," and he was taking issue with comments being posted to his website.[4] *"The Castle Doctrine does NOT give anyone the right to become a vigilante in the street. Within the walls of your home, you and your right to self protection reign supreme."* Concerning the Joe Horn shooting of two Mexicans, he said: *"...if your conscience isn't bothered, if your moral feelings aren't hassled, if YOU want to allow some old fool like this to jeopardize our gun rights, great, go for it, and when Joe Horn is used as the example of WHY the American citizen shouldn't have guns, I hope you'll remember this...".* Indeed, that is what chapter 6 of this book was about. And he also said: *"If MURDER and a vigilante America is the way we need to go, some of you are well on your way!"*

Some people think the castle laws allow them to be vigilantes, and that is what Texas Fred was addressing. His views on the castle laws are more representative of the average Texan and

Oklahoman (and the author's). Most individuals will avoid dangerous confrontations and are not quick to resort to violence, so they shouldn't be stereotyped with the hotheads. They are not the problem. Another anonymous writer said it well: "...'*Castle Law', despite what some people think, doesn't allow murder just for tresspassing. You need to prove the perpetrator was trying to break into 'an occupied home, business or car (occupied too: an empty car doesn't count)'; also the law doesn't include 'land', other restrictions might apply. Castle Law it's not a free ticket to shoot and kill anyone. Most people that brag about that law never took the time to actually read the law; like the guy who shot a high school girl in the head for walking into his property at night, he claimed Castle Law but now he is in jail.*"

The kind of language buzzing around out there is not a bit comforting.

REFERENCES CITED -- Chapter 8

1. Dale Lezon, "Liberty couple indicted on murder charges in boy's death," *Houston Chronicle*, June 5, 2009.

2. Linda Falkenberg, "Burden of truth lies with Horn," *Houston Chronicle*, June 30, 2008.

3. Staff writer, "Homeowners armed with right to shoot," *The Dallas Morning News*, January 19, 2008.

4. Texas Fred does not fit the stereotype that all Texans are hotheads where guns are concerned. In fact, most Texans and Oklahomans show a great deal of restraint and common sense. In a thread of July 2nd, 2008 at 12:39 PM he had this to say about offensive comments being posted to his website (quoted by permission):

http://texasfred.net/

"I am going to say this ONE MORE TIME and after that some of you can keep on blathering like the ignorant and uninformed *jail-house lawyers* you think you are:

1. Joe Horn is a murderer
2. Joe Horn is an old fool
3. Joe Horn placed himself in the position to be killed
4. Joe Horn was told, repeatedly, STAY IN YOUR HOUSE, police are on the way.
5. Joe Horn made an open declaration that said, "I am gonna kill em"
6. Joe Horn, at that very moment in time, became a PREMEDITATED murderer. Adrenaline and *heat of the moment* be damned, Horn was in a place of his own choosing, he was armed and extremely dangerous, he was untrained in law enforcement, as are MANY that are making the most ludicrous comments on this thread and if the psychology that I have studied is any indicator, Joe Horn had a latent desire to KILL and saw this as his opportunity to act on that desire."

Chapter 9 - What lawyers and others associated with criminal justice say

"No one is without fault." - A Roman proverb attributed to Seneca the Elder

This very brief chapter is necessary for an understanding of how the criminal justice professionals think. Probably most prosecutors see serious problems in the castle laws. But make no mistake about it, others have no difficulty with the laws, and they apply them to the letter rather than take the more arduous path of proving motives other than genuine self-defense. The legal profession needs to realize that its already tarnished reputation is being further damaged.

The following sampling of comments made by district attorneys, criminologists and others associated with criminal justice comes from more than one source.*(1)*

Many prosecutors are skeptical

"They're basically giving citizens more rights to use deadly force than we give police officers, and with less review."
- Paul A. Logli, president of the National District Attorneys Association.

Indeed, when an intruder is in your personal territory and you are living in a castle law state such as Oklahoma or Florida, even an *unarmed* intruder can be killed. The actual degree of threat may range from none at all, through crimes that would never get a death sentence in a court of law to genuine cases of deadly intent. Only in the latter instances should deadly force ever be warranted. But the reality is that self-defense shootings have already encompassed the entire range of threat levels, including "*...none at all.*"

We have legalized abortion. The act of abortion *does* involve terminating a human life, in most cases where no physical threat to the mother exists (such as a medical condition) and certainly where no consent from the one killed is possible. In fact, an aborted fetus is not legally a victim. There are those who would do the same thing with aging humans, *even those still sentient*, i.e., by carrying out euthanasia *for the good of all* rather than accommodate the associated health care costs. If a self-defense law allows someone to get away with killing another who was not actually an immediate threat, especially where there might have been a motive, then the outcome was convenient to the one who did the killing. Such cases are very much in league with those other two kinds of homicides. All of these might be described, collectively (and sarcastically), as *convenience homicides*, and they stand in sharp contrast with legal executions, where the state punishes someone for committing a reprehensible crime. But the point here is that regular murders are convenient to *someone*, and making distinctions between homicides does not change the nature of the act.

One author used the term "*throwaway lives*" for the victims of such homicides.[2] Such killings show us "...*how cheap human life can be viewed in some quarters...*" and how the nurturing of humanity "...*has more or less evaporated in modern times.*"[2] However, other societies have been making exceptions to what we would call outright murder, and that has been happening for a long time. The "honor killings" of certain Islamic cultures come to mind, where a woman's family can murder her to restore "honor" to her family without fear of retribution, even if the woman was only the unwilling *victim* of a sexual assault! There is no honor in killing *anyone*, certainly not someone already victimized. Nor is it an honor in a genuine case of self-defense, when armed intruders enter a home. Replace the word "honor" with "survival," and you'll have a better description of what was done.

Are we creating a death culture, one that solves some of its problems by killing? It looks as if we are; we are trivializing homicides. We already have too much of the mentality of rogue states. Nazi Germany always comes to mind, and it wasn't the only state that practiced genocide; it's still happening. In Hitler's Germany you could die for merely disagreeing with the politics of the state, even if you did not belong to a group labeled "*untermenschen.*" The same was true in Stalin's Russia. *Is that where we're heading?*

"*It's inconceivable to me that one in a hundred Floridians could tell you how the law has changed.*" - Gary Kleck, criminologist, Florida State University.

That has been the author's position throughout this book. Comments made by ordinary citizens in the previous chapter show it clearly. Police officers and soldiers operate under strict rules of engagement, and they usually know their limits. If they deviate they face internal reviews or a court martial. But ordinary citizens have been given a license for "legalized killing," and the majority of them cannot tell you what their limits are.

"*The Legislature's intent was to allow good people to use deadly force, but the reality is you can't write that law perfectly...the result is you might have killings where people should be prosecuted but you can't because of the law they've given us."* Shannon Edmonds, legislative director for the Texas District and County Attorneys Association.

The author agrees, but Edmonds has a kinder way of portraying the motives of court officials. Add to it that some prosecutors are only too happy to evoke the law to reduce their workload or stay in good favor with the voters. Politics *does* get into their actions in various ways, and there might even be corruption. Think deeper; there are *several* bad motives, and they were described in this book's Introduction. One has good cause to doubt that prosecutors always have noble motives:

"Keep this in mind about what you're being told by prosecutors: They don't like this; it's a limitation on their power. I think that they're muddying the waters a little bit here." - Keith Hampton, legislative director for the Texas Criminal Defense Lawyers Association.

If the prosecutors were so adherent to the concept of justice, the laws would not be allowed to apply in ways not intended. Keith Hampton also noted: *"The castle doctrine refers to your own castle. Not somebody else's. You can't take weapons and start hunting down people that you think did something wrong."*
His statement refers to the deed of Tommy Oakes, who shot a man because he thought the man was breaking into a *neighbor's* home. None of the castle laws allow you to do that. This is an

example of a killing where the threat to the killer was "...*none at all.*" But amazingly, instances like that have been allowed to pass as self-defense. Some prosecutors even ignore the *exceptions* of the law, which in any reasonable mind would have required pursuing a case of murder rather than self-defense.

"*The problem that I perceive is that this is not going to protect the law-abiding citizens...It's going to protect the criminals.*" - Jana McCown, an assistant district attorney for Williamson County in Texas.

The author of this book believes that is exactly what is happening. The situation examined in detail in chapters 1 and 2 is not without precedent, and the following chapter will cite others of a similar nature. The detailed wording of the law, especially that overriding presumption of innocence, *works for criminals.* It is sure to be abused, and it already has been.

"*In effect, the law* [meaning castle law] *allows citizens to kill other citizens in defense of property.*" - Anthony J. Sebok, a professor at Brooklyn Law School. The intent of the castle laws was self-defense against an intruder who posed a deadly threat. Unfortunately, what has actually been happening justifies Professor Sebok's assertion. Those doing the shooting have killed when their own lives were *not* at stake, claimed to have been defending a neighbor's property, created a confrontation when it could have been avoided, etc. It should not be about saving property but *saving lives.*

The main issue with many prosecutors is that presumption of innocence

"I think, not purposefully, but unaware of what they were doing, the folks who passed the so-called castle doctrine used that same concept of a <u>defense presumption</u>..." -- Shannon Edmonds, legislative director for the Texas District and County Attorneys Association.

Attorney Edmonds was referring to a previous failed gun law when he mentioned, *"...that same concept..."*. The presumption of innocence forces prosecutors to not charge even in the face of evidence damaging to the killer, or if a Grand Jury is convened, requires instructing them that they, too, have to presume innocence. In such cases the prosecutor would likely be reluctant to let the general public see any contrary evidence, so one could expect terse comments to the news media. The incident might then be accepted as an uncomplicated case of self-defense. Or worse, the killing might even be held up as an example of a brave citizen defeating some criminal ogre. *San Antonio Express News* writer Robert Crowe[1] reported that *"Experts fear that hidden in the stories about heroic homeowners killing intruders are untold numbers of criminal cases.*" It was said that in Texas the number of justified homicides tripled in 2007, when the new law went into effect. None of them went to a grand jury, because the investigators concluded that they happened in self-defense. Some of those investigations were probably not thorough.

"*We have some very good defense attorneys in Harris County, and they are going to have an absolute field day with this.*" - Bill Delmore, Harris County Assistant District Attorney Delmore said that to Texas legislators. He also told them, "*The existence of this presumption is so scary to prosecutors, that we would prefer to see the bill not passed than passed in the present state that we see it today.*"

But we ask in 2010, where are those challenges to the castle doctrine? They haven't happened thus far.

A very gray area exists in the *stand your ground anywhere* language of the doctrine. When there has been a homicide that would not qualify as true self-defense, witnesses tend to scatter (if they even exist); they often don't want to be involved and may have some fear of the one who did the killing. As Delmore put it, "*In these situations, the defendant will always have a reason in his mind that he needed to shoot somebody. Either someone pulled a knife, or someone showed a gun, or someone was breaking into his vehicle."*

The reality is that you end up having to rely on the word of the killer in such incidents, and unless a careful investigation is carried out you will have no insight into the kind of person you are dealing with. That takes time, human efforts and use of technology (computer resources, etc.); it translates to money. Nevertheless, if we want to be sure that justice prevails, we have to know the nature of the shooter *and* the victim. As Delmore noted, *"It's going to require the state to sort of prove a negative, which is very difficult to do."*

"A lot of it comes down to the background and character of the <u>victim</u> and the background and character of the <u>defendant</u>," - Deputy District Attorney David Greenberg, supervisor of the district attorney's office in Vista California.

The laws are indeed not being used in the way intended. States that do not have what we are calling a castle doctrine still do it the old way, so you have standards that vary a lot as you go across the land, but no matter where you are, the excuse of self-defense is common among those who commit murders. It is offered even if the one killed was not armed when the incident took place, and prudence suggests that the nature of *both* the victim and the one who killed him should be examined carefully.

Greenburg noted that in a third of all the pending murder

378

cases, self-defense is being claimed. The stated figure did not count cases of gang violence or domestic homicide. But things are different in a state like California, where a precedent established that "...a simple assault does not justify a homicide." In Oklahoma or Texas or Florida it apparently doesn't matter if the shooter doesn't take precautions (e.g., by keeping doors locked and calling 911), or even if the one killed had no weapon. You thus have a situation where premeditated murders are almost invited.

Even in California there are cases where a prosecutor didn't file a murder charge, because there was good reason to believe the killing was a clear-cut instance of self-defense. David Greenberg said: "*The reality is, yes, there are cases we do not file because of self-defense*" He also noted that the district attorney generally doesn't make a public statement as to why charges were not pursued. But that kind of policy will not instill much public confidence. Secrecy of judicial action is what Associate Justice William J. Brennan (U.S. Supreme Court) disdained; his opinion was quoted in the introduction to this book.

"*You have to look at each situation and the totality of the circumstances to decide if they* [meaning homicides in self-defense] *are justified.*" Bill Flores, a former assistant sheriff in the San Diego California area, offered that comment. It just doesn't happen that way in Oklahoma and other castle law states. But in the long run the outcome will be damaged reputations and the public's perception that something is seriously lacking in their criminal justice system.

So that is the existing situation. Prosecutors claim they don't know what to do with the mess, but some of them have screwed around with the intended limits of the laws. Legislators apparently don't know how to write a law that's perfectly clear in the jurist's mind; maybe legislators should re-take English Composition 101 for minimum competency! The public *thinks* it knows what it wants and demands action but is getting something else in the process. Who is to blame? *Everyone.*

All laws need to be applied with great care, because the misapplications make a mockery of justice and erode public confidence.

REFERENCES CITED -- Chapter 9

1. Scott Marshall, "Self-defense claims common in murder, assault cases," *North County Times (San Diego, CA)*, Sunday, June 17, 2007; Steve Thompson, "Prosecutors fear castle law's 'presumption' will allow real murderers to go free," *The Dallas Morning News*, March 16, 2008; John Liptak, "15 States Expand Right to Shoot in Self-Defense," *New York Times*, August 7, 2006; Robert Crowe, "Critics fear law could protect aggressors," *San Antonio Express News*, April 19, 2009.

Steve Thompson's article in The Dallas Morning News summarized the basic features of the Texas castle law: "*It presumes you are reasonable in using deadly force if someone – illegally and with force – enters or is attempting to enter your occupied home, car or workplace. You are not given this presumption if you provoked the person or were engaged in a crime. It removes your obligation to retreat if possible before using deadly force if you are anywhere you have a right to be. The previous law obliged you to retreat if a 'reasonable person' would have, except in a situation where someone unlawfully entered your home. It gives you added protection from lawsuits by injured attackers or their families. The previous law granted this protection if someone illegally entered your home, but not in other situations.*" You don't have to be a lawyer to see how this opens up some very gray areas. The Oklahoma law doesn't even make a clear statement about prior provocations.

2. George Forbes, "Throwaway Lives," *Scottish Memories*, p35, March 2007.

Chapter 10 - The Darker Side Examined

"If something can go wrong you may be sure that it will."
- That is one way of stating Murphy's Law.

The weakness of a self-defense law is revealed when it either doesn't have the intended effect, or when it is used in a way that is not appropriate. In searching for cases that illustrate problematic examples the author found it helpful to *imagine* situations involving such weaknesses, from which appropriate search keywords could be selected. The available literature[1] was then consulted to find out if anything even remotely like the scenario had ever happened. The approach worked surprisingly well. As it turned out, most of the imagined situations had actually occurred in one form or another.

The term "alleged" applies to the real cases examined in this chapter because some of them had not been resolved through legal process at the time of writing. Another reason for keeping an open mind is that in most of the cases presented here, even those supposedly closed, we depend on journalistic quality which may or may not exist. Finally, the courts make mistakes, and that should be kept in mind.

When things go wrong and innocent people die

We will first look at what might be called the *baseline situation*. There have been many cases where a self-defense law never came into consideration, although it might have, because the intruders prevailed over the innocent people. An effective defense was lacking and/or resulted in a bad outcome. If you watch the day-to-day news, you will eventually come across a story of the following type:

A rural <u>family</u> of six was taken by surprise at about 5:30 PM on a hot July day when three armed intruders searching for money, firearms and other valuables entered their home through an *open* door. Things got out of control, and the <u>intruders</u> started killing. Three of the children managed to flee from the home and took refuge with a neighbor a quarter mile down the road (they had gone through a wooded area, not actually alongside that road), but the other child, a teenage boy, was murdered along with his parents. The mother had been raped. The <u>killers</u> made a run for it and have thus far evaded the police. [Note the underlined words]

This could have been a valid self-defense situation according to state statutes, but there was no apparent resistance on the part of the victims. The existing law in our state allows the use of deadly force against intruders. Proponents of the castle doctrine argue that this is yet another good reason for an armed public; other groups think we need strict gun registration, claiming that it would keep guns out of the hands of such criminals. Neighbors reported that the father had told them that he had considered arming himself but that he didn't like the idea of having a gun in his home because of the children. One of the surviving children said "Our doors were not locked when it happened, but Dad always locked the doors before he went to bed." It is full daylight at 5:30 PM on *any* July day, and this incident shows us that intrusions are not necessarily midnight things.

Even if the father had a gun, would it have been available for use when the violent intruders came in? In this scenario the problem was more in the realm of lax security (the "open door") than not having a gun, although a gun could have prevented the crime if the door had been battered in, assuming that the gun could have been retrieved in time after the sounds of a break-in were heard. Some intruders certainly do force their way into homes. Those last two paragraphs were made up, but a *Google* internet search using just three keywords from the scenario, family intruders killers, turned up the following four *real-life cases* on the *first* Google search results page:

The wife of a San Francisco surgeon answered a knock at the door of their home and was immediately shot in the chest by one of two men standing outside. An intrusion followed, and Dr. Kim Fang, who was known to be a skilled marksman, engaged them with his *legally registered* handgun. A gunfight followed, and both the doctor and one of the intruders, Mesa Kasem, received mortal wounds. The wife survived her injuries. The family nanny and the second intruder also received non-lethal wounds. Two of the children, ages 10 and 13, managed to escape without injuries, and they took refuge with neighbors.[2] The doctor was justified in what he attempted to do, but this case shows the uncertainty of who lives and who dies in a gunfight. The district attorney involved with this case never had to deal with a castle law decision, because the one attempting to defend his home perished.

An old military proverb applies, "Remember this: when the enemy comes into range, so do *you*." When the bullets fly you can usually count the dead and injured on *both sides*, maybe not in every minor skirmish, but it averages to both sides when you look at a lot of skirmishes.

Another fatal intrusion took place in Aurora, Colorado, and it did not involve a gun. Deadly force can mean a number of things, and in this case the intruder came armed with a blunt object, perhaps a hammer, and somehow acquired a knife at the residence. Bruce Bennett, age 27, tried to defend his family but was bludgeoned and slashed to death. The killer sexually assaulted his 26-year old wife and their seven year old daughter before killing them, too. The only survivor was the three-year old daughter, who was also brutally beaten and left for dead. Her jaw had been crushed, and bone fragments were driven into her windpipe; but she survived.[3] Use of a gun against such a monster (or perhaps monsters) would have been entirely justified. One wonders how the killer gained entry. This remained a cold case in 2009, but the killer did leave his DNA behind. As in the previous example, a district attorney never had to deal with self-defense law because the husband died in his attempt to defend his family.

The castle doctrine generally doesn't apply to cases where the one killed lives in the dwelling where the homicide occurred. Such situations involve people who have a right to be there and thus any violence in that setting fits into the category of domestic assaults and homicides. However, there are cases where domestic murder and self-defense could be confused. An Army medical doctor, Jeffrey R. MacDonald, has been called the "Green Beret Killer" because of the murders of his wife and two daughters at the family home within the perimeter of Ft. Bragg, North Carolina. The doctor had injuries, too and he claimed that intruders had attacked the family.

Army investigators concluded within the first hour of their arrival at the crime scene that the doctor had stabbed himself seventeen times and clubbed himself three times after killing his own family, to make it look as if they were *all* victims of outside intruders. The crime was thus attributed *to the father*, and he was tried and convicted and has spent decades in federal prisons.⁽⁴⁾ But was this really a domestic homicide?

Stabbing one's self seventeen times to create an alibi is a bit much to swallow. Who can be sure of what really happened? This case is controversial. One Fayetteville, North Carolina narcotics investigator heard an account from an informant that supported MacDonald's claim that intruders had indeed perpetrated the murders. The Harvard legal scholar, Alan Dershowitz, has been quoted as saying that MacDonald is the most victimized person in the history of United States jurisprudence. If the alternative view is true, then it's just another example of the variability of justice in the United States. If the court's conclusion was correct, this was an example of an attempt to conceal a murder by attributing it to self-defense (see further down).

Joseph Kallinger and son Mike Kallinger posed as salesmen on January 8, 1975 to gain entrance into a New Jersey home, where they robbed and terrorized eight people. A nurse who happened to be there to help an elderly friend was taken to the basement, sexually violated and murdered.[5]   Kallinger was demented -- he heard voices that told him to kill and mutilate young boys. His second victim was a Puerto Rican boy and the third was one of his own sons.

Truman Capote wrote the popular book "*In Cold Blood*," which was about the Holcomb, Kansas murder of a father and mother and their two children -- the Clutter Family.[6]   The real-life setting of the Kansas mass murder was very similar to the one of the imagined scenario. Use of deadly force by a family member supposedly would have been entirely justified, but such reasoning is by *hindsight*. The existence of a self-defense law cannot save people who are unprepared to defend themselves. Imagine a different scenario:

Supposing we could enter a parallel universe, where there *had been* a successful fight for survival at the Holcomb, Kansas dwelling in 1959.   Would a *revised* casualty list lead to a clear-cut conclusion of right and wrong? What if the district attorney decided that Herbert Clutter did not have a valid reason for using his pump-action shotgun to kill one of those two "*unfortunate young fellows*?" Richard "Dick" Hickock showed up at the Clutter home with Perry Smith and was killed. In that case the 10 PM news might have quoted this statement from the prosecutor: "*Herbert Clutter shot both of the men, killing one of them. The other is now in serious condition but is expected to survive, and he has told the investigating officers that they came to the Clutter home seeking help. The father leveled a gun at them, and -- without warning -- began shooting. Herbert Clutter is being charged with manslaughter."*

The point here is the *variability* of the outcome regardless of the wording of a law, and that includes the castle laws. In the first chapter of this book a case was cited where possible criminal motives were simply ignored. Another prosecutor might have handled the matter differently.

In Donalsonville, Georgia a mass murder that took place during May of 1973[7] was distinctly different in character, a sort of inversion of what is generally thought of as an intrusion into a home. Donalsonville is over in the southwest corner of the state, in Seminole County. The setting was fairly rural in 1973. Four men, three of them escapees from a Maryland minimum security work camp, entered a vacated mobile home looking for guns and money. While their burglary was in progress, members of the Alday family, who lived there, started showing up. The burglars, Carl Isaacs and his accomplices, then forced the arriving Aldays *indoors* at gunpoint and proceeded to kill them one-by-one. The dead included five male members of the family and a woman.

The woman was the wife of one of the family members. She was raped, then dragged out of the house and forced into a car, where she was raped again and finally murdered. Carl Isaacs, the one who instigated the Alday murders, was not executed until the year 2003.[7]

The odds of an effective resistance in Donalsonville case was slim to none, but if one of the Aldays had managed to produce a gun and start shooting, his actions would have been justifiable under Georgia's current castle law. Considering that the intruders were escaped convicts, an Alday probably would have been exonerated for killing or injuring the intruders even without a castle law. *Or at least that is what we think ought to happen,* but again, that's speculative logic. Being wary and driving off upon seeing strangers at their home -- simply fleeing -- was another option, but when normal individuals come up on something like the situation in Donalsonville a sense of danger does not sink in right away. A soldier or a police officer living daily with mortal threats might be ready for it, but the ordinary citizen isn't.

The point being made here is that not everyone will benefit from the castle laws because they don't pay enough attention to home security and are not prepared to defend themselves when trouble finds them. Just having a gun for defense if often not enough; you might not have a chance to reach it in time. However, if the laws put a damper on burglaries and other kinds of intrusions, then everyone will benefit through a *herd effect* due to falling crime rates. This kind of reasoning assumes that intrusive criminals will be deterred by the existence of such laws. The death penalty never deterred all murders, so it is safe to assume that the some will continue to take the chance, no matter what the consequences are. No doubt, others will be intimidated. Proponents of the Oklahoma castle law claimed almost a 50% decrease in burglaries, but even if the correlation is statistically valid, the remaining half is still a large number.

One has the feeling that justice varies considerably in these situations, as it does in other crimes. Hanging Judge Isaac Parker sentenced 160 criminals to die on the gallows, yet he was on record as being personally against the death penalty. Parker had some wisdom for the fine mess we find ourselves in today. He said: "*...in the uncertainty of punishment following crime lies the weakness of our halting justice.*" It is true. Present-day lawyers can rationalize it however they please, but *justice varies wildly.* The situation may never change, and what is written in very old books tells us that the problem has been around for quite a while:

"But his sons did not walk in his ways. They turned aside after dishonest gain and accepted bribes and perverted justice."
- From the Holy Bible, I Samuel 8:3

The verse was about Samuel's wayward sons, whom he had appointed as judges over the people, and that was millennia ago. In this context the modern way of saying "perverted" is "corrupted."

Four immediate thoughts come out of the examples thus far considered:

1. Pay more attention to locked doors, especially sturdy metal doors with heavy locks and other security measures.

2. There is some merit in running like hell, if possible, in spite of those "stand your ground" rights.

3. There really are situations where homeowners and apartment dwellers are justified in using deadly force, and that is true with or without a castle law; thus, none of this rules out the consideration of having a gun for self-defense.

4. The castle law of your state may or may not work the way you think it should, because justice is not consistent and sometimes it is corrupt.

Equitable force

Some of the self-defense laws of the various American states allow you to shoot an unarmed intruder if you merely *think* that your life is threatened. In such situations, the concept of *equitable force* does not apply. Actually, it should, especially if you have an advantage, *i.e., ascendancy.* The word *ascendancy,* meaning being dominant or in control, applies to the cases where the homeowner already has his gun in his hand -- ready to shoot -- when the intruder is encountered. It is genuinely intimidating to the one looking straight into the bore of a firearm, but the desired outcome will not happen if the intruder is the one with *ascendancy.* Consider this fictitious encounter scenario:

Mike McCoy was in his study doing some paperwork when he heard his wife let out a throaty yelp from the living room, "*Who are you?*" That didn't sound right at all, so he took the 9 mm semiautomatic pistol out of the desk drawer and headed down the hall toward the living room, flicking the gun's safety to *off* as he went. Then he pulled the slide back and let it snap forward to chamber a round from the magazine. When he reached the living room he found two punks trying to flank his wife, and she was doing a good job of dodging, throwing chairs, sofa pillows, etc. One of the assailants had a switchblade knife. Mike then did something unexpected: He pointed the gun at the ceiling and yelled one word very loudly, "*GUN!*" The two punks turned, saw the black handgun very clearly against the background of an ivory white wall and bolted for the open door. The armed one dropped his knife when he tripped on a sofa pillow lying on the floor, and that was his undoing, because he left his fingerprints behind. And Mike never once pointed the gun at the intruders. He just stood there like a statue with the gun pointing up. When the door was secured and after the rest of the house had been searched he flicked the safety *on*, pointed the gun downwards and removed the magazine; then he ejected the live round that was in the chamber. His wife was already calling 911.

There have been many real-life incidents like this one. Yelling "GUN!" or "SHOTGUN!" and scaring an intruder away before any shooting starts is commendable, although it can be risky. People have even bluffed assailants with pellet guns, which definitely isn't recommended. In *hindsight*, Mike used good judgment in the confrontation, applying the concept of equitable force. If one of the intruders had charged him, or produced a gun, he could have started shooting. Of course, he and his wife might have died if the other assailant had a gun and the situation *had* turned into a shootout There was a more fundamental problem: an unlocked door, which allowed the intrusion to happen in the first place. City dwellers usually know better, but in the more rural areas there is tendency to think that off-the-street intrusions never happen. Unfortunately, it is wrong to think that way *anywhere*.

It doesn't always have to end in bloodshed. Real-life examples of crimes being stopped without recourse to violence are fairly common. Seabrook, New Hampshire is on US Highway 1, not far north of the Massachusetts state line. Near noon on April 13 of 2009 a Seabrook woman was taken by surprise when a "loud crashing" was heard. A burglar had kicked her door in, and he came into the house. The woman retrieved her weapon, and -- gun in hand -- confronted him. The man fled the house and took off across US 1, but she had gotten a good look at him and recognized him as the friend of a family member. Given that information and other descriptions of the intruder, the police were thus able to track him down.[8] This was a case where the intruder had a drug habit and was stealing to support it.

A Colorado man heard a sound downstairs and went looking with his gun at the ready. It turned out to be a burglar. He chased the intruder out of his home and fired the gun into the ground.[9] You can almost hear the burglar a few minutes later, out of breath: "*He...he...shot at me!*" Would that make a burglar rethink his choice of a career? It might make him more inclined to kill in future burglaries.

Sometimes the intruders really do get shot at. An example

found through the "Armed Citizen" column involved three robbers kicking in the door of a Houston, Texas area home. The homeowner produced his gun and shot at the criminals, hitting one of them. Police caught the suspects when they took their wounded cohort to a hospital.[10] What do you bet that the homeowner installed a better door after that experience?

So even when gunfire is involved the outcome is not always fatal. For every home intrusion that ended disastrously there are many more cases where an armed citizen defended successfully, often without having to fire a single shot. The National Rifle Association's publication *American Rifleman* has for years carried the column "Armed Citizen," which reports the experiences of ordinary citizens who used a gun in self-defense. In going through these reports one is impressed by the many cases where the defender did not have to kill an intruder or even fire a gun at all. Another good resource is the online Civilian Gun Self-Defense Blog:

(www.claytoncramer.com/gundefenseblog/blogger.html)

The same pattern of non-fatal encounters is found through the latter reference. There is a whole range of outcomes in armed confrontations, from non-violent to tragic. Thus, a new point is added to the four already noted:

5. A rule of equitable force ought to exist no matter what the castle laws say we can do.

Police versus armed but innocent citizens

The following imaginary incident considers what happens when police go to the wrong address:

Slim Reed was a 27-year old police investigator, operating in plain clothes with the narcotics division of a large city. "Plain clothes" did not mean a business suit; the officers looked a lot like punks and drug addicts, because they had to blend into the street scene. Reed was a good man with a clean record, and he had a wife and two young children. He and two other investigators were en route to a site where they intended to set up a surveillance, but an emergency call came through: "...gunfire at 1035 Nesbit Lane heard by neighbors. The lieutenant advises that a suspected drug dealer lives there and has been investigating the case." It was a terrible screw-up. The address intended was 1835 Nesbit Lane; somehow an "8" was confused with a "0", and how that actually happened was never pinned down to satisfaction during the following internal investigation; speculation centered on the possibility that the dispatch simply misread the computer display. Reed's narcotics unit was closest to the address, but it was diverted to a wrong address eight blocks down Nesbit Lane. To make it even worse, carpenters were starting work on an addition to an outbuilding in a nearby back yard, and the sound of a Ramset nail gun driving concrete anchors through a sill plate echoed through the neighborhood just as Reed reached the door. The heavy nail guns work just like a firearm. One of his men headed around the house.

The front door proved to be tough. Reed yelled "*Police! Police! We're coming in!*" The first attempt to batter through failed, and it alerted the homeowner, Bill Hastings, who had served time as a special forces sergeant in Vietnam. He had been decorated for valor. Hastings was a good man, too, and he had pursued a second career as one of the managers of builder's supply outfit after twenty years of honorable military service. Hastings had heard someone shouting outside his door followed by a forceful bump, but the words didn't register as *police*, because his hearing had become badly impaired over the years (an M-60 going off near him in firefights had a part in the deafness). Thinking thugs were breaking in, he grabbed his shotgun from the hall closet, chambered a shotshell and brought the sights into alignment on the middle of the front door, which was only eighteen feet away. It was just Hastings and his wife in the house; the kids were already adults with families. When the lock broke on the second try Reed came through first with his 9mm ready.

In a bygone year Hastings would have fired first at the armed man with a ponytail wearing a scruffy-looking leather jacket, but age works against fast reflexes. Officer Reed got off the first shot when he saw the shotgun. The round was not well placed, because Reed had stumbled, and it wounded Hastings non-fatally in his left side, about on a level with his navel. But the aging veteran was no stranger to combat. The pain from a bullet striking spoiled his aim, but he came back on target while Reed was recovering from the stumble, and the full force of a high brass 12-gauge goose load from eighteen feet impacted Reed right above the bridge of his nose. Reed was dead before he hit the floor; part of his skull had been shot away. Hastings never got off a another round. The second officer in line shot Hastings two more times; one round penetrated Hastings' aortic arch and the second struck his solar plexus. He was dead by the time the EMT team arrived. It was the kind of irony that defies understanding. The decorated military veteran had never been seriously injured in Vietnam even though he had survived several deadly firefights, and officer Reed went out that day thinking it was going to be just another covert surveillance among the street people, certainly not anything *confrontational*. Hastings' wife was hysterical, and she was promptly handcuffed; she believed she was being kidnapped until the uniformed officers showed up.

There is more to the scenario:

The reported gunfire at 1835 Nesbit Lane also turned out to be real, and it was drug-related. After realizing that a team had been diverted to a wrong address, another unit went to the intended location, thirty minutes late, and they found a bullet riddled body there, apparently the result of a squabble over territory between drug traffickers. And this had happened in a decent-looking middle class neighborhood.

Although this situation is offered as an *hypothetical* case, it is not without precedent in real-life incidents. It does not actually fit into the castle law scenario because the wording of self-defense statutes generally contains something like this: "...*the intruder must be acting illegally.*" A law officer is not acting illegally when he is, with good intentions, doing his job. But even with that exception, some of the state castle laws require that the officer clearly identify himself, or else *he* can be counted as an intruder.

Law enforcement officers are not acting illegally when evidence indicates that a residence or business needs to be entered and investigated. Police are usually very careful about keeping addresses straight, but sometimes they make mistakes. The error of going to a wrong location because of a confusion of address numbers or street names is very real.[11] Too much reliance on informants is often a cause of those mistakes.

In the scenario, Hastings died believing that a physical threat was at his door. This looked like a castle law situation from Hastings' viewpoint, because he was defending his own home; technically, it was not, although it is the kind of thing that starts internal investigations. In both the scenario and the real-life examples of that kind of situation[11] the loss of life is a tragedy for all concerned. Officers generally try to do what is right in delicate situations, acting on their instinct under conditions known as *Exigent Circumstance.*[12] When that happens, sometimes the outcome is good and sometimes it is not. Police and soldiers alike have dangerous, depressing jobs, and the pay scarcely compensates all the risks.

Keywords from this imagined scenario turned up a surprisingly large amount of material. The CATO Institute conducted a study of botched SWAT-type raids between 1985 and 2008 and found 333 erroneous intrusions, of which 173 were raids on what turned out to be innocent individuals.[13] Consider the following questions:

Did the legislators that promoted the state's castle law foresee this kind of situation? Real life tragedies come in more forms than legislators ever could imagine. Is there a provision for such convoluted situations? A re-examination of the selected castle laws in chapter 3 leaves one with the feeling that the laws try to simplify what can't be simplified.

How might the District Attorney treat this shooting incident if Reed had died and Hastings had not? How would it have been treated if Hastings had died and the Reed had not? Add a sixth point to the five already considered:

6. Complexity can enter the picture; gun battles at private

dwellings are not always about the good guys and criminals.
The Armed Forces are keenly aware of this phenomenon,
which is known to them as "friendly fire."

A gun in the wrong hands

Let us now consider the novice with a gun scenario, which of course is fabricated:

The newspaper headline read: "*Man Shoots Self Defending Home From Intruder.*" Leland Qualls was aware of several break-ins in his town, and he bought a .45 caliber semiautomatic pistol from a reputable gun dealer. This involved the usual waiting period, but Leland was a decent guy and did not have a criminal record. Going through the gun's manual, he convinced himself that he knew how to operate every feature of the gun. Then he moved the safety to the safe position (*or so he thought*), loaded the magazine with cartridges and put the magazine in the gun, chambered a round, then removed the magazine, added another cartridge to replace the one that went into the chamber. Finally, he put the fully loaded magazine back in the gun. He said aloud, as if there was someone standing beside him: "Now I'm ready for war." The loaded gun was put in the drawer of his bedside table and forgotten for the next 27 months. He grew up in a family that did not keep guns, and incredible as it seems, Leland had never actually fired a gun -- not even once -- even after he bought that .45 caliber pistol. His first pull on a trigger happened on that awful night.

There was a "thump" in the dream. Leland woke up at

about two AM and heard muffled sounds. He also thought he felt movement through the floor, which was possible because it was an older home with a pier and beam structure. He lived alone and had no pets, so it had to be someone in the house. In fact, *it really was a prowler.* The gun was removed from the drawer, and Leland tiptoed barefoot down the hallway, which was dimly lit by light filtering indoors from a full moon. The gun was in his right hand, and he tried to take the safety off using his right thumb according to what believed he'd read in that manual. It didn't budge. He stopped, and bending over from the waist up and looking downward, with the gun pointing approximately straight down, he reached over with his left hand and put three fingers on one side of the slide, to oppose his left thumb, which touched the safety on the other side. He thought "Lemme see, it should go *this* way." Yes, he knew the right direction, but *the safety was already off!* It couldn't move any further in that direction. Not realizing that or the highly relevant fact that his right index finger was already curled around the trigger, Leland gave the safety a hard jab with his left thumb. The maneuver caused Leland to nudge the trigger, and there followed a flash of light and a deafening "BAM!" that left his ears ringing. "YEOW!!!"

Leland was startled by the intense pain in his right foot. The onset of pain coincided with the gun going off, and after a second or two came the realization of what had happened. A young medical doctor later informed him that the heavy bullet had shattered a metatarsal as it plowed its way through his foot and into the hardwood floor. There had been another source of pain, not quite so bad, because the recoiling slide had torn off part of a fingernail and lacerated two fingers.

At least the shot had the desired effect. The burglar sincerely *believed* he'd been the target and moved with the dedication of someone full of adrenaline. He knocked over several potted plants on the back porch as he reversed his path of entry. The police didn't get him that time. Leland spent what was left of the night receiving medical care and explaining what happened to the police. He was still limping six months later, but it was those teasing remarks that he found hardest to bear: "You shot yourself in the *what?*"

Didn't the legislators wonder about what would happen when *everyone* was given a green light to take on a Dodge City style shootout? The consequences of gun accidents range from minor to tragic. The scenario is entirely plausible, and it could have been fatal if the bullet had severed an artery. There was a real life humiliation which happened in 1960 to a certain Batesville, Arkansas native, someone well-known in his time, who slid a loaded .22 rifle toward himself across the bed of a truck, muzzle first, while sitting on the tailgate. The rifle went off when he did that, and a bullet tore a diagonal gash across *both* cheeks of his butt when the trigger snagged on something (When you move a gun in *that* direction a snag *can* pull the trigger!). Fortunately the grazing bullet didn't go deep. It was a really stupid accident because the gun shouldn't have been loaded under the circumstances. This person was going fishing, and he always carried the gun to "*...shoot water moccasin snakes.*"

It has been pointed out that most gun owners don't hunt or have concealed carry permits or participate in target shooting sports (see the comments of Daniel McElrath in reference 7 of chapter 7). McElrath seriously doubts that all of those individuals are gun collectors! The guns are probably kept for self-defense. That fact is a little disturbing if those people are keeping guns without doing the things that improve competence and safe practices.

Superficial familiarity with a gun is a formula for trouble. Even experienced police officers and members of the armed forces have gun accidents from time to time. The author knows of specific cases where individuals have firearms but never practice with them. He has even test-fired firearms for a few owners who were reluctant to shoot *their own guns*!! What are they thinking? *"I'll make up my mind when a burglar breaks in."*

A discharge caused by unfamiliarity with a gun can kill one's self, a family member or even a neighbor, and this is why anyone who intends to use a gun for self-defense needs to spend plenty of time learning about the weapon, learning gun safety and developing marksmanship on a shooting range. Those who drafted the castle laws did not fully comprehend the possible consequences of the situations they have created. The following incidents are real life examples of people who couldn't control their own gun:

First, it's nice to know that a bad guy can make the same mistake Leland did. When would-be robbers attempted to take on a Chicago Southwest Side convenience store one robber pointed a gun at the owners and demanded cash, but a young employee attempted to disarm him. In the struggle *the robber shot himself in the foot.* Then the store owner stabbed the injured robber in the back! The robbers fled, but police apprehended them when the one who shot his own foot tried to get medical help at the Provident Hospital of Cook County.[14]

The owner of La Nouvelle Fine Cleaners went to his business to check on a security alarm and found two robbers inside. He grabbed a handgun that he kept in the store and fired a shot at the two intruders, then chased them out the front door. But as he chased them he tripped and shot himself in the chest with his own gun (*there's that finger-on-trigger problem!*). Fortunately, the wound was non-fatal.[15]

An Elgin, Illinois man was startled by his wife coming home in the early morning hours, and in the dim light he took her for a burglar. He fired a round, hitting her in the thigh. Fortunately, the wound was not fatal, although it probably would have been if the bullet had opened the femoral artery.[16] Shooting at a dimly-lit shape in a home is equivalent to an irresponsible hunter shooting at vague form moving behind a bush. It simply should not be done. You should hold fire if you can't see well enough to identify an object of concern along with whatever else is out there in the line of fire.

In a similar incident in Natchez, Mississippi the outcome was fatal. A man awoke to the sound of a barking dog. Getting his pistol, he went to investigate, but he didn't realize that his wife had moved into the kitchen. He went into the kitchen, and he thought she was an intruder. He shot and killed her. It was a dim-light situation. [17]

This was a classical "friendly fire" accident, the kind that also gets soldiers killed. *Know where everyone is -- that's the rule.* It is wiser to stay put even if you are armed. Let the intruder do the moving. The eye is a marvelous motion detector, and if you are hunkered down, quiet and not moving, odds are good that you'll see him before he sees you. That might give you a second or two of edge.

But something else needs to be said about the latter two incidents. Intentional domestic killings -- outright murders -- have been attributed to an intruder, and these always present the possibility of being *purposeful, premeditated murders,* (see below). Prosecutors tend to be suspicious of such incidents and rightfully so. The following case was treated as an accidental shooting, but it got the shooter charged with manslaughter:

Josh Beasley claimed that he was playing a kind of war game with a shotgun, pretending that he was "clearing" his home of *imaginary* intruders. His wife was in the kitchen, and when he bounded into the kitchen he leveled the gun at her in mock combat and pulled the trigger. There was a live shot-shell in the chamber, and she was killed. [18]

Unless you are in a genuine life or death situation you *never point a gun at anyone, loaded or not, unless that person is threatening your very life.* If there is no evidence of imminent violence, then you certainly have no moral right to take that person's life.

The Beasley incident was treated as an accidental homicide caused by negligence, and doesn't fit into the category of self-defense. It just shows you what carelessness with a gun can do. But such killings also make you wonder about the possibility of a more sinister motive.

We want to live in a free society, and there is no way to keep that freedom if we take away someone's right to have a gun unless he or she is a felon or psychologically unstable. That freedom doesn't remove responsibility: gun owners need to know a lot about their guns and gun safety. A new point may be added:

7. Those who choose to use guns to defend themselves need to be in control of their guns, which means familiarization and practice at a shooting range. Ownership of a gun demands skill, responsibility and adherence to a set of safety rules.

Grudge murders passed off as self-defense

The grudge murders attributed to self-defense may become common occurrences. Here is an imagined example:

James and Richard had an ongoing squabble over a particular girl, one that both had cohabited with in sequence. They had already been in two fist fights over her, once in a bar and again at a carnival, when Richard caught James with the girl. One day James came to Richard's place to slug it out and even the score, but in Richard's mind this was the perfect situation he'd been hoping for. He grabbed the aluminum baseball bat that he always kept in the corner and used it to kill James in his living room. Richard put everything he had into just one blow, and it worked. Then he reported the incident and claimed self-defense when the police arrived. "*Use of deadly force*" does not have to mean a gun, and the authorities believed this was a castle law situation. Richard was released after a brief investigation, but he should have been charged.

It was a murder, not self-defense, and a superficial investigation allowed Richard to get away with it. If the police had asked the right people they would have known that James and Richard were fighting over a girl.

This scenario, and variants of it, will probably be the most common type of abuse of the castle laws. It will almost always be two men fighting over a woman, but female perpetrators are not excluded. Drugs such as meth cause irritability, and killings of this kind are more likely to happen among drug users.

Methamphetamine-induced aggressiveness was probably a factor in the York murder (chapter 2), but there was also a question about jealousy over a girl who had been at the home earlier in the evening, who left before an argument between Charles Bussey, Bobby Don Mullinix and Tristan York culminated in a murder. York's murder had nothing to do with self-defense, but it does illustrate how passions and drugs might be the driving factor in *any* murder, including those attributed to self-defense. That is why the castle laws will lead to error if existing jealousies and drug-involvements are ignored.

Rick believes that Faron's shooting death (chapter 1) would easily fit into the category of grudge murders, at least if one ignores that nasty problem of Faron's status as a prosecution witness! Jealousy over a girl was there for all to see, and Bud had been trying hard to get into a confrontation with Faron. Rose said Bud had been drinking in the final hours before he killed Faron, and there was indeed a background of involvement with marijuana, even though the Durant police denied it. There had been prior provocations when Bud went to Faron's home.

A similar incident happened in San Antonio.[19] Those who knew both John Herbert (the killer) and Christopher Hewett (the one killed) said it was over a dispute concerning two girls, and drugs were involved. It was known that John Herbert was trying to provoke a fight with Christopher Hewett, and he eventually succeeded. Hewett came unarmed to Herbert's place, and he kicked the door in. In the ensuing struggle, Herbert overpowered Hewett and stabbed him to death. This happened on February 27, 2008. But this killing was allowed to pass as self-defense. It was a murder by any other standard. Notice again that a killing in self-defense doesn't have to involve a gun.

The San Antonio Police apparently ignored an exception to the Texas castle law. Quoting from the cited source:[19] "One [exception] is that deadly force is not justified if a killer is the person who *provoked* the initial confrontation. [italics added for emphasis]. The other is deadly force isn't justified if the killer was committing a crime greater than a Class C misdemeanor." Both of those exceptions applied in this case. Herbert later confirmed that he and Hewitt had been on the phone throughout the day, exchanging violent threats. Herbert had even gone after Hewett, seeking a confrontation, and there was a comment by Herbert, stating that he avoided an earlier incident with Hewitt, because he feared police would find up to 10 pounds of marijuana inside his apartment. A party was in progress. Hewitt came back later, and he got in that time; so the marijuana was gone by the time the police arrived on the scene. The San Antonio Police apparently also ignored the fact that there was an *"unrelated"* warrant for his arrest on a drug charge! *What were they thinking?!!* Maybe an anonymous writer pinpointed what was in their minds: *"This* [the shooting after an argument] *is not even an issue, who really cares if the criminals are weeding each other out?"*

You hear comments like that from ordinary citizens and even from law officers. But if we accept such conditions *there is no rule of law.* Such thinking leads us right back to the wild west mentality. Another anonymous writer put the problem in perspective: *"... 'I had heard he was a Marine, so my first instinct was to kill him,' Herbert said in a recent interview. My question is this, why then if Herbert was in fear of this Marine then why did he provoke him as well as round up his friends to go fight Chris?*"

Crimes of passion, grudge killings, etc., are likely to multiply dramatically in the castle law states because all the closet psychopaths, the individuals with grudges and those with any other nefarious motive will see the law as a golden opportunity to fulfill their desires. Texas legislators know about this mood and are currently taking a hard look at their castle law. The loose ends need to be tied down right away. Meanwhile, the court officials could be using better judgment, which is what we expect of them, but they aren't. The essential point is this:

8. Ongoing feuds cannot be accommodated. They do not qualify as self-defense situations. The involvement of drugs and prior hostilities should not be ignored.

Purposeful, premeditated murders

Conniving minds will not fail to overlook the potential for perverting the castle laws. Here is a fictitious plan that someone might follow to disguise *your* murder as a self-defense incident (it assumes that *you* are male):

What if your neighbor thinks you are having an affair with his wife and is mad enough to kill you? Let's also suppose that he's being paranoid and it isn't actually true. So he phones you and says, "Come over for a beer and bring that new golf club you told me about. I want to see it." Like a fool, you take the club with you, and he shoots you dead! He tells the police that you tried to kill him with a golf club and that he defended himself. He is questioned about that phone call he made to your place just before the shooting incident, and his answer is "Well, I think that's what made him mad -- I was griping about him not keeping his grass mowed." (Yes, you were being a little lax!) A detective looks across the street and sees a yard that needed mowing two or three weeks ago and says "...Hmm...It checks out." The prosecutor is swamped with work and doesn't press for much investigation. The police are swamped, too, and they could care less at the moment; so the fellow is turned loose. The wife actually believes that their neighbor went nuts. After all, he did seem a little strange at times. The scary thing is that this seemingly absurd hypothetical situation could actually happen in a castle law state.

That was a simple plan thought up by an hypothetical, homicidal loner, and it worked because of its simplicity. We may be sure that organized crime figures will not overlook opportunities for carrying out a murder conspiracy. Consider the following fictitious incident:

A man known as 'Skeeter' Dyson was a scrufulous-looking criminal, and he had a background that included burglary, car theft and a certain amount of violence. He had a meth habit, too. In a lapse of good judgment he double crossed his boss, Ricardo "Ricky" Torres. Ricky said, "I want that son of a bitch dead," and he sent a messenger to look up a man named David Burris. Ricky was collecting a favor from David, something owed from a decade ago, and there was a workable plan for eliminating Skeeter. As a youth, David stole cars for Ricky and was involved in numerous thefts in San Antonio Texas. He was never caught or even suspected. One time a man came up on a car theft in progress, and David had hit him with a socket wrench, which turned the man into a vegetable. This caused David to re-think the hazards of car theft, so he went into hiding, later took up a real estate career and actually prospered. But his life-style change was driven by the visible realities, not conscience, because David still did things that crossed the boundary of decency and legality. His deeds continued to evade detection.

David now lived in a nice home down a secluded rural lane about half of a mile from his nearest neighbor. This was in the Texas hill country, roughly an hour's drive north of San Antonio and not far west of US 281. By pure chance, Ricky had run into David about six months before Skeeter fleeced him. The first thought was, "I ought to take David down here and now for giving me the brush," but another thought crept in: "Naw, he might be useful. I need to think about that." Ricky was a true opportunist, good at getting people to do things for him, and a use for David came soon enough.

The plan was simple: "Texas has a castle law. Skeeter's MO is there to see, but you, David, are squeaky clean. I'll send Skeeter to rob your place, and he doesn't know you once worked for me. He'll go there thinking you will not be home. I'll tell him the home contains an expensive coin collection. You do the rest." David knew he had to do it to avoid becoming a scattering of bleached bones in some rural ditch. Just to be nice, Ricky was paying him $2,000 in cash to carry out the task.

David made sure that his BMW was in the garage with the door closed and locked. The home certainly looked vacated. Skeeter arrived in the middle of the night. He was allowed to break the lock and move into the middle of a room before the ceiling light was turned on. Then David killed Skeeter with just one blast from a 12-gauge shotgun. *Keep it simple.* David called 911, and when the Sheriff's deputies arrived the shotgun was confiscated and David was handcuffed. They noted that a door had been forced open. But their subsequent investigation found that while Skeeter had been twice convicted of burglary, absolutely nothing turned up for David. David had been asked why he shot an unarmed man, and his reply was that, 'He was coming at me. He barged into my own home. I feared for my life, I believed he meant to kill me.' He stuck to that simple explanation -- never changed his account of what happened in any way, and of course the castle law had the provision of not requiring the homeowner to retreat. His story was thus accepted, especially because a concealed loaded gun, one that had been stolen, was found in Skeeter's cargo pants. *That* bit of information had been kept from David during the questioning, and he actually didn't know about it. The district attorney thus considered all of the available evidence and said, "Here is a clear case of a homeowner defending his life and turf against a criminal intruder." David was thus not charged, and he was released the day after the shooting. And that was the end of the matter for another decade.

But to the embarrassment of all, David's connection to Ricky Torres and the murder of Skeeter Dyson was eventually uncovered after David bilked more than

$800,000 from an elderly client in a highly fraudulent real estate deal. The feds caught him that time. The crime was not related to the earlier murder in any way, but when an investigator noticed that David had previously killed a man in "self-defense," intuition caused her to probe more thoroughly into David's past. All the rest came tumbling down when a prison inmate told her what he knew about David.

There is no statute of limitation for murder. The castle laws cannot protect you if at some later time it is shown that what was treated as a self-defense homicide was in fact a premeditated murder; at least that is how it ought to be. The hypothetical example presented here might actually work in real life. First appearances can be very misleading, and that is how some will get away with it.

Under the castle doctrine the presumption of innocence is applied to the homeowner, the one defending, and there is a strong tendency to not do much investigating if things seem to fall into place. The police *are* overloaded with work. Courts are overloaded, too, which means too many crimes and not enough prosecutors, judges, accommodations for prisoners, courtroom space, etc. Prosecutors have to get *dispositions* one way or another, and traditionally that has meant *plea-bargaining*. The presumption of innocence is a *new option -- even easier than plea-bargaining* -- if the case falls into the castle doctrine category. But while the burden of proof falls on the prosecutor, the castle laws do not actually prevent a prosecutor from going after someone if there is reason to think it was a murder and not self-defense.

There are many variants of schemes that can be used to disguise a premeditated murder as a killing in self-defense. The laws are sure to be manipulated to cover hotheaded arguments and more thought-out schemes that lead to murders. *But those need to be identified for what they actually are and treated as such, not protected by a castle law.* Unfortunately, they are also more likely to be the most difficult to prove. Criminals and their defense lawyers have a way of making the laws favor the criminal.

Faron's shooting death (chapter 1) looks like a murder to keep a witness from testifying. If the court was correct in sentencing Jeffrey MacDonald for the murder of his family[4] the case stands as an example of an attempt to disguise a murder by claiming that intruders committed it. In "*A gun in the wrong hands*" (above) there were two examples of shootings said to be in self-defense situations.[16, 17, 18] Murder charges were not pursued in those cases, and maybe they were just tragic

418

accidents. But shootings of that type are not unlike the MacDonald case and could raise a suspicion of premeditation. Some are more obvious than others.

It is probably easier to get away with murder in Texas and Oklahoma, but those who plot homicides in those states will want to come up with a better blueprint than Nikolas Kotsopoulos did. Nikolas was convicted of murdering his wife in 2003, and that happened in Manhasset, New York. Manhasset is located on Long Island. The shooting took place on Orthodox Easter, while his wife was preparing dinner. *During his trial in 2003 he had insisted that he was innocent and that an intruder had killed his wife.* His story changed in 2009 when, seeking a new trial, he told a federal judge that he had in fact killed his wife accidentally. As he put it, "I was taking the bullets out of the gun. Suddenly it went off. Boom. I saw my wife go down. I ran over. I said, 'Honey, are you all right?"

But the autopsy photograph of his wife not only showed a bullet hole in her face but also two black eyes. The son testified that Nikolas Kotsopoulos beat his mother, and Nikolas admitted on the stand that he had pistol-whipped her before trying to "scare her" with the gun. Nicholas was a bit dense, but others much more clever lurk out there. There was a recent fatal backyard shooting in Ft. Worth, Texas,[21] and self-defense was claimed by the shooter. Here is how the incident was described: "*The 37-year-old man told police he fired approximately five times at the suspect and then went back inside the house to protect his children. The 24-year-old man who was shot stumbled to the front yard, where he was found dead. He was identified by the Tarrant County Medical Examiner's office as Pierre Bullock of Fort Worth.*" This was one of those in-the-yard things, not an actual home intrusion. Some thought it might be justified because the law says you can shoot 'em under the circumstances, so go ahead and do it; for example: "*Depends if he's cutting thru your yard to steal something. I'm not a lawyer but I believe its legal in TX to shoot in defense of your property as well as you[r] life.*" Others were more reserved: "*In most states, that would not be self-defense. Even in TX, I'm worried that this guy will find he regrets his actions. I hope it turns out to be a dead career criminal and not a dead drunk neighbor.*" As a matter of fact, it turned out that the man did not have a criminal record. There appears to be a seed of doubt in the minds of some of those familiar with the situation. One individual, apparently a neighbor, had this to say:

"*Having read the commentary on the demise of Mr. Bullock, I can only conclude that there is much need for an in-depth investigation. Someone needs to look at land line and cellular phone records of the deceased and the shooter. It appears that a connection is possible. Did the deceased know the killer or perhaps he knew his wife or girlfriend. Was the deceased invited into this backyard for the purpose of being executed under the guise of the 'castle law?' This all sounds very misleading and full of holes...sounds like premeditated murder to me."*

Maybe so; maybe not, but it is right to be very wary of those situations. As Robert Crowe of the San Antonio Express put it:[19] *"Experts fear that hidden in the stories about heroic homeowners killing intruders are untold numbers of criminal cases."*

Researching the material for this book was an eye-opener for the author. As he dug into the accounts of shootings categorized as being in self-defense, he started noticing the suspicious-looking cases. It's hard to put a percentage on the questionable shootings, but it could be as high as a third of the total. That's just an intuition because there are too many subjective assessment factors. The killings that plant a seed of doubt are in a kind of legal limbo; the shooter has been "presumed innocent," and the incident thus becomes *legally untouchable.*

If the prosecutor got it wrong, we are left with what amounts to a cold case of murder. If the surviving family or other victims of the shooting can't open a civil lawsuit, is there even a criminal law option? Being realistic, it's at best only remotely possible, and the associated litigation costs will be beyond the reach of most individuals. After the presumption of innocence has been applied, very few critics will want to say, "*It is alleged that he (or she) might have murdered the intruder...,*" one reason being that the prosecutor who made the decision will be offended. As an example of what can happen when egos are wounded, the Ada, Oklahoma prosecutor brought a lawsuit against John Grisham because his book "The Innocent Man" was considered slander. How does that fit with laws that set no time limitation for the crime of murder? The absurdity of the logic should be evident to the reader.

Maybe if we have enough ill-advised castle law killings all of those old, filed-away cases will have to be re-examined. *Let the ones that murder in plain view and apparently get away with it worry about that for the rest of their lives. Indeed, their case could be re-considered. Maybe it will never happen to them, but they can't be sure about that.*

As a matter of fact, reassessments of earlier incidents *do happen* occasionally, perhaps because DNA evidence proved that a court's decision was wrong or for a variety of other compelling reasons. In February of 2010 a female professor of biology at the University of Alabama in Huntsville suddenly began shooting her colleagues at a faculty meeting. The group had been working at a conference table when the professor allegedly produced a 9 mm semiautomatic pistol and began firing with accuracy and purpose. Her shooting spree left three dead, and three more were wounded, two of them critically. Apparently the violence ended only when the gun jammed. The woman, a Harvard graduate, had been denied tenure at the university, and that may have been the motive: brooding hostility fueled by rejection.

There was more to account for. The tragedy brought immediate attention to the fact that in 1986 the professor had shot her teenage brother to death in Massachusetts;[22] he was hit in the chest by a blast fired from a shotgun. The incident had been attributed to an "accident," and no charges had been filed. It was especially disturbing to learn that the professor's wealthy and influential mother had served on the police board, raising suspicions of a possible cover-up. The shooting spree in Alabama thus brought calls for a reinvestigation of the earlier Massachusetts shooting. Such reassessments not only identify overlooked crimes but also ruin the reputations of the officials who made the erroneous or corrupt decisions in the first place. For the sake of justice and legal integrity we should not want the so-called self-defense shootings to be exempt from future reassessments. *"It was self-defense"* and *"It was an accident"* are the two explanations used most often by murderers.

A lot can go wrong in those millions of house or property-sized legal vacuums we've created. Some domestic murderers will try to claim that an intruder came in, killed the wife (or the husband) and then fled. Others will set someone up by simply inviting them in or creating some other reason for getting the victim into the home, then kill them and claim self-defense. Add another two points for the realm of premeditated murders:

9. In all castle law shootings the possibility of a murder must not be treated lightly, which means that backgrounds and connections have to be examined carefully. Drug and alcohol abuse, criminal records, gang associations, etc. -- everything potentially relevant -- are signals that say "dig deeper." Unfortunately, the rules of evidence often work against such scrutiny.

10. The castle laws should not prevent a reversal of a prosecuting attorney's decision if new evidence comes into the picture. After all, there is supposedly no statute of limitation for murder, and we shouldn't be creating one. A situation of legal secrecy is especially likely to be abused.

Trigger-happy shooters

An hypothetical situation was not needed to find this category, because examples of trigger-happy shooters turned up with the other searches. The author believes these kinds of tragedies will only continue to accumulate because the castle laws that have weak or missing safeguards actually encourage people with bad judgment to do the wrong thing. Ignorance of what the laws allow abounds out there, and those anonymous comments cited in chapter 8 reveal the misconceptions.

The senseless shooting death of a seven-year old boy at a Trinity River levee near Houston, Texas was cited in chapter 8, and more should be said about it. A seven-year old boy named Donald Coffey, Jr. needed to "use the bathroom," and his people stopped their off-road recreational vehicle to let him relieve himself. Then a man and a woman took turns shooting at him and his people. This happened roughly 40 miles northeast of Houston, Texas, beside the Trinity River.

A sign warning that "trespassers will be shot" was posted near the dwelling. If nothing had happened the sign might have been viewed as a bluff, but this was a case where two people were all too willing to pull the trigger. The wife, Sheila Muhs, was holding the 12-gauge shotgun. She fired the first shot, then handed the gun to her husband, Gayle Muhs. He fired the next round. Donald was hit in the head, and he died not quite two days later. Other members of the family were also injured by shotgun pellets in that incident, one of them seriously, and these individuals apparently were not even on the homeowner's property when the homeowner and his wife took turns shooting at them. Sheila then called 911, and this was said to be from the transcript of the voice recording: *"They're running over our levee in big-wheel vehicles, and I shot them."*[23] A levee is usually on waterway property.

A similar shooting of two illegal aliens that were burglarizing a neighbor's property in nearby Passadena, Texas was cited in chapter 8 as an example of what *isn't allowed* by the Texas castle law, although in that case a grand jury found the shooter, Joe Horn, justified in what he did![24] The transcript of Horn's dialog with a 911 operator actually documented a premeditated murder. A very similar incident happened in 2008 in central Texas, in the hill country at Kingsland, when Tommy Oakes gunned down Casey Rowe when he thought Rowe was breaking into a *neighbor's* property. Rowe died two months later. In that case the Llano County grand jury handed down an indictment against Tommy Oakes. The district attorney charged Oakes with criminally negligent homicide.[25] A comparison of the Passadena and Kingsland incidents illustrates the variability of justice in our land, and anyone who is inclined to push the limits of a statute or shoot to kill when it isn't absolutely necessary should take a warning.

Alabama's castle law is very rigid, and the one who killed Matthew McLain will never be held accountable. McLain was not a burglar. In fact he was a law student at the Cumberland School of Law of Samford University in Birmingham, Alabama, and he was returning from a celebration of his acceptance into a legal honor society when he was killed. He made a mistake that is familiar to apartment dwellers: he thought he was going into his own apartment, but it was a wrong address -- an identical end unit. Matthew had been having trouble with his own apartment's lock, and this time it just wouldn't yield. He moved to the patio door and tried it. It was open, so he walked into the kitchen of Saafir Asaad Malik's apartment. Malik was in another room. He had guns, and he first tried to get a magazine into a 9 mm automatic but dropped it. Then he grabbed a .357 magnum revolver and went into the kitchen, where he shot McLain in his left eye. Because of the honor society event, McLain was wearing a business suit. The shooting may have been in semi-darkness, but wound characteristics (stippling, etc.) indicated a close-up shot.[26]

The Alabama law is very rigid, and Malik's criminal record could not be taken into account. Malik had a former name, Shawn Jones, and he had been charged with felony assault in Florida. In 1991 he had pleaded guilty to misdemeanor domestic battery. But he had beaten his pregnant wife, and it was the same tendency to violence that showed up later in the apartment shooting. Federal prosecutors didn't charge him with firearm violations at that time, because he refused counsel. There were anabolic steroids in his apartment (the police found them), and those hormone substances are known to cause aggressiveness. Even more disturbing were the accounts of Malik's neighbors. Malik falsely portrayed himself as an undercover FBI agent and often brandished weapons. This kind of behavior points to a serious psychological disorder. And yet, the Alabama law enforcement and court system could do *nothing* about the situation.

While McLain's killer, Saafir Asaad Malik, has escaped accountability for a senseless killing, voters might apply a harsher standard to those who wrote the law if this kind of insanity continues to repeat. Jurists can be aloof and point to rules of evidence and statutes and say, "It had to be done that way." A normal individual would have a conscience about it and worry that one he turned loose might commit further violence. Malik has been charged with felony possession of steroids. That's how the court handled Malik's case! *"There's not one thing we can do to right this. All we can do is get up and share his story,"* said Beth Boswell, Matthew McLain's mother. Indeed, that's all Rick can do concerning his grandson's shooting death.

Once again, you see the wild variations of justice at work. By their actions the courts have shown that they are more protective of the criminal than they are of innocent individuals. The castle doctrine could be called a rule of lawlessness in some cases, and it shows the error in a law that allows someone with a record of prior criminal activity, notably assault in this case, to escape scrutiny. The need to account for prior criminal activity was stated in point 9, above. That will never happen unless the Supreme Court rethinks its rules of evidence.

Part of the problem with trigger-happy shooters is, unfortunately, ingrained into their minds. It's like rape; there is a compulsion to *dominate* others. The rest is a lack of understanding of what their limits are. Thus a new point:

11. The public needs to be better educated, but even with that accomplished, wrong-headed shootings will still occur. Some individuals refuse to be educated. Good judgment cannot be legislated.

Recommendations

Those eleven points (above) in bold italic print may be collected and further summarized. The following summary is addressed to the individual, the private citizen:

- *Secure your property better. Lock up.*
- *In the choice of fleeing or defending (if there is a choice), never rule out fleeing.*
- *Use equitable force. Use force only when there is no other alternative.*
- *Gun owners should be proficient with their gun(s).*
- *Gun owners should know what the law allows and forbids.*
- *Citizens should be aware that the courts can be capricious.*

And these points are respectfully addressed to the legislators and the courts:

- Intrusion related situations involving injury or death can be deceptively complex.

- All homicides including accidents and those claimed to be in self-defense are worthy of thorough investigation.

- There is no statute of limitation for murder, and homicides in self-defense should not be an exception..

- Homicides resulting from feuds and provocations do not qualify as self-defense.

Everyone -- legislators, lawyers and private citizens alike -- should review the *criteria for validity* presented in chapter 3. Some of the castle law states, such as Georgia, require homeowners to inform themselves of what the law provides, and the concept is a good one, but -- to use a military proverb -- *"Three percent never get the word."* The actual figure may be more like 30 percent in this situation, or worse, and some of the comments from the general public (especially those quoted in chapter 8) support such fears. The public needs to *know* what's required rather than what it thinks the law ought to mean. One option would be to offer an educational booklet and then test for comprehension. The law would protect a citizen only if he or she successfully completed the test. That's draconian, but nothing else comes to mind. It's probably a bad idea.

The focus comes back upon the ones that are supposed to show good judgment: the court officials. Prosecutors should be held to a standard, and police likewise, if they fail to investigate thoroughly. And that's how it's supposed to be, but it isn't. If drug testing and thorough background checks of all concerned is not carried out after a shooting incident, then we are going to see a rash of murders carried out in the name of self-defense.

But we do need self-defense laws that protect a homeowner under siege while weeding out the imposters. It is probably better to revise laws appropriately than to discard them.

REFERENCES CITED -- Chapter 10

1. Meaning the internet, newspapers and libraries. You have to be careful with internet materials because some of it can be misleading. That is also true of the media -- what you read in newspapers and what is said during radio and TV newscasts and commentaries.

2. Michael Cabanatuan, Henry K. Lee, Jaxon Van Derbeken, Erin Hallissy, Chronicle Staff Writers, "Killer Had Visited Home To Deliver Furniture: Robbery of Alamo residence may have been plotted in November," *San Francisco Chronicle*, January 7, 2000.

3. Kirk Mitchell, "Aurora family killed by intruder with 'taste for violence'," *Denver Post*, August 11, 2008.

4. Jerry Allen Potter and Fred Bost, "Fatal Justice: Reinvestigating the Macdonald Murders," W. W. Norton, New York. "Fatal Vision," a bestseller

book by Joe McGinniss portrayed MacDonald as being guilty, but McGinniss later recanted his position and admitted that he fabricated some of the information in his book, notably that MacDonald was a drug user. The prosecuting attorney's career began to fall apart after the trial was concluded.

5. A sketch of Joseph Kallinger is found in the *Serial Killer Crime Index* (*www.crimeZZZ.net*). The *Index* is of itself a valuable resource for finding home intrusion crimes, although its scope is much broader and the database is international.

6. Truman Capote, "In Cold Blood," Random House, 1966.

7. Bill Torpy and Bill Montgomery, "Alday killer executed 30 years later," *The Atlanta Journal-Constitution,* May 7, 2003. The murder happened on May 14, 1973, and Isaacs held the record for the longest delay between sentencing and execution. He was arrogant and expressed his contempt for the Aldays. The crime was one of the worst in Georgia's history.

8. Elizabeth Dinan, "Gun-toting homeowner scares burglar," *Sea Coast On Line*, April 17, 2009. Intrusions are often drug-related; see chapter 5.

9. Felix Doligosa Jr., "Homeowner fires gun, scares off intruder," *Rocky Mountain News*, December 28, 2005.

10. Paige Hewitt, "Three arrested after robbery attempt northwest of Houston," *Houston Chronicle*, May 20, 2009.

11. When police raid a wrong address the outcome is terrorized citizens. Sometimes the raid turns into a shootout. Consider the following examples: Staff writer, "SWAT raids wrong home, calls error 'mistake'," *WSVN TV 7 News*, April 10, 2008. This happened in Northwest Miami-Dade Florida. The raid's intended target was 2627 NW 49th St., but they went instead to 2627 NW 49th Terrace. It's not hard to see how the addresses were confused, but the occupants of the dwelling, a woman, her sister and young children, were thoroughly traumatized. Apparently, two concussion grenades had been thrown into the apartment, and the officers came in pointing guns. A potentially lethal raid took place in Minnesota: Staff writer, "Minneapolis SWAT team raids wrong house," *Associated Press*, December 18, 2007. Gunfire was exchanged between the police and the homeowner, who believed he was defending against criminal intruders. It is a miracle that no one was killed. The man living at the house shot two of the SWAT officers! Their

bullet proof vests saved them from serious injury. Misinformation from an informant caused the incident. The same article cited a tragic incident that took place in Atlanta, Georgia in 2006, where police killed a woman aged 92. She had fired one shot at them, thinking they were criminals breaking in, and she went down in a hail of returned gunfire. In all, almost 40 rounds were fired by the police officers. This botched raid was the result of false information from an informant. In 1999, in Denver, Colorado, Police officer Joseph P. Bini gave a SWAT team a wrong address, which resulted in a man being killed. Bini turned out to be a renegade cop. In 2009 he pled guilty to charges of sexual misconduct with underage girls: Staff writer, "Former Denver cop on sex offender registry," *KUSA TV 9 News*, March 2009.

12.   "*Moral authority*" is an old military term with a similar meaning. "*Exigent circumstance,*" as used by police and the courts, exists when an officer unexpectedly encounters a situation of imminent danger, especially one that could result in loss of life or property. *Immediate action*, is necessary. Examples include terrorist attacks, a bank robbery in progress, a burning home or the sound of gunfire coming from a home. In these examples there is no time for a search warrant, and the officer has to use his own judgment, doing what he thinks is right. See also: United States v. McConney, 728 F.2d 1195, 1199 (9th Cir.), cert. denied, 469 U.S. 824 (1984): "Those circumstances that would cause a reasonable person to believe that entry (or other relevant prompt action) was necessary to prevent physical harm to the officers or other persons, the destruction of relevant evidence, the escape of a suspect, or some other consequence improperly frustrating legitimate law enforcement efforts."

13.   Radley Balko, "Overkill: The Rise of Paramilitary Police Raids in America," *CATO Institute White Paper*, July 17, 2006; the specific CATO website is: http://www.cato.org/pub_display.php?pub_id=6476.
Some police sources dispute the accuracy of Balko's study (see reference 11, above).

14.   Staff writer, "Would-be robber shoots himself in foot, gets stabbed, then arrested, police say," *Chicago Tribune*, August 26, 2008.

15.   Staff Writer, "Man shoots self when aiming for robbers," *Denver Post,* September 11, 2007.

16.   Staff writer, "Elgin man mistakes wife for burglar, shoots her," *WGN*, March 16, 2009).

17. John Koob, "Natchez man shoots wife in mistaken home invasion," *The Natchez Democrat*, January 1, 2008.

18. Leslie Reed, "Husband shot wife during intruder game," *Omaha.com*, February 6, 2009.

19. Robert Crowe, "Critics fear law could protect aggressors," *San Antonio Express-News,* April 19, 2009.

20. Ann Givens, "Manhasset man admits he killed wife - by mistake," *Newsday*, March 26, 2009.

21. Staff writer, "Police say Fort Worth homeowner shoots, kills backyard intruder (Texas)," *WFAA TV*, May 31, 2009.

22. Kristin M. Hall and Desiree Hunter, "Accused Alabama professor shot, killed brother in 1986," *The Associated Press*, February 13, 2010; Martin Finucane, "Two different views of a single tragedy," *The Boston Globe*, February 13, 2010. See also the commentary and links at this website:

http://riverdaughter.wordpress.com/2010/02/22/amy-bishop-and-massachusetts-politics/

23. Dale Lezon, "Liberty couple indicted on murder charges in boy's death," *Houston Chronicle,* June 5, 2009.

24. Lisa Falkenberg, "Burden of truth lies with Horn," *Houston Chronicle*, June 30, 2008.

25. Staff writer, "Kingsland man indicted in shooting at neighbor's home," *KVUE News*, January 7, 2009.

26. Scott Sexton, "A Right Goes Wrong: Man's killer is protected by Alabama law," *Winston Salem Journal,* December 21, 2008.

Closing Thoughts

The need for self-defense statutes that favor innocent individuals caught in deadly situations is not disputed, and the existing castle laws probably work correctly *most of the time.* However, those statutes should not be an excuse for using deadly force without a clear need for it, or for committing outright murder. The reader should be aware of the fact that the *other* type of failure of justice can and does happen: individuals who are actually forced to shoot or die are charged with manslaughter or even murder. With the passing of time the misapplications of the new laws will accumulate, and something will have to be done.

After Rick's own terrible experience, whenever he reads of a situation where someone was wounded or killed and a self-defense law was evoked, skepticism takes hold, because he knows from what happened to Faron that newspaper and TV reporting is typically superficial and often tilted -- even full of errors. Sometimes media sources seem to hold back the real story. He wonders what really happened when he reads about those cases. The court, aloof as it usually is, certainly did not gain his confidence.

After things settled down a bit in the wake of Faron's death a certain girl who numbered among those who knew Faron heard a chilling story. One of the young men that accompanied Faron to Bud's place that fateful night told her that Faron simply walked into the house and Bud had shoved or kicked the door shut. Then he heard Faron saying, "*Why is your hand behind your back...are you holding a gun?*" then: "*No! We're not going to handle it this way.*" After that came the gunshots. The account is hearsay, and the one who told that to the girl has been involved in criminal activities. He even stole things from Rick. Nevertheless, it could have been the truth. Only Bud knows what really happened.

Faron was just one example of a castle law tragedy. His I.Q. was well above average. He could have pursued a difficult professional career such as medicine *if* he had made it his priority. He had a healthy sense of humor. He was curious about many things, and he loved going on adventurous trips. His grandfather was a pilot, and during Faron's brief life the two often flew together; he was being taught about flying and navigating. They hunted and fished and hiked deep into wilderness trails. They did what grandfathers and grandsons were supposed to do.

It is often said that "...if you spend time with your children the outcome will be good." *Be careful with that cliché; it's not always true.* Faron yielded to the influence of a reckless crowd, and he didn't heed the warnings about drugs. He lived in a community that is not coping with its drug problems. He had been abandoned by his own father, and *that troubled him considerably.* He made mistakes. But he didn't deserve to die the way he did.

Now his daughter will also grow up without her biological father. How will that affect her? The permanent loss of a parent can be devastating. Rose, the mother, was adopted; she searches for a parent. Is there a remedy for people who have been separated from their real parents, who wonder how it came to be that way? Some circumstances cannot be made better, and because of Faron's death one has to conclude that in the daughter's situation,

"It is not a case of finding the key to a locked door. There is no door." - From *Beyond Belief*, by Emlyn Williams

Rick will be haunted by the perceived injustice for the rest of his life, and his wife was in turn subjected to the trauma. His daughter still pines about Faron's death and is suffering from very serious complications of post traumatic stress. Faron's maternal grandmother took the full brunt of the thing, which included Bud's stalking at her place. Faron was still living with his grandmother when he was killed. His brothers say they will never get over the loss. Even some of Faron's friends have emotional problems because of the tragedy.

There will be more shootings without cause. Another child will be killed for being in the wrong place at the wrong time, caught up in a drive-by or maybe for wandering onto someone's property. Murders will be attributed to self-defense or accidents. There will be gun accidents in homes due to carelessness. Many of these situations could be avoided, but the effects they leave behind can't be avoided. They are permanent when someone dies. They cast a very dark shadow over the lives they affect.

"It has been said, 'time heals all wounds.' I do not agree. The wounds remain. In time, the mind, protecting its sanity, covers them with scar tissue and the pain lessens. But it is never gone."
- Rose Kennedy

www.ingramcontent.com/pod-product-compliance
Lightning Source LLC
Chambersburg PA
CBHW060614290326
41930CB00051B/1498